Workers' Playtime

Theatre and the labour movement since 1970

ALAN FILEWOD & DAVID WATT

Currency Press, Sydney

First published in 2001 by
Currency Press Pty Ltd
PO Box 2287
Strawberry Hills NSW 2012
www.currency.com.au
enquiries@currency.com.au

Copyright © Alan Filewod and David Watt, 2001.

National Library of Australia – Cataloguing-in-publication Data
Filewod, Alan D. (Alan Douglas), 1952- .
    Workers' playtime : theatre and the labour movement since 1970.
    Bibliography.
    Includes index.
    ISBN 0 86819 631 2.
    1. Workers' theater - Great Britain. 2. Theater - Political aspects - Canada. 3. Workers' theater -Australia. 4. Theater in propaganda - Canada. 5. Theater in propaganda - Great Britain. 6. Workers' theater - Canada. 7. Theater - Political aspects - Great Britain. 8. Theater - Political aspects - Australia. 9. Theater in propaganda - Australia. I. Watt, David, 1947- .
    II. Title.
    792.0941

Publication of this title was assited by the Commonwealth Government through the Australia Council, its arts funding and advisory body.

Book and cover design by Kate Florance, Currency Press
Cover photo: The March to the Future performance in Frog Hollow, Darwin, 1989. (Photo: Peter Matthew)
Printed by Hyde Park Press, Richmond, SA

Contents

Illustrations

Acknowledgements

A great number of people have contributed generously of their time and work to help our research and ensure we get the facts right. They sat for interviews, opened their files, answered our emails and extended their hospitality. In each case they took us on board in the spirit of solidarity and friendship. We wish to thank the following in particular. In Toronto: Don Bouzek and Bob Moher. In Melbourne: Patricia Cornelius, Steve Payne and Mark Wilkinson. In Birmingham: Jan Bessant, Rhoma Bowdler, Stuart Brown, Joyce Canaan, Jacqueline Contré, Richard Hamilton, Kevin Hayes, Aidan Jolly, Dave Rogers and Fiona Tate, and in London Frances Rifkin. In Darwin: Mark Crossin, Janet Crews, Gillian Harrison, Didge McDonald, Barbara Pitman and Trevor Surplice. Thanks are also due to our colleagues and students, who have had to listen to us talk through the material on more occasions than could be reasonably expected. Mark Gauntlett in Newcastle is owed a particular debt of gratitude for editorial advice, as is our Currency Press editor Victoria Chance.

Thanks are also due to the Social Sciences and Humanities Research Council of Canada and the Research Management Committee of the University of Newcastle for supporting portions of this research, to Scott Duchesne who worked as research assistant on the Ground Zero material, and to the staff of the Northern Territory Archive Service in Darwin and the Birmingham Central Reference Library Archives Service.

A more personal debt of gratitude is owed to Julie Pavlou Kirri in Newcastle for love, support and the occasional judicious application of an incisive and unsentimental intelligence, and Clem Filewod in Guelph.

We dedicate this book to the memory of our fathers, Donovan Filewod and Alan Watt, who may not have approved but did, after all, spend their early years actually fighting fascists, and to our children, Alan, Sally, Clement and Elena.

Introduction

From Political Theatre Companies to Strategic Ventures

This book arises out of our shared interest in exploring contemporary theatre work that engages with the organised labour movement. Ten years ago this might have quite happily been called 'political theatre', and there would have been little dispute about our object of study. 'Political theatre' was then defined by both content and aesthetic form, it used staging techniques appropriate to specific, probably 'working-class', audiences in a range of non-theatrical spaces, had an allegiance to a set of identifiably 'popular' or 'working-class' dramaturgical forms, and was undertaken by 'companies' with a declared 'political' objective. A number of factors have intervened to alter that simple description.

Firstly, in Baz Kershaw's words, 'the political has become ... promiscuous', and therefore 'the traditional category of "political theatre" may no longer make much sense, except, perhaps, as an historical construct' (Kershaw 1997: 255). The emergence of 'identity politics' and 'difference politics', with their multi-focus on issues of ethnicity, gender and sexuality among other things, has almost pushed class politics off the agenda, or at least eroded its claim to primacy. At the same time, changes within the trade union movement have made it increasingly difficult to sustain the common left-wing assumption of twenty or thirty years ago that the labour movement represented a monolithic working-class consciousness (or an even vaguer working-class 'culture'). This rethinking of 'the political' has disturbed assumptions about the nature of 'political theatre', which has altered the nature of our analysis.

Secondly, the notion of a 'company'—a consolidated group of individuals with shared theatrical and political objectives working to develop a yearly program of plays—has also been unsettled. 'Company' is an ambiguous and always problematic term in the theatre, referring to both the corporate productive structure and the creative team (so that the company hires the company). Historically, consolidated companies, or 'ensembles', concentrate on refining a particular style within a small repertoire of theatrical forms and a defined set of methodologies for generating performances. Much of the work we survey began in this way and flourished at a time when funding made this a natural way to proceed, with a high point in the mid-1970s in Britain or the mid-1980s in Australia and Canada. The decline of public arts funding in all three countries since then, however, has forced politically-engaged theatreworkers into new ways of operating. In the field of work we examine, the theatre ensemble with an annual season has been replaced by teams who work together only for the duration of a specific project.

The erosion of funding which has led to the collapse of the 'company' as an ensemble has also contributed to the disappearance of another feature once thought central to the viability of a theatrical venture—the theatre building itself. For funding bodies, critics and indeed for many potential theatregoers, a physical playhouse confers both identity and proof of community support; hence Theatre Workshop's presence in London's Stratford East validated its working-class credentials by virtue of the neighbourhood audience it 'serviced'. But labour-engaged theatreworkers, in order to survive, have since repudiated the deeply entrenched notion that the playhouse embodies the society that attends it. They have discovered that to intervene in union-defined issues they had to go where the issues were unfolding, so they could research and play in the field. While they were sometimes encouraged to do this by a romanticised desire to 'play the shop floor', more often it was a pragmatic necessity. As union interventions became more instrumental, artists had to produce shows for specific audiences making adaptability and flexibility key tools for their success. And while the initial point of contact may have occurred at moments of public struggle, most artists found that ongoing work with unions took them behind the picket line, into the meeting rooms and canteens where day-to-day union work took place.

This process clarified for artists and unions alike a deeper reason for repudiating the designated performance space. As our case studies show, performance in a worker-defined space is not so much representational as transformational. Touring to union halls and community centres, or performing in the streets, is not simply a matter of taking theatre to 'the people' but rather of enacting the dynamics of social change, in which space is both the process and means of contact. Often the immediate reasons for touring are material—the need to play a quick show for workers on their lunch-break, or to fit into the agenda of a union meeting—but it also reflects an ideological commitment to the principle that public space is site and means of social change.

This grounding in public or non-theatrical space inverts the conventional view of theatrical viability. It is no longer the theatre building that validates a company's credentials, it is the work itself, and the work is constantly adapting to the needs of the moment. Similarly, the performance space, the theatrical tools of style and technique and the administrative tools of company structure and management are all variables.

The most effective politically-engaged artists are those who understand the historical changes affecting their working environments because they are best able to develop appropriate new structures to meet those changes. Two of our case studies, Banner Theatre in Britain and Ground Zero in Canada, operate like small businesses, or even labour contractors, hiring a workforce for a contracted project. Another, the Northern Territory Trades and Labour Council (NTTLC) in Darwin, organises performance-based work through a shifting group of individuals hired by a purpose-formed committee. Consequently, our case studies do not follow a conventional pattern analysing texts and performances as fixed and final entities to reveal genealogies of style and performance technique.

A third factor that has unsettled easy categorisations of 'political theatre' results from the relationships between the artsworkers and their labour movement constituencies. Often the latter are closely involved in the artistic processes, becoming collaborators rather than simply audiences for 'political theatre'. This work is not best viewed as theatre in search of new audiences but as attempts to find ways in which performance (rather than just 'theatre') can serve the political and social objectives of a specific sector of the organised labour movement at a particular moment in time. Instead of a form (or even a spectrum of forms) which can be described as 'political theatre', each project invents its own forms for its individual circumstances. In most cases, loose, temporary and contingent alliances of like-minded artsworkers and political activists engage in a constant process of negotiation and adaptation to changing contexts.

For all these reasons—the rethinking of the political, the demise of traditional notions of a theatre company and the changing relationship between performers and audience—we believe a new description is needed. Since the components of theatrical production are constantly reworked, we prefer to use the term 'strategic ventures' rather than 'companies' to describe the case studies that follow.

We come to our task from a shared interest but bring the different contexts of our respective countries, personal histories and separate yet convergent academic backgrounds. We both resist the fiction of a theatrical world that stands outside the lived world of material culture. While the case studies we have chosen arise out of different historical and cultural specificities, they are all responses to a shared political crisis. We do not want to (in fact, could not) write a categorical survey or a master narrative sustained by totalising concepts of nation and class, or essentialist notions of an international 'political theatre'. Rather, we focus on particular problems that map a set of historical crises. Since the history of theatre in the labour movement is discontinuous, fractured along very different national and theatre histories, we initially expected that our case studies would largely consist of close analyses of exemplary performances, or even 'plays'. We soon discovered, however, the need to detail the strategic decisions (political and aesthetic) which the ventures themselves entailed.

There were a number of considerations in selecting which ventures to analyse although, in a notoriously undocumented area, our personal knowledge was inevitably a factor. We sought ventures which manifested a long commitment to work with the labour movement rather than sporadic opportunism, and which had therefore embarked on a dialogic relationship with their chosen constituency. We also wanted to examine ventures in our respective home countries, Canada and Australia, settler societies with related histories in which social and cultural developments transmuted an essentially Anglo-European political, intellectual and theatrical heritage. These two factors led to three of our case studies. Firstly, Ground Zero, which has a history of involvement with the union movement dating back to the early 1980s, and a pre-history in the Canadian popular theatre movement of the 1970s. Secondly, Melbourne Workers Theatre, probably the most significant theatrical product of the Australia Council's Art and Working Life Incentive Program and the only theatre company in Australia devoted exclusively to working with the trade union movement. Thirdly, the Northern Territory Trades and Labour Council, which revived the Darwin May Day rally in the late 1980s by enthusiastically embracing the possibilities of community-based performance.

We also wanted to include an example of union-based work in Britain, although not perhaps for the usual reasons. British political theatre work in the 1970s was a powerful influence in Australia, largely through a publication record that makes it the best documented in the English-speaking world. And although the American guerilla theatre scene was a well-documented and powerful influence in Canada, British work also made its mark there. We wish to stress, though, that we do not subscribe to a dominant historiography which relegates 'minor' histories to the peripheries of discourse—so that, for example, Australian and Canadian theatre history are merely regional histories given coherence in the interstices of British and American experience. Rather our interest stems from the fact that Britain offered a more fertile ground for experimentation and public debate around questions of politics and theatre, and for the establishment of relationships between theatreworkers and elements of the labour movement. This intellectual and political context was the product of a more consolidated tradition of left-wing thought, left-wing theatre and overtly class-based politics than was the case in either Canada or Australia or for that matter in the United States. It allowed theatre practice to develop more fully, even though not much has survived the crisis of British unionism in recent years. The company we concentrate on does not even rate a footnote in the most compendious source on political theatre in Britain, Catherine Itzin's *Stages in the Revolution*. We have chosen it not just because it deserves its place on the record, or even because it has outlived many of the companies Itzin included, but because it is tied to a tradition which goes back to the 1930s, and also to a related project of the New Left in the 1950s and 1960s, the British folk song revival. These connections illustrate the fertile ground that characterised British theatre work in the 1970s and 1980s.

Although there are major differences between these ventures, their ignorance of each other displays a sad sense of fragmentation endemic in contemporary practice that is not helped by the fragmented history of labour movement theatre. Despite this fragmentation though, they share a common set of problems.

In the period we examine, developments in technology revolutionised the nature of work, while a transnational corporate economy decimated union movements as they globalised the workforce. The steady shift in union membership in the three countries studied here from blue-collar workers in private sector manufacturing industry towards white- or pink-collar workers in the public sector has altered the notion of the working class, particularly the industrial working class, the traditional site and target of left-wing theatre. Further, the rise of a casualised service sector has forced the union movement to find ways of recruiting in traditionally difficult areas. These shifts are not a temporary aberration, but spell the demise of the 'working class' as left-wing thought has constructed it for at least a century. Jeremy Rifkin's *The End of Work* represents the most apocalyptic version of this change. Rifkin notes that we are now well into 'the Third Industrial Revolution' or 'the third and final stage of a great shift in economic paradigms, marked by the transition from renewable to nonrenewable sources of energy and from biological to mechanical sources of power', particularly as technology moves into 'the last remaining human sphere—the realm of the mind' (Rifkin 1996: 59–60). The most alarming element of this, he claims, is already clear:

> In virtually every major manufacturing activity, human labor is being steadily replaced by machines. Today, millions of working men and women around the world find themselves trapped between economic eras and increasingly marginalised by the introduction of new laborsaving technology. By the mid-decades of the coming century, the blue collar worker will have passed from history, a casualty of the Third Industrial Revolution and the relentless march toward ever greater technological efficiency. (Rifkin 1996: 140)

For Rifkin, this 'disappearance of work' is not restricted to manufacturing industry, but is equally apparent in the service industries that, it is often claimed, will pick up the slack. And it is not merely a national phenomenon. Global corporations, now more powerful than national governments, are able to 'transfer production and markets quickly and effortlessly from one place to another, effectively controlling the commercial agenda of every country' (Rifkin 1996: 237).

Rifkin's 'Third Industrial Revolution' is more generally seen as an epochal shift from a 'Fordist' to a 'Post-Fordist' phase of capitalist development. The mass production exemplified in Henry Ford's huge Detroit factory in the 1920s shaped both the structure of industry and the labour movement response to it. With the introduction of Taylorist time management practices, semi-skilled workforces engaged in minor, repetitive tasks in the production process, earning 'higher wages in return for managerial control of production' (Murray 1989: 40). These were determined by collective bargaining over wages and conditions between employers and industry-wide unions with the power to disrupt the production line. The central strategy of the Left was the mass organisation of the working class that lived in essentially class-homogeneous areas surrounding the factory. Fordism, in a real sense, constructed or consolidated class, even 'working-class consciousness', as the central locus of political activism.

Yet as mass production gave way to the production of a diversity of goods, flexibility and adaptability to the market became defining features of production. This has had far-reaching effects on the organisation of the workforce as manufacturing industry moved to smaller, more technologically sophisticated workplaces and subcontracted component manufacture. The geographical and administrative decentralisation of industry has loosened the correspondences between working life, community and class position. The workforce divided into 'core workers' with strong bargaining positions and a huge pool of unskilled, casualised labour in danger of becoming a new poor beyond the reach of the union movement. This has created new social divisions, especially those between 'public' and 'private' sectors and between the two-thirds with rising expectations and the remaining 'new poor' who are left behind on every significant dimension of social opportunity. (Hall 1989: 118)

This epochal shift beyond Fordism is most clearly seen in the developing areas of western economies. Now, the argument runs, the focus of employment is shifting 'from the factory to the office and the shop.' (Murray 1989: 38) The new workforce in the public and service sectors does not, on the whole, see itself in class terms. To recruit in these areas unions have been forced to take more activist roles in social issues beyond the Fordist battles over wages and conditions. The massive change in the gender balance of organised labour has brought with it a host of issues such as pay equity and sexual harassment, while the rapid growth of multicultural demographics has forced unions into areas of social policy covering minority rights, workplace language and racism.

As a result, union movements have had to rework their long-held assumptions about class identity, eroding their commitment to a class-based politics. In its place, provoking Kershaw's charge of promiscuity, are the new politics of 'identity', of gender, ethnicity and culture, and of single issues, like race, sexism and environmentalism.

'Identity politics' was, of course, implicit in the counter-cultures of the late 1960s when the theatre work we examine had its beginnings. It also has an intellectual history that coincides with the shifts towards Post-Fordism in the sphere of economics. One of the most concerted left-wing attempts to embrace it was the 'New Times' project initiated in the late 1980s through the British Communist Party journal *Marxism Today*. For the 'New Times' project, the erosion of class consciousness was reflected in the 'proliferation of new sites of social antagonism', 'new subjects, new social movements, new collective identities' and it needed a new 'unified counter-hegemonic force as the agency of progressive change' (Hall and Jacques 1989: 17). 'Class', instead of being the focal point, was just another site of resistance.

These changes present enormous challenges to unionism, and the union movements are struggling to meet them. As they battle to maintain their membership amongst the new 'core' workers in manufacturing industry, the unions must search for new ways to recruit those on the fringe who have been thrown into casual and part-time work. The Australian union movement, for example, has responded by initiating its largest restructuring process this century, on the one hand consolidating smaller unions into huge super-unions and on the other hand developing a grass-roots system of enterprise bargaining in individual workplaces. Unions in the three countries we survey are embracing the new politics of single issues, although very unevenly, in a program known in Canada as 'social unionism'. Social unionism widens the scope of organised labour's concerns to the full range of political concerns that surround working people, including gender equity, ecology, peace issues, homelessness and social welfare. The difficulty for traditional unionists is to understand that while these issues affect their members, the unions themselves have to acknowledge the expertise, and often leadership, of non-union coalition partners. Although he acknowledges its importance, Canadian labour historian Bryan Palmer is critical of social unionism:

> It actually understates working-class power by accepting the current conventional wisdom that class as the central agent of socio-economic transfiguration has been undermined, and new social movements of women, ecologists, and peace advocates are more potent than class because they can more easily mobilize masses of supporters. (Palmer 1992: 372)

Palmer's warning is clear: unions can become so embroiled in social politics that they lose ground in their fundamental struggle for workers' rights. His critique draws us back to the overwhelming issue that continues to transform the labour movement and the work of its partnered theatrical ventures, namely, the explicit anti-labour program of the New Right which transforms nations into markets and labour into a global workpool. The rhetoric of a 'global marketplace' disguises a systematic move to restructure national economies to suit the needs of transnational enterprises which, 'anxious to remain mobile and flexible in the face of global competition', as Rifkin has argued, 'are increasingly going to shift from permanent to contingent workforces in order to respond quickly to market fluctuations' (Rifkin 1996: 201).

The setting up of 'free trade' zones in cheap-labour countries; the intervention of the International Monetary Fund in currency crises; the establishment of a European currency; the North American Free Trade Agreement (which is restructuring national economies throughout the Americas); and the Multilateral Agreement on Investments (which although defeated in 1998 is far from dead) all contribute to the destabilisation of the fundamental principle of the right to work, and erode protective labour legislation. This has been compounded by the deregulation of tightly regulated industries, from airlines to broadcasting, a lifting of conservation and ecological protections, and concerted attacks since the late 1970s by the 'business sector' on the welfare policies that have dominated politics in Australia, Canada, the United States and Britain.

The rightist push has destabilised labour-engaged artists from two directions. First and most critical has been the attack on the labour movement, sometimes explicitly brutal (as in the defeat of the National Union of Mineworkers in Britain in 1985, the suppression of striking air traffic controllers in the United States in 1981, and the violent confrontations between waterside workers and the state in Australia in 1998) but usually more gradual, such as the decertification of unions and a rollback of protective labour laws governing collective bargaining, closed shops, replacement workers and union elections. These crises provide opportunities for artists to work in solidarity with unions, but render unions less capable of resourcing them. Further, while unions increasingly need every kind of public support they can muster, they fail to take imaginative advantage of the opportunities on offer. Even in the best of times the prevailing attitude of labour organisations to artistic work has typically been indifference, tempered by occasional enthusiasms for local projects that promote instrumental ends. And these are not the best of times.

Secondly, the same forces attacking unions have undermined social programs of every kind, including the cultural policies sustaining artists. The decentralisation of the arts councils in Britain, the drastic cuts to arts funding in Canada and the retrenchment of incentive policies in the Australia Council have pushed radical and fringe theatres, already marginally funded, closer to the edge.

Therefore when we focus on the development of direct work with unions, we must also look at the ways theatreworkers have adapted to external and internal pressures in order to continue working. Theatrical work is an ongoing play of planning and improvisation in the administrative office as well as in the rehearsal hall. Artistic methods must respond to the political and structural needs of the moment with the available resources. There is no stable moment of organisation or artistic expression; each moment is a crisis and a critical response in a process of change governed by forces that artists themselves cannot predict; engaged theatreworkers are constantly revising their previous plans in the fog of political change. Adaptive flexibility is more than a political principle, it is a means of survival.

While we believe that the working class remains a central structural feature of western capitalism, working-class consciousness has perhaps never been further in abeyance and the term has almost disappeared from public discourse. As the old narratives of working-class consciousness have lost purchase, and the central issues for the union movement have expanded beyond workplace wages and conditions, the notions of class politics which have underpinned the whole narrative of theatre and the Left have become destabilised. These shifts have forced the strategic ventures we examine far beyond the simple agitprop forms with which most of them started. They have done this by painstakingly establishing dialogic relationships with a union movement struggling with change.

We have chosen to approach our case studies in a similar spirit of dialogic solidarity. This approach accentuated the reflexivity of our research, and led us to a better theoretical understanding of it. In this we are grateful for the advice of Joyce Canaan (whom we both met through her partner Dave Rogers of Banner Theatre). Joyce is an anthropologist who pointed out that we were engaged in 'ethnographic research'. This leads us to confess that we are not neutral observers. We write about this work because we share its political commitments, and many of the socio-cultural experiences which shaped it. We are drawn towards these theatreworkers by similar life trajectories and social formations: we, like most of them, are products of the middle-class dissidence of the 1960s and 1970s. We see ourselves as 'involved' in the same political project, and thus as participant observers rather than simply recorders and interpreters of objective data. In sociological terms our research is qualitative rather than quantitative, and concerned with analytical description rather than universal laws. Our book is not an objective, universalising account of a 'movement', or even a small sector of it.

Nonetheless we began with the conventional techniques of the theatre historian in accordance with our academic training. We researched the socio-historical contexts of the work we intended to examine, reading literature on the cultural history of the period, the history, forms and nature of the trade union movements of Britain, Canada and Australia, and the theatrical practices which have coalesced around these movements. Our next step took us to conventional searches of primary documentary material, albeit in some unconventional settings and circumstances. We commenced work on our case studies by sorting through playscripts (which, when they existed, tended to be incomplete and very scruffy things defaced with cigarette burns and coffee stains and stored in the back of a filing cabinet), grant applications, minutes of company meetings, publicity material, correspondence, tour itineraries, private papers, and so forth. While our access to these documents was contingent upon what companies would show us, we found them all open, generous and candid, surrendering any initial suspicion they may have had as to our motives and intentions. We were usually left alone with a filing cabinet and a photocopier. Our next step, though, took us into the world of the ethnographer, wherever possible 'participating, overtly or covertly, in people's daily lives for an extended period of time, watching what happens, listening to what is said, asking questions' (Hammersley and Atkinson 1995: 1).

The fact that we were researching the 'not-yet-dead' gave us an advantage to be envied by many theatre historians: the possibility of conversation, both informal and taped interview, with the people involved in the ventures. Our intuitive inclination was towards 'naturalistic' interviews, free-form dialogues rather than standardised questionnaires, and these formed a central component of our research. We immersed ourselves in the social, cultural and intellectual milieus of our sites of study. We wandered around unfamiliar cities, had conversations in homes and pubs and, on one memorable weekend in Cornwall, sat around a campfire till 2.00 a.m. with a bottle of duty free Scotch after a day on a nude beach talking about Ewan MacColl. Our practice was to go away and write the chapter, then take the drafts back to those we had 'researched', and rework them on the basis of their comments, sometimes quite substantially. In one case, a response to a draft entailed a company member taping a long interview on our behalf with a former key participant, whose perspective he felt was unrepresented. In another, it led to a protracted email correspondence between researcher and researched, some of which forced its way directly into a chapter, and more of which served to reinflect it. The case studies as they appear represent our takes on the work we analyse, and can only be partial and even partisan accounts. We have, though, filtered them through the responses of each other and our interviewees, making them, to differing degrees, our collaborators in the process.

Of course, researching the 'not-yet-dead' introduces complexities as well. It is a research method that alters its object. (Indeed, in one of those rare moments when research feels useful, we are delighted that Dave Rogers of Banner Theatre and Don Bouzek of Ground Zero came to know one another through our research. Ground Zero has already hosted a Canadian visit by Banner and the two companies may collaborate on a joint project on globalisation.) We hope that our knowledge and experience might be useful to the people we spoke with; that the serious attention of an outsider to the continuing history of a venture provoked reflection, and led to a re-inspection of its history or a reappraisal of present strategies. Most obviously, we are acutely aware that what we write could assist or damage a venture's reputation with its funding bodies, and thus that we could influence the careers of people we regard as friends. Our objectivity is clouded by that friendship, and it means a possible complicity with particular factions within a company, or even with the mythologised histories which companies or factions within them can construct for themselves to legitimise strategic decisions in the present. We have learnt from Ric Knowles who has written, insightfully from personal experience, about the dangers involved in this sort of research (Knowles 1992). We are now unavoidably implicated in particular narratives of the histories of these ventures. Such complicity is an inevitable consequence of engaged research. We want our book to intervene in the debates which give this field of work its vitality (in an unfashionable parlance, to be an act of solidarity) rather than be a definitive, totalising description.

The structure of the book mirrors our research process. Chapters 1 and 2 describe the broad contexts, and are the result of a conventional process of literature searches. Thus Chapter 1 offers an account of the emergence of new, self-consciously 'political' theatres from the counter cultures of the 1960s and 1970s, and their initial attempts to embed themselves in the culture of the labour movement. Chapter 2 delineates the specific national contexts of the dialogic processes that helped to shape the ventures represented in our case studies. The next four chapters are the product of our field work, the case studies themselves. We then attempt to draw together the strands emerging from the case studies, and to delineate what they may imply for a continuing practice in the constantly changing context of what we still perceive as, at base, a battle between capital and labour, however confused that battle may have become.

Chapter One

Gravediggers of Capital: From Counter-Cultures to Worker-Student Alliances

The case studies we detail were ventures initiated almost entirely by artists whose political and cultural formation was in the 1960s and 1970s. This theatrical activity 'emerged' neither from the labour movement nor a tradition of left-wing theatre, but from *decisions* by people outside the labour movement whose political and social formation was very different from those within it. These ventures are thus generationally situated rather than a continuation of a consolidated tradition.

Counter-Cultural Protest

In Australia and Canada (the British situation is different, and will be discussed in Chapter 2), the founding figures of counter-cultural protest were predominantly the disaffected children of the bourgeoisie, thrown up by a postwar economic boom which led in turn to an explosion of tertiary education. This was a generation offered the opportunity during adolescence, that prime period of intellectual formation (when their parents had joined the workforce), to live the liminal life of the student. Their lifestyle helped to attenuate the connections with their parents' generation, and created different patterns of social alliance. Their parents, whose caution and social conformity was instilled by the Depression and World War II, saw their children's adventurous sense of social and political possibilities as a feckless disregard for the 'realities' of social life.

The boom in education offered large numbers the opportunity to think about social reality, and the intellectual and cultural wherewithal to do it. The affluence that made unemployment more a life-style choice (for some) than an affliction created the conditions for a middle-class bohemian radicalism to flourish. In rejecting the perceived conservatism of their elders, baby boomers constructed communal lifestyles built around music and modes of dress, re-occupying the run-down inner-city housing which their parents' generation had worked hard to escape. Once removed from the middle-class suburbs where most of them grew up, they were better able to perceive the moral ugliness that sustained 'the system'. The nodal point was the protest movement, which began in the United States in the mid-1960s, against the Vietnam war. This was particularly notable in Australia where the possibility of being drafted into the army, if less pressing than in the United States, was nonetheless real. It was also true in Canada, where the war was brought home daily on American television channels and which was deeply implicated in the business of war production while, at the same time, home to thousands of American draft dodgers.

As these bohemian radicals became more analytical, the war came to stand for more than just the threat of death in a foreign jungle for no convincing reason. An ambient opposition to war in general became more specific. The Vietnam war was revealed as an imperialist capitalist drive to secure resources, cheap labour and markets in South East Asia and this led to support for the nationalist struggle of the Viet Cong, and its leader, Ho Chi Minh. In Australia and Canada this meant a shift from the soft politics of opposition to war to the hard politics of a public (and in Australia, treasonable) support of the enemy.

In addition to the war there were a number of more locally-determined single issues (racism, the politics of gender and sexual preference, and ecology, for example) that galvanised the baby boomer generation. Their views, however, were not widely shared nor were they politics as conventionally understood, particularly by most of the labour movement. Indeed the anarchistic libertarianism that characterised their outlook eschewed the politically programmatic and resisted organisational structure almost as a point of principle. This gave rise on the one hand to an amazing inventiveness and strategic imagination. On the other, there was a continuing tendency for the loose alliances characteristic of the counter culture and the communalism built around lifestyle rather than party discipline to fragment and collapse when push came to shove. This inevitably led to the disillusionment, in effect a loss of innocence, which followed the worldwide defeats of counter-culture political activism in 1968. While the counter-cultural high points of that turbulent year have been mythologised in some circles as triumphs, at base they display the impotence of a politics unable to obtain purchase beyond the confines of its own loose membership.

As protest action stepped up, most famously in Paris but elsewhere in the western world as well, it was put down with increasingly brutal policing by states genuinely concerned that something untoward was happening. The naive assumption that partying in the streets and refusing to conform would produce social change by altering consciousness quickly gave way to one of two broad responses. The first was a retreat into 'opting out', either through the establishment of communal havens made possible by the economic boom or via the oblivion offered by a proliferating drug culture. The second was a radical rethinking of political activism. The relative impotence of counter-cultural activism became obvious as boom turned to bust in the mid-1970s, and economic realities began to assert themselves. Hippies began to discover their lack of influence on the 'straight' world that they had hitherto been able to disregard. When the counter-cultural movement appeared to have run its course, new political alliances were sought.

Guerilla Theatre

The clearest examples of this search for new political alliances emerged throughout the industrialised west in 'worker-student alliances' which were particularly noticeable from 1969, and from an increasing, if initially somewhat romantic, tendency towards Marxist analysis. Of particular attraction were Trotskyism and Maoism, especially the latter which offered the example, in retrospect greatly misunderstood, of the Chinese Cultural Revolution. Here were models for alliances between the intellectual and the downtrodden peasant, somewhat awkwardly and patronisingly applied to very different circumstances in the developed west, and converted into some tentative and fairly unsuccessful approaches to the organised labour movement. The widely circulated image of dancers *en pointe* with clenched fists and rifles in the Chinese revolutionary ballet *The Red Detachment of Women* held a romantic fascination for would-be revolutionaries in the west.

While revolutionary romanticism projected images of heroic third world students and workers joined in mass struggle, the reality in Australia and Canada, where the organised Left had been almost purged from the labour movement, was somewhat different. The points of mismatch were clear: while some left-wing unions and a few on the Left of the Labor Party in Australia had embraced the anti-Vietnam cause, many more unionists were hostile to feckless hippies not just because they were morally transgressive but also because they were middle-class outsiders who displayed little understanding of the labour movement and even less of the realities of working-class life. From the student perspective, the working class displayed a disappointing lack of revolutionary fervour. The most conspicuous of its members were just as likely to be arguing about sports results and swapping racist and sexist jokes in pubs as manning the barricades. In Australia workers stood on the side of the road during anti-Vietnam marches hurling abuse, and more, at the marchers. They looked nothing like heroic Vietnamese peasants valiantly throwing off the yoke of US imperialism. They seemed unimpressed by students, dressed in the style of Che Guevara in army surplus store clothes and berets, who wanted to lead them in the battle for a socialist utopia. They were even less impressed by the more romantically desperado activities of the 'guerilla armies' (the Symbionese Liberation Army and the Weathermen in the USA, the Baader-Meinhoff Gang in Germany, the Angry Brigade in Britain, the Red Brigade in Italy, for example) which began to engage the attention of student activists in the early 1970s.

The formative discovery, or rediscovery, of this period was the performative nature of the street demonstration. Locked out of conventional media channels, protesters discovered the 'theatrical' power of taking to the streets to demonstrate dissent, just as they discovered the power of the underground press. Street demonstrations moved from sombre displays of numbers marching in serried rows to theatricalisations of a lifestyle. Increasingly they took on the atmosphere of mobile street parties, inspired by the widely televised anarchistic guerrilla tactics of the Yippies and the spectacular effigies of Peter Schumann's Bread and Puppet Theatre towering above jubilant crowds in the United States, as well as the cunning media manipulations of the Situationist International in Europe.[1]

'Performance' became a natural mode of communication, which led to the discovery of a cheap theatrical means to disseminate dissident views, from street theatre to music (always music) to performances designed for non-theatrical venues, usually counter-culture gathering places, again inspired by American work, from the San Francisco Mime Troupe and Teatro Campesino to Bread and Puppet Theatre and the Living Theatre. Their work was promulgated through the pages of The Drama Review, the most

---

1. These street 'performances' are now the subject of academic attention. See Schechner 1992, Kershaw 1997 and Cohen-Cruz 1998.

self-consciously radical of the US academic theatre journals (which, because it carried photos of naked performers, was often banned, and therefore immensely attractive, in Australia).

These new dissidents well understood performance as media opportunity. By the early 1970s, the explosion of guerilla theatre in the student movement had generated a dazzling variety of forms and texts, mostly untheorised and unrecorded. In 1973, Henry Lesnick published a mass market paperback anthology of several dozen guerilla theatre texts from the United States in an attempt to document its range and at the same time argue its limitations. Critical of 'the antiworking class bias of middle class students', Lesnick argued in his introduction that:

> Many young middle class radicals have not had the experience which might contradict the dominant bourgeois assumption that we can transcend the fundamental facts of social life merely through isolated, individual effort. This kind of experience, coupled with an understanding of the power of collectivity, as it is seen in the organized production of modern industry or in the history of American and European labor struggles, would probably provide the basis for repudiating the classic bourgeois view of the transcendent role of the individual. But the middle class, in the absence of these experiences, in the absence of a class analysis and in the absence of a politically conscious mass working class movement turns to the much touted individual effort. (Lesnick 1973: 17)

The transcendental leftism that held sway within much of the counter-culture was obvious from its beginnings, and was particularly notable in the libertarianism of the politicised avant-garde theatre. In the year prior to Lesnick's book, Karen Malpede Taylor had tried to place street theatre in this context, which led her to valorise the most famous of these politicised avant-garde theatres, the Living Theatre, in her collection, *People's Theatre in Amerika* (Taylor 1972: 206–233). The notion of 'the people' as something apart from the class structures of social formation was clearly spelled out in the polarisation that *Village Voice* drama critic Arthur Sainer noted in his 1975 work, *The Radical Theatre Notebook*, which, like Taylor's book, saw the fruit of revolutionary activism in the interiorised collectivities of the avant-garde. In his conclusion, written as an open letter to the 'radical theatre community', Sainer records a meeting of radical artists which polarised discussion between Julian Beck and Judith Malina (of the Living Theatre), who argued that theatre must go to the 'poorest of the poor' and 'teach them our techniques so they can make their own theatre', and those including Richard Schechner who argued that artists first need to liberate their own psyches and souls (Sainer 1975: 361).

This politically sterile individualism was not just confined to the United States, although it had particular resonances in an American culture in which class politics had little purchase. At much the same time in Britain, where class politics was important, Howard Brenton saw a similar futility:

> I think the fringe has failed. Its failure was that of the whole dream of an 'alternative culture'—the notion that within a society as it exists you can grow another way of life, which like a beneficent and desirable cancer, will in the end grow throughout the western world, and change it. What happens is that the 'alternative society' gets hermetically sealed, and surrounded. A ghetto-like mentality develops. It is surrounded, and, in the end, strangled to death. Utopian generosity becomes paranoia as the world closes in. Naive gentleness goes to the wall, and Manson's murderousness replaces it. The drift from the loving drug scene in Amsterdam in the late 'sixties to the speed and wretchedness five years later illustrates this process. The truth is there is only one society—that you can't escape the world you live in. Reality is remorseless. No one can leave. If you're going to change the world, well, there's only one set of tools, and they're bloody and stained but realistic. I mean communist tools. Not pleasant. If only the gentle, dreamy, alternative society had worked. (Brenton 1975: 10–11)

The failure of the alternative was glaringly obvious to others as well, especially in the United States, where, as Lesnick argued, it died on the streets of Chicago in the police riots of the 1968 Democratic National Convention. After the riot:

> it was apparent to everybody that the reality which we had planned to make more vivid in our skits was, itself, more painfully immediate, explicit and grotesquely dramatic than any theater we could hope to present. ... No art could achieve the drama, intensity or scope of the reality—there could be no aesthetic 'heightening of reality'—and none of us at the time saw any alternative function for guerrilla theater and so we abandoned it. (Lesnick 1973: 21)

The Search for 'Working-Class' Theatre

The attraction of what Brenton bluntly called 'communist tools' was that they offered a way out of this impasse; to be effective, revolutionary theatre had to align with the working class (configured as 'the people', or sometimes 'working people', in North America and Australia, but very much the 'working class' in Britain), and for that tools had to be found. Or rediscovered, as Lesnick argued in his book:

> Though there might be some exceptions, people generally do not have to be told their reality is oppressive. Rather what is required is an analytic perspective on their oppression—knowledge of its causes, relatedness to other people's oppression, and correct strategies for ending it. The 'agit prop' theater of the thirties, which is the major American progenitor of contemporary guerilla theater, almost always attempted to provide this kind of analysis. ... Agit prop is a form of propaganda leading to action. (Lesnick 1973: 21–22)

Lesnick appended a selection of documents from the American Workers' Theatre Movement (WTM) of the 1930s to his collection of street texts. In so doing, he followed the example of Taylor, who had included the WTM as part of the 'people's theatre' she documented, in order to establish historical continuities of theatrical technique and political engagement:

> People who work in the theatre have a tremendous opportunity right now. For the first time we have the artistically convincing means to accomplish our revolutionary purpose.
>
> I couldn't have understood this without first going back to the 30s. It's this concrete knowledge of the painful, step-by-step advances in techniques—from activist endings to simultaneous texts—that gives me some hope for the future. (Taylor 1972: 2–3)

Lesnick and Taylor were not alone in their recognition that the 1930s offered a prehistory of radical theatre. In 1974, Jay Williams added another link in his sentimental narrative history of the New York theatre scene of the 1930s, *Stage Left*, in which he described meeting Left theatre groups in London in 1969:

> They spoke about abolishing the proscenium and taking theatre to the people, about performing in the streets, and they used words like 'agit-prop' and 'improvisation'. Their plays were heavy-handed and their acting often amateurish, but they were bursting with energy; they were irrational and sometimes incoherent, but along the way they fired off salvos in the most high spirited way at Church and State and any other institution that offered itself.
>
> It must have seemed new and fresh to them and to most of their audience. To me, however, it had all the nostalgia of a Currier and Ives print. It was

like a trip back to Grandma's house for Christmas, or watching kids play one o' cat in a school playground. Thirty-five years before, but in another country, I had been a member of a group something like these and we had used much the same language in describing what we were doing.

There was a profound difference. We had been at the hub of change. In America, we had been part of a metamorphosis; after us the American theatre was never the same again. (Williams 1974: 2–3)

Even if Williams' rather grandiose claim were true, there is little to indicate that the broad structures of American *society* were significantly changed, but myth-making usually entails a little looseness with mundane matters of fact.

British researchers analysed their own discontinuous tradition in an attempt to clarify the fundamental problem of a seemingly successful radical theatre that nevertheless failed to bring about the revolution. From its inception in 1971, *Theatre Quarterly* systematically recuperated the 'lost' history of the radical theatre, publishing articles on Unity Theatre, Theatre Workshop, the Workers' Theatre Movement in America, the Living Newspaper Unit of the Federal Theatre Project, and of course, Brecht. In its fourth issue, Roger Hudson wrote a lengthy editorial, under the title 'Towards A Definition of People's Theatre', in which he made an initial attempt to impose categorical coherence on the recuperated material. Although his definition showed the impossibility of systematising such disparate historical examples, it began the process of constructing a historical narrative. Hudson divided 'people's theatre' into five intersecting categories: '*Popular Theatre*' ('the area of popular culture'); '*Social Theatre*' ('culture for the masses' including 'Revivals of folk culture, folksong and dance'); '*Working Class Theatre*' ('aimed at working class audiences ... seen mainly to consist in romantic forms of naturalism and revivals of melodrama and music hall'); '*Political Theatre*' ('to encourage political awareness') and '*Revolutionary Theatre*' ('to create new revolutionary forms of theatre freed from the restrictions of feudal or capitalist society') (Hudson 1971: 100–1).

Of these, 'Political Theatre' was the most complex, because it was the theatre of instrumentality. Hudson subdivided it into a series of aims:

a) To describe 'objectively' or communicate a political interpretation...
b) To portray what is happening in other countries, other parts of the same country, or events in working class history.
c) To arouse emotionally or intellectually to action...

d) To strengthen solidarity...

e) To make aware of the possibility and desirability of change...

f) To demonstrate strategy and tactics... (Hudson 1971: 100)

Theatre with these aims was a vanguardist instrument for education. Hudson, though, warned his readers 'you may have to align your interpretations with those of the organisation calling the meeting or demo'.

The Discovery of Agitprop

Following the efforts of *Theatre Quarterly*, researchers sought to uncover not just the historical data but the buried debates on aesthetics and class form which surrounded the texts. Typical of many, but more diligent than most, were Richard Stourac and Kathleen McCreery, who took time out from work with Red Ladder and Broadside Mobile Workers' Theatre in Britain to engage in the research which produced their 1986 book, *Theatre as a Weapon*, a valuable account of the radical theatre movements of the 1920s and early 1930s in the Soviet Union, Germany and Britain. Similarly, in 1976 Robin Endres and Richard Wright excavated a lost history of Canadian workers' theatre texts in their collection *Eight Men Speak*, and in the United States Ira Levine's *Left-Wing Dramatic Theory in the American Theatre* (1985) attempted to delineate the contours of a long debate within the political theatre movements of the 1930s.

The perceived failure of the guerilla street theatre movement indicated a need to *engage* with a broader struggle, and the academic project of recuperating precedents offered theatrical methods. As guerilla theatre-makers carved out a niche on the fringes of the theatrical profession, they resituated their work; what had been guerilla street protest was now historically legitimised agitprop. But the awareness of precedents, abetted by heavy doses of Brechtian theory, was not in itself sufficient to forge links with working-class struggle. That could only be learnt on the ground, and it wasn't easy. A generational hostility to authority was often coupled with a naive, occasionally arrogant self-righteousness. The central assumption of too much of this early experimentation was that working-class people needed to be made aware of their exploitation. They needed Marxist analysis to understand its sources, and a young, middle-class intelligentsia to explain it to them. Approaches to them were sometimes as patronising as this sounds. Clive Barker has described the ethos that sometimes resulted in fairly scathing terms:

The Alternative Theatre in England during the early 1970s had too many examples of groups of students explaining to car-workers how the car-workers were exploited, a subject on which the car-workers were experts and the students were not. (Barker 1992: 32)

The response of unionists to the Melbourne-based Australian Performing Group's *Doctor Karl's Kure* may stand as indicative of a failure to connect. This was a popular theatre piece designed for outdoor performance which attempted to explain the ways in which Marxism offered a panacea for the systematic exploitation of the working class. The group which wrote and performed the play were mostly left-wing students from Monash University, who formed the 'political' faction of a large conglomerate of students who, as APG, became one of Australia's most important alternative theatre collectives. The piece was memorably performed before a May Day march in Melbourne in 1970, where it was announced by an aging union leader in a three-piece pinstripe suit as a bit of entertainment for those who didn't mind being late for the march.

What audiences saw (and workers more often ignored) in these agitprops were clever pastiches that lampooned authority and communicated attitudes rather than analysis through gags and slogans which Kershaw describes as a 'carnivalesque agitprop' quite different from its programmatic 1930s precursor (Kershaw 1992: 78-84). A representative example, which shows the anthology of cultural sources typical of agitprop, is this 1972 piece staged in a shopping mall in St. John's, Newfoundland, by the Mummers Troupe ostensibly to support striking cinema projectionists:

The Coronation of Cecil B. DeMille

NARRATOR: [*with drum*] This is the story of the Coronation of Cecil B. DeMille [*boom*].
Once when Cecil was a little boy, he saw a film.

Cecil appears as actor with cigar and rattle. Scene from Gone with the Wind *or something. Punch and Judy appear, do passionate love scene. Finally Judy talks.*

JUDY: Wait darling. I must go get something before we go any farther.
PUNCH: Hooboy this chick is hip.
NARRATOR: Little Cecil thought to himself, this is an X film.

Judy returns with stick clobbers Punch with some jabber, much chasing & off. Judy gives V sign, down.

Little Cecil felt something was wrong. He felt he could make bigger, better films. So [*boom*] when Little Cecil grew up, he was called Big Cecil [*Fatso appears*] Now, he became a director.

Big Cecil swaggers, is decorated with a sign that says 'Director'

And he made bigger & better films.

Frame up with sound (bugle blown, or pistol).

With a cast of thousands

A lot of paper cut-out faces, come up with a sudden 'AAAAH' sound, down.

And thousands [*same*] and thousands [*same*]. But of course the important part of the film was the about the star, the great Charlton Heston.

Punch appears.

PUNCH: Hi folks.

NARRATOR: Who was especially adored by audiences for his fine profile.

Punch turns, preens.

And his stunningly beautiful co-star, Carole Lombard.

Judy rises with a sign around neck saying 'Doris Day'.

Cecil B. DeMille told them all what to do. And he got bigger and bigger.

Cecil stands on a box.

He told the great Charlton Heston what to do.

PUNCH: AAAH. Heil.

NARRATOR: And CBDM told the great Carole Lombard what to do.

JUDY: AAAH. Heil.

NARRATOR: And CBDM told the cast of thousands what to do.

JUDY: AAAH.

NARRATOR: And Big Cecil B told everyone what to do.

All puppets up 'AAAH', also frame holder does 'AAAH'.

PUNCH / JUDY / FRAME HOLDER: AAAH.

NARRATOR: And Big Cecil got bigger & bigger.

Cecil stands on a box or on stairsteps.

Then Big Cecil ran out of people to tell what to do. So he bought theatres. Thousands of them. And he told audiences what to do.

Sign: 'Prices for this engagement $1 more'. Sign: 'All passes & senior citizen tickets to be suspended'.

And Big Cecil got bigger and bigger. Until finally Big Cecil is crowned King of the Movies [*music, etc*]. And he got HUGER and told everyone what to do. Everything and everybody was part of Cecil's movie. Until someone got tired of being in CB's movie

> *Frame holder quits and pickets around with strike sign.*

And the films stopped.

> *The Curtain turns around or Punch and Judy hold up banner and on it is written, 'Whose movie are you in?'*

> *Play 'Star Spangled Banner'. Over the banner rise signs saying 'only 58 shopping days til Xmas', 'Support the air cadets', etc*[1]

For the Mummers, the abject failure of their intervention was a critical lesson. Chris Brookes recalled in his memoir:

> We intended it as a strike support piece but it was a failure: sloppy, preachy and pretentious. Passers-by thought we were just another bunch of hippies doing silly street theatre. They were right. (Brookes 1988: 46)

Richard Seyd, a founder member of the London-based Agitprop Street Players (which later became Red Ladder, one of the most important of the left-wing touring groups which appeared throughout Britain in the 1970s), describes a similar salutary lesson during a strike in Dagenham in 1969:

> On our own initiative we constructed an outdoor play, *Stick Your Penal Up Your Bonus* (the title was its only redeeming feature), and took it down to Ford's to show to the workers collecting their strike pay. There we tried, unsuccessfully, to get the attention of the workforce. We had no organisational relationship with the workers at Ford's or their trade unions. We might just as well have been selling cut-price carpets as trying to put over socialist ideas within a theatrical framework (in fact we might have got more attention if we had). (Seyd 1975: 36)

Red Ladder's response to this experience, their first of trying to play to industrial workers, was to seek closer links with the labour movement which would legitimate their performances for union audiences: 'We realised ... that we had to relate to working people through their own organisations and not stay on the outside of the labour movement' (Seyd

---

1. The scenario of 'Cecil B. DeMille' survives in handwritten draft in the archival files of the Mummers Troupe, kept by Chris Brookes in St John's, Newfoundland.

1975: 36). The company thus embarked on a year of discussions with union contacts in the process of devising a play, then spent 'weeks of delicate negotiations' for permission to perform it at a union conference.

Hippies Meet Unionists

Red Ladder were not alone in deciding not to 'stay on the outside'. In Australia, the APG in Melbourne and the Brisbane-based Popular Theatre Troupe (PTT) formed close informal alliances with particular union officials to establish touring circuits of working-class venues, particularly workplaces. This set in train the slow process of breaking down the distance between theatreworkers and the audiences they aspired to influence. In Britain and Australia, this movement towards the unions as the site of working-class organisation was facilitated by the public presence of trade unions in politics, in the British Labour Party and the Australian Labor Party. The route was more or less directly charted, although the journey wasn't always quick or easy, and the resistance was not all on the side of unionists. Allen Lyne, originally from the Popular Theatre Troupe, was still complaining of an 'us' and 'them' attitude in companies by the mid-1980s:

> Most people working in the field know nothing about their own union, let alone anyone else's; or about the trade union movement generally—its history, its direction, its strengths and weaknesses. In two supposedly political theatre companies I've had to insist that the staff become unionised. (Lyne 1987: 48)

In North America, the route to union solidarity was less direct but equally inevitable. Canadian groups like the Mummers Troupe came into contact with unions as the consequence of reaching out to 'the people', part of a widespread postcolonial quest for cultural authenticity which sought popular sources. The Mummers Troupe went from agitprop to revivals of traditional Newfoundland mummers plays, and from there to documentary 'people's histories'. This brought them into a direct contact with local unions in small communities.

The differences in national context, which we outline in the next chapter, gave rise to particularised strategies, as our case studies show. But in each case we see aspects of the political education of a generation, as hippies became political activists, bringing their different politics to the elaborate and extensive organisational structures of a class-based movement with a long history.

Exhuming 'Working-Class Theatre': The Second International

The working-class culture that theatre activists sought in their initial encounters with labour was comprised of diverse, often tenuous practices and expressed a vast range of local and regional traditions which frequently intersected with other spheres of popular culture. Within labour traditions, cultural activism showed the formative influence of the Second International Workingmen's Association Congress in Paris in 1889, a loose worldwide alliance of trade unions and social organisations. The intellectual orthodoxy established by the Second International held sway within the labour movement until its collapse with the outbreak of war in 1914, and vestiges of this orthodoxy have never gone away. The short term plan was that the affiliated groups would organise themselves into political parties to fight for reform through conventional political channels. While this would not produce socialism in itself, it would prepare the working class to take power when the revolutionary moment inevitably arrived. A characteristically simplistic reading of Marx suggested this would happen when the proletariat was sufficiently consolidated, organised and, above all, *educated*, and once the European Depression of the 1890s had deepened into a 'crisis' of capitalism.

Essential to the Second International was an assumption spelt out by Polish historian Leszek Kolakowski: 'Workers who were left to the mercy of capitalists, deprived of education and stupefied by toil, would never be capable of playing their part in the socialist revolution' (Kolakowski 1978: 8). This placed an immediate stress on the educative role of an intellectual vanguard that had not been 'stupefied by toil', in short, a disaffected bourgeois intelligentsia, or what in Canada were referred to as 'brainworkers'. In Britain, Australia and Canada, it also led to the formation of political parties which saw socialism as a matter of gradual social reform through parliamentary means. In Germany, on the other hand, where the biggest socialist party in the world, the Social Democratic Party, was essentially illegal, it produced a much more radical line, led by a formidable group of bourgeois intellectual Marxists. In all cases, though, the task of education was taken on in full seriousness, and the late nineteenth century saw the emergence of an elaborate network of workers' education organisations, self-education groups, social clubs, amateur drama clubs, workers' choirs, debating societies and the like.

Art and culture viewed in a very particular way had a central role to play in all this. As British historian Raphael Samuel has claimed, the Second International 'worshipped at the shrine of art; it conceived itself as a messenger of high culture, bringing education and enlightenment to the masses' (Samuel, MacColl and Cosgrove 1985: xvii). Art, thus envisaged, was largely the province of a bourgeois intellectual vanguard, that brought to its task high art models, reflected in the iconography of the union banners of the period. Samuel argues that the literary and artistic origins of British socialism in particular were characterised by a 'vision of the socialistic future' oddly linked to 'the Golden Age of the past' revealed in the visual art of William Morris and Walter Crane (whose iconography dominated the earliest banners), and the enthusiasm of socialist orators for larding their speeches with citations from Shelley, Whitman and particularly Shakespeare. Socialism, like art, 'exalted the masses; it transported them from the mean conditions of their everyday existence to a state of imaginary transcendence' (Samuel, MacColl and Cosgrove 1985: 4). Art and culture, and theatre other than 'popular' forms like melodrama, were seen as a means of emancipation from working-class experience under capitalism. This was not a case of art recruited to the cause of class struggle, but of art as a means of humanising a degraded class.

The theatre which emerged as part of this project was essentially amateur, and modelled on the high art theatre which working people could not afford to see. It was seen as an antidote to the more affordable populist melodrama, on the grounds that popular culture was corrupting and intellectually demeaning. The strongest manifestations of this reformist zeal can be seen in the attempts by theatreworkers on the fringe of the labour movement to establish various forms of 'People's Theatre', particularly in France, during the period of the Second International (Bradby and McCormick 1978: 30–44). These were predominantly the work of bourgeois sympathisers rather than party activists, often more concerned with the rejuvenation of the theatre and the consolidation of 'the nation' than with furthering the cause of the working class (Kruger 1992: 31–82). Similar projects in Germany produced the *Volksbuhne*, a vast organisational structure of union-based subscriptions to the mainstream theatres. Although this was not the source of a distinctly radical theatre, it did help the construction of an audience for the work of new playwrights like Ibsen and Hauptmann (Davies 1977). Most of the theatre generated by these movements has disappeared, and was, in any case, of little interest to theatre practitioners in the 1970s who sought specifically working-class traditions of performance. They were drawn towards the more radical tradition produced when, following the collapse of the Second International and the disappearance of the international solidarity it was meant to reflect (or at least sustain), it became clear that socialism had to be made rather than just waited for. This meant that working-class consciousness had to be rebuilt, consolidated and maintained. Under the influence of these new felt imperatives, a more radical and instrumentalist view of culture emerged, nowhere more clearly than in the theatre.

In the 1970s, artsworkers exhumed or inspired the exhumation of this material, largely to discover radical labour movement traditions within which to work. The substantial literature that emerged on a hitherto neglected area of theatre history coincided with a new interest in the experimental theatre practice of Brecht and Piscator, with the former becoming a theoretical touchstone for most left-wing theatre practice and the latter revived as the principal prophet of a theatre specifically aimed at militant working-class audiences. What emerged was a picture of a vital and radical cultural tradition which reached its zenith in the 1930s.

A significant feature of this new work was that it rejected the notion of theatre as a civilising extension of a national culture to which the working class had been denied access. Instead, the value of theatre lay in the extent to which it expressed a distinct transnational working-class culture. Under such a notion, 'high' art became—as popular culture had been for the Second International—a means of ideological control, an apparatus for the generation of the 'false consciousness' which legitimated the dominance of a ruling class. There are signs of such a view emerging towards the end of the period of the Second International, for example within the *Volksbuhne*, which constantly split and reformed over the issue of whether art should be viewed as a means of spiritual and moral uplift, on the one hand, or more instrumentally as a means of political activism on the other. By 1910, the *Freie Volksbuhne* journal published an internal debate, which prefigured some of the major debates on the Left in the postwar years. In it a member proposed 'proletarian art' as an antidote to the *Freie Volksbuhne*, which, he claimed had become a 'consumer association for retailing bourgeois art' (Davies 1977: 74). While this position received little support at the time, and the *Volksbuhne* held to the orthodoxy of the Second International, it signalled a growing tendency to view theatre as part of a broader, class-based political project.

Proletkult, the Popular Front and the Rise and Fall of Agitprop

In Russia, the *Proletkult* movement was the focal point of a huge network of proletarian cultural and educational organisations which briefly (1917–1920) achieved the status of a government agency following the Revolution of 1917 (Ermolaev 1977: 9–54). *Proletkult* was, among other things, committed to the destruction of professional theatre in Russia, advocating instead a participatory form of theatre with some similarities to the People's Theatre movements of France (Russell 1988: 25–51). Most importantly, it formalised the notion of constructing an international proletarian culture from within the working class in opposition to bourgeois culture. This notion, if not *Proletkult* itself, produced the two main offspring behind the radical theatre of the 1920s and 1930s, namely, the large scale outdoor pageant and the agitprop movement.

The pageant took off in Germany in particular, (Davies 1980: 79–84) and has been documented as part of a British Communist Party cultural strategy from the 1930s through to the early 1950s (Wallis 1994, 1995). Mass spectacles such as those Piscator staged for the German Communist Party may be seen as one of the precursors to the processional performances of the 1970s, although there is little to suggest that their influence has been particularly strong. Our Darwin case study shows that the performances of May Day celebrations in recent years, for example, owe more to the work of Welfare State International in Britain and Bread and Puppet Theatre in the USA, which have drawn on much older, carnivalesque performances. The communist pageants in Europe did not survive as a model for the radical theatre groups of the 1970s, in part because this sort of mass spectacle requires resources and organisation far beyond the reach of small theatre troupes, and because the form was so successfully appropriated by the Nazis in Germany and Mussolini in Italy, effectively disproving the assumption that the mass proletarian spectacle was inherently revolutionary.

The other, more successful offspring was the agitprop movement. In the English-speaking world agitprop troupes emerged as loose amateur groupings around the edges of the communist parties. They found audiences at marches and rallies during the 1926 General Strike in Britain and at those provoked by the worldwide Depression which followed the Wall Street crash of 1929. By the late 1920s the troupes were tied into a transnational network through the International Workers' Dramatic Union (by 1932 the International Union of Revolutionary Theatres), centred in Moscow, although local styles developed in each country, and even in particular cities. Agitprop attracted theatreworkers in the 1970s, often with a degree of romanticism. This was an unsurprising response to the stories of commitment, courage and resourcefulness, and to the stirring photographs of youths in overalls striking heroic poses that filled the books about the movement which appeared at this time. Even if it wasn't the full picture, this inspirational history was quickly accorded the status of centrepiece of a radical theatrical 'tradition'.

Closer inspection might have helped avoid some humiliating mistakes about the supposed homogeneity of working-class culture at this time. In fact, agitprop was the small tip of a large iceberg of labour movement theatre. In Britain, for example, amateur productions of the plays of Shaw, Ibsen and Shakespeare sat side by side with the agitprop of the Hackney People's Players or the Salford Red Megaphones. Douglas Allen, writing on the Glasgow Workers' Theatre Group, offers a useful corrective to common conclusions about a consolidated radical culture. He writes about a Communist Party initiative on a Glasgow winter evening in 1937, advertised in the *Daily Worker* and taking place in the Trade Union and Workers' Club:

> What is on the agenda? A trade union discussion on the latest unemployment figures? A Left Book Club meeting to analyse Hitler's latest moves and promote the case for a Popular Front? A film show with the latest scenes from war-torn Spain? Not exactly. Tonight's attraction is a 'Gramophone Recital', with, as featured items, Leoncavallo's *Pagliacci* and Mascagni's *Cavalleria Rusticana*. It is for this that dozens of men and women—after maybe ten hours at work, and with only a hurried tea—are making their way through the Glasgow streets.

Allen argued for the need to 'penetrate the popular received picture of 1930s activity [with its] ... concentration on the romantic, the dramatic, the picturesque, the extraordinary'. In 'mythologising and romanticising' the agitprop moment, Allen wrote in 1980, activists were indifferent to, and ignorant, or simply dismissive, of 'the "great art" produced by bourgeois culture' which the Glasgow Workers' Theatre Movement embraced, albeit selectively. For Allen this exemplified 'the gap between the contemporary bourgeois intellectual world view and the self-educative, culture-hungry outlook of the old working-class community' (Allen 1980: 45, 53).

The inadequacies of the view that there were essential working-class forms that stood outside the specificities of social context can be seen in the ideological realignment of agitprop in the 1930s. The theoretical defence of agitprop as a new working-class aesthetic for the machine age was domesticated, as Communist Party politics changed, and reconciled with the bourgeois humanism which earlier it had militantly opposed.

Agitprop had been proposed in the 1920s as a transnational form that modelled the historical process of revolutionary change in the international proletariat, whose class unity and industrially reconfigured social relations would render national cultural differences obsolete. Theatre was a weapon, the movement's motto proclaimed, and like all weapons, it was a transcultural technology that erased differences. But agitprop was never an unmediated practice. It is commonly ascribed to the Blue Blouses of the Bolshevik revolutionary period, yet its template in the west was the highly disciplined, German-style mass drill, especially after the emigration of the German Left once the Nazis came to power. We can see this in the texts written by the German émigré John Bonn of the New York *Prolet Buehne* which were characterised by numbered performers and a mathematically arranged mass declamation (Samuel, MacColl and Cosgrove 1985: 301–315; Taylor 1972: 43–47). Although the severe, machine-gun style of the German agitprop had been adapted as the international template for agitprop, it had been challenged from the beginning by regional and local forms, drawing on vaudeville, sideshows, 'red puppets' and 'revolutionary circus' (to cite only a few American examples).

These local practices were, however, partially written out of the theory and historical writing because their artistic anarchism contradicted the industrial values of what might be called theatrical Taylorism, after the American time and motion expert whose ideas greatly influenced Meyerhold's theories of biomechanics and had currency in the Soviet Union in the 1920s. In the theatre, these industrial values foregrounded proletarian principles of craft, discipline and rigour; in a fairly obvious analogy, theatrical work was seen as replicating the dynamic and physicality of industrial labour, and the artistic form it produced was, like the automobile rolling off the lines in Detroit, a technological artefact. And like an automobile, its properties were defined by its method of production and social function. When radical troupes in the 1930s spoke of agitprop as a 'weapon' they weren't simply romanticising the political stance of the artist, but describing the depersonalised industrial quality of the work they produced, just as a later development of community theatreworkers would refer to their artistic forms as 'tools'.

The Popular Front

The proposal that agitprop was a proletarian instrument that embodied the aesthetic of the machine age evaporated as the communist parties— agitprop's chief sponsors   laid down the tools of revolution to join the

Popular Front. This move to the mainstream was the central principle of an international strategy, which was formally ratified by the Communist International in August 1935, under which communist parties around the world were advised to drop the 'class against class' struggle that had dominated revolutionary politics since the onset of the 'Third Period' of Communism in 1929. Theatreworkers, along with activists across the whole spectrum of political and cultural struggle, were enjoined to replace the revolutionary stance of agitprop with a 'theatre of action' designed to cement alliances with sympathetic factions of the middle class in the fight against fascism. The Popular Front also rehabilitated the notion of national culture, so that local and popular traditions were increasingly seen as the culturally resistant voice of the majority, rather than the rarefied tastes of the elite. This was an important step because it allowed radical theatre activists to pursue careers in the professional theatre, it enabled artists like Joan Littlewood to recruit Shakespeare and Ben Jonson as 'people's theatre', and it recuperated stage realism (oppressively so in the Soviet Union) as an artistic mode. In the late 1920s, radical theatre debates focused on the relative merits and class affinities of the mobile and stationary stage (mobile good, stationary bad, of course); by the mid-1930s the dialogue had moved away from questions of form and class property to engage with the issue of social value.

This push to solidarity in the theatre had been building since the early 1930s (Goldstein 1974: 37–38; Levine 1985). It was first noticeable in the changing terms of critical reception, which increasingly equated artistry with realism and introduced the narrative of the crude, the inartistic and the politically futile that detractors still use to de-legitimise agitprop. In Britain and Australia the move to the mainstream produced Unity Theatre and New Theatre respectively by the end of the 1930s, both ventures which increasingly eschewed touring in favour of in-house performances in their own theatre buildings, and moved towards a position that reproduced some of the attitudes to art and culture which had characterised the period of the Second International. Colin Chambers indicates the shift:

> Unity wanted to overcome the working class's historical exclusion from the dominant culture by appropriating and transforming the 'best' that the bourgeoisie had developed whilst trying to create its own tradition too. Within this intention, partly in reaction to the extreme attitudes and isolation of the WTM and partly following the Popular Front approach, there was a strong current of thought that believed Unity should be taken

seriously as a 'proper' theatre, a tendency that became more overt as Unity became more successful. (Chambers 1989: 51)

As a result, the work of these Popular Front ventures became increasingly indistinguishable from the theatrical mainstream, and certainly less attractive to those in search of a class-specific theatrical tradition, despite their continuing but increasingly tenuous labour movement connections. Chambers points out that both the 'new wave' of socialist playwrights of the 1950s and 1960s in Britain (such as Arnold Wesker and John Arden) and the groups which emerged in the early 1970s saw Unity as 'an irrelevance' (Chambers 1989: 386). Thus when John McGrath catalogued the theatrical precursors of his own practice of political theatre in his highly influential book on popular political theatre, *A Good Night Out*, he excluded Unity altogether (McGrath 1981).

Popular front dramas offered little to those in search of a specifically working-class theatre: Unity actually expelled Roland and Claire Muldoon, the founders of Cartoon Archetypal Slogan Theatre (CAST), the first British foray into working-class theatre in the 1960s. In 1977, when a consortium of some new companies presented a proposal designed to keep Unity's London theatre alive as a venue, the Unity membership rejected it at the Annual General Meeting (Chambers 1989: 396).

Agitprop was thus put aside in the mid-1930s, gradually in some places, abruptly in others, as the Popular Front came to the fore. The values of craft and artisanship were translated into the new vocabulary of aesthetics via the adoption of methodical creative processes—of which Stanislavsky provided the most widespread, enduring and misunderstood. Stanislavsky's techniques were circulated originally through Left theatre companies, for whom his pseudo-scientific psychology, his emphasis on the actor's work, his defence of realism and the not insignificant fact that he was Russian, blended together in an irresistible package. Stanislavsky provided the means by which modern socialist artists could build on the cultural resources of the past.

Despite the alignment with national culture, Left theatres still believed artistic technique was a transnational practice that modelled and reflected an international working-class experience, coded in terms of 'discipline', 'craft' and 'method'. But by the 1960s, the embedded industrial values of the old Left theatre came under attack as conservative and reactionary. A striking example of this inversion of the meaning of working-class culture can be seen in Canada in Toronto Workshop Productions, where George

Luscombe (who had worked with Joan Littlewood's Theatre Workshop at Stratford East and had returned to Canada and continued working in that tradition for 25 years) produced brilliant work that strictly adhered to a notion of popular high art. Like Littlewood he theatricalised nontheatrical sources to produce collective creations and verbatim documentaries (on subjects like the Spanish Civil War and the Depression), and staged popular classical literature. Luscombe's allegiance to high art traditions and a notion of artistry was firmly grounded in the work of Stanislavsky and Rudolf Laban.[1] He equated this notion of rigorous artistic discipline with a mastery of industrial craft. Like Littlewood before him, he believed that political theatre needed the resources of a sophisticated theatre plant to express its fullest artistic possibilities. To accept less (as most political theatreworkers do) is to accept marginalisation, and deprive the artistic worker of the necessary tools for the job.

One of the unfortunate results of this was a theatre which became increasingly indistinguishable, on a superficial level at least, from the mainstream theatre which had been the enemy in the early 1930s. It began to draw audiences from a wide social spectrum rather than play to the working class in a theatrical language which emerged from a distinctly class-based culture—even as the notion of class culture was supplanted by a less essentialised idea of class as practice.

Hasty Panaceas

As much as theatreworkers wished for it in the early 1970s, there was no ready-made class-specific theatrical form waiting to be rehabilitated to capture the attention of working-class audiences. What Douglas Allen describes as the 'socialist counter-culture' of the 1930s—'a body of activities as diverse and comprehensive as the "counter-culture" of the late 1960s, but with a more specific socialist ideology underpinning and unifying it' (Allen 1980: 54)—offered a bewildering plethora of theatrical styles and forms, many of which indicated a more ready accommodation with middle-class culture than the new generation of political theatreworkers wanted. Agitprop was the exception, but its valorisation was not entirely useful.

---

1. For an account of Luscombe's theatrical background and methods see Filewod 1987: 52-79.

The attractions of agitprop were obvious. It was a populist form designed to be performed anywhere, which meant it sat well with the guerilla street performances of the late 1960s. It favoured the presentation of broad representative figures over the naturalistic portrayal of surface reality, giving it an explanatory force attractive to a movement which saw itself as a radical intellectual vanguard. It constituted an oppositional form to the mainstream theatre, as much dominated by the naturalistic habit in the 1960s and 1970s as it had been in the 1930s, and also to the ascendant forms of the period, popular television and film. Its tactical interventionism, and the rhetoric which constructed it as a class-specific weapon of political struggle, appealed to a movement concerned to make cultural work a tool of political activism. Research was beginning to reveal the extent of a hitherto forgotten body of work, which gave credence to attempts to see it as a buried manifestation of a quintessentially working-class culture that, if revived, would allow access to working-class audiences in the present.

The initial rush to discover hasty panaceas, however, obscured some awkward facts. Agitprop was not a class-specific form, but a brief attempt to impose one on the broader labour movement by a communist faction, whose influence had waned substantially since the 1930s. As Douglas Allen has made clear, the labour movement was never as culturally homogeneous as some 1960s and 1970s romanticisations suggested, and even if the 'working-class consciousness' upon which agitprop relied could be assumed in 1930 it could not in 1975. As Richard Seyd pointed out in Britain, '[i]f people don't think that capitalism is an absurd and damaging way of organising society then very little that one does in an agit-prop piece is going to change their minds' (Seyd 1975: 40). Further, the 'tradition' of left-wing theatre that artsworkers sought to tap via agitprop in the 1970s was at best a tenuous one, and its connections with the trade union movement could not be assumed. The discovery of traditions of cultural activism within the trade union movement awaited a period of protracted dialogue with theatreworkers. This process proceeded differently, and produced different results, in each of our four case studies. We shall discuss the contexts which shaped these differences in the next chapter.

Chapter Two:

Coming to Labour Culture

'The recovery of a radical past, it was felt, could in some way confirm a contemporary radical practice'.

Ian Burn (Cited in Kirby 1996: 61).

The strongest initial impulse of political theatreworkers in the early 1970s was to make theatre for 'the people'. Few radical populist theatre groups at the time engaged with unions (although funding opportunities led more of them to do so in Australia), and their construction of 'the people' commonly led to a populist sense of community framed by region or cultural localism. They repudiated mass market stereotypes and sought to revive what they saw as the suppressed 'real' culture of popular life, and create models of 'people's theatre'. Not surprisingly, such groups, particularly in Canada, often found their evidence of populist culture in rural and regional areas. A much smaller group who brought a Marxist-inspired construction of 'the people' as 'working people' or the 'working class' (like the Red Ladder that Richard Seyd describes) sought organised labour with its promise of the articulation and organisation of class consciousness.

Theatre activists and unionists met at flashpoints of struggle, especially on picket lines in media-inflamed strike actions. Although street theatre and agitprop were welcome signs of public solidarity for unions at these times, such struggles were the exception rather than the rule of union work, and thus provided an illusionary beginning. That first generation which looked to unions as the site of revolutionary activism quickly found a different reality. While some unions were more radical than others, all shared the same day-to-day work of membership drives and collective bargaining, and they were more committed to pragmatic reformism than revolutionary change. When theatre activists discovered that most union activism happened around a table, rather than on the picket line, many dropped by the wayside; those who didn't learnt how to accommodate the realities of union work and to work within labour culture.

For many, this process clarified the differences between labour culture and working-class culture, two formations that have often been confused. The differences are crucial, because as Canadian labour historian Bryan Palmer notes, working-class culture is not a 'transhistorical culturalist class essence of unambiguous unity' but 'the connective tissues of an ambiguous realm of everyday life that bridged the chasm separating class as a silent structure and class as a potent force of revolutionary change' (Palmer 1992: 20). The idea of a more historically specific and localised 'labour culture' provided artists with a frame that highlighted the intersection of what Palmer calls 'indigenous local manifestations of a popular, as opposed to a truly mass, culture' and the practice of an oppositional class politics (Palmer 1992: 20).

This entailed a process of learning. The construction of the militancy of the late 1920s and early 1930s as a norm, and of agitprop as its clearest artistic reflection, led to assumptions about union cultural traditions that did not bear close scrutiny. When artists and researchers began to excavate the 'lost' history of the radical theatre, they embarked on a somewhat romantic search for a labour arts tradition, and made some valiant attempts to recuperate it. This happened on the local level, as we see in the work of Ian Burn and Sandy Kirby in Australia, and Carole Condé and Karl Beveridge in Canada. It also happened on the institutional level, as witnessed by the establishment of the Workers Cultural Heritage Centre in Hamilton, Ontario, and in Britain, the Working Class Movement Library in Salford (Ewan MacColl's first stomping ground), and the National Museum of Labour with branches in London and Manchester.

These searches uncovered a rich but fragmented cultural history, initially apparent in traditional ceremonials, such as Labour Day, May Day and Eight-Hour Day processions, which, although languishing, were nonetheless honoured. Such events drew attention to the iconographic history of the labour movement revealed through the banners occasionally brought out for the marches. Artsworkers and young labour historians uncovered more of these, often dragging them out of dusty store-rooms after years of neglect. With them came badges, membership certificates, old copies of union journals, photographs and memorabilia, attesting to a strong, almost all-encompassing social life centred on the union movement, a network of sporting and social clubs, workers' education organisations and libraries. The banners in particular revealed an extraordinary heritage, as Ann Stephen and Andrew Reeves document in their book on the Australian labour movement, *Badges of Labour, Banners of Pride: Aspects of Working Class Culture*. But the fact that most of the banners hadn't been seen for thirty years should have been as revealing as their existence in the first place.

The recuperation of labour culture in the early 1970s, then, owed more to visual artsworkers, folk singers, theatreworkers and a new generation of labour historians than it did to the labour movement itself. Reeves admitted that, as 'with most other aspects of union history, cultural activity has enjoyed years of strength and weakness. Currently, union cultural activity is enjoying a resurgence that commenced about 1970' (Reeves 1988: 31). In fact Reeves himself helped to produce that resurgence in Australia through his work at the Museum of Victoria and the organisation of the travelling exhibition that *Badges of Labour* accompanied. Others like Sandy Kirby and Ian Burn were similarly diligent. Their work uncovered the history of labour arts as 'always already' invented, always in the process of being rediscovered, or re-articulated. This recuperative work showed that there was no one essential 'moment' of paradigmatic labour art by which modern work might be measured and authenticated. Instead, labour art was a process of historic invention in which 'contemporary radical practice' (especially banners and music) could be confirmed as part of a 'radical past', rather than standing outside this tradition as a modern revisionist wish fulfilment.

While the visual art 'tradition' could be reconstructed through the old banners, there were no equivalent artefacts in the search for a theatre tradition. The death of agitprop some forty years earlier should have meant something. Theatreworkers didn't find a living tradition of performance activity within the movement, or anything which bore comparison to the romanticised picture of class-based radicalism. The recuperated literature of the workers' theatre movement evoked a vision of labour mobilised through cultural action but contemporary labour practice failed to confirm the myth. Some vestiges of a performance tradition remained—labour movement rituals were still happening—but all were moving into a decline, and the movement showed little interest in revitalising them.

Even in the 1930s, the union movement had no homogeneity, no single 'culture' and no real unity of purpose, despite mostly communist-inspired attempts to define them. Like the union movement of the 1970s, it was predominantly impelled by a pragmatic concern with immediate ends (wages and conditions in particular industries) rather than a commitment to broad social change. Artists had expected to find in the labour movement a repository of working-class cultural artefacts, or even a living working-class culture; what they found instead was a fragmented history of tactical deployments and antiquated ceremonials and, except in pockets, no perception of the potency of cultural work.

More than anything else, it was the discovery that labour culture was a contingent set of responses rather than a formal archive of methods and structures that shaped the way theatreworkers found a place in the sphere of union work. Their stage was not class, but class consciousness. They learned through their work the fundamental principle that class, as Palmer argues, is:

> nameless, faceless, a fundamental but inarticulate social entity. It produces, by definition, although the understanding of what production is and how it is valued has undergone shifts and transformations over the course of the nineteenth and twentieth centuries. But beyond this production, class as a structured objective socio-economic relationship does nothing. It takes on voices through what it does out of this material situation. It speaks, not so much with words of surplus produced, profits generated, and labour forces restructured (for these are, after all, more capital's words than labour's) but with languages of resistance and accommodation. (Palmer 1992: 23)

The working class was obviously not something one could simply join; it was a social structure in which one was positioned by economic relations. How artists came to an understanding of the complexities of class consciousness as something to be recuperated, or even manufactured, and defined their place was shaped by the specificities of their routes to labour engagement in Australia, Canada and Britain, which we will now examine.

Australia: From Community Arts to Art and Working Life
Australian Unionism and Cultural Activity

The Australian labour movement emerged with the formation of craft-based unions in the early nineteenth century, the not particularly radical 'aristocrats of labour'. Their ascendancy was superseded by a huge influx of unskilled workers in the 1870s and 1880s, most notably rural workers in the Shearers' Union. But the radical unionism which resulted had all but collapsed by 1892, following a series of disastrous industrial defeats. It was a rearguard evacuation of industrial militancy in favour of action in the political sphere that produced the Australian Labor Party (ALP) at this time. This awkward alliance of socialists, union activists, radical nationalists and middle-class reformers actually held the balance of power in the New South Wales parliament in 1891, and further electoral success did much to give Australian unionism its characteristic forms and strategies.

Australian labour at first glance appears to be enviably strong until the end of the 1980s. Union organisation of the workforce was the highest in the world in the 1920s and it remained close to 50% until well into the 1980s. Yet the 'Australian variant of labourism' was characterised by 'a peculiarly narrow conception of working-class interests' with a social and economic policy restricted to 'A high level of employment (for white, unionised males) and good wages and conditions for those in employment':

> Broader notions of social justice, and of a powerful welfare state in aid of it, were conspicuous by their absence. Under the banner of labourism, unions lent their support to White Australia, protectionism and compulsory arbitration.
>
> These three pillars of early labourism illustrate the latter's character as the political expression of craft unionism. (Ewer, Higgins and Stevens 1987: 8)

Compulsory arbitration, a feature of Australian industrial relations until it was effectively dismantled in the 1990s, delivered comparatively high wages through legally binding agreements known as 'awards' and facilitated high union density by virtually rendering union membership compulsory. But compulsory arbitration also centralised union activism, weakening shop-floor involvement and rendering it, at worst, pragmatic, self-serving and politically unimaginative. An elaborate organisational structure emerged, centred on the Australian Council of Trade Unions (ACTU). While the ACTU remains a powerful and occasionally radicalising influence on the ALP, it has mostly been a reformist ALP which has shaped the movement's political agenda. Radical unionism built on a consolidated sense of working-class culture has been the exception rather than the rule, and often brutally suppressed.

Union density remained as high as it did in the 1970s and 1980s because of the unionisation and affiliation of large numbers of white-collar workers from public sector clerical officers and service industry employees to university academics, which compensated for the decline of the older industrial unions. (It is significant that the immediate past President of the ACTU was not a man from one of the older manufacturing industry unions, but a woman of non-English-speaking background from the Teachers' Federation, Jennie George and that her successor, Sharan Burrow, also has Teachers' Federation and Australian Education Union credentials.) These demographic changes have further eroded the sense in which the labour movement may be seen as a repository of an unproblematised working-class culture based in manufacturing industry. They have also given rise to a drift towards 'social unionism', which is characterised by a concern with causes beyond pragmatic issues of wages and conditions in particular industries, although this can also be attributed to the continuing activities of radical factions within the movement, like the Builders' Labourers' Federation's espousal of issues of ecology and urban development, and consequent alliances with groups far beyond the union movement, in the late 1960s and early 1970s.

The movement's ninety-year reliance on compulsory unionism made it particularly vulnerable to international changes in the nature of work especially with the rise of casual service sector work, in which unions have always struggled to recruit members. Most importantly, though, Australian unionism has been unable to counter the effects of what David Peetz has referred to as an 'institutional break' in industrial relations, an internationally-driven 'decollectivisation of the employment relationship' which, in Australia, has spelt the end of compulsory unionism, particularly since it became a central target of employer groups and conservative state governments in the 1990s, and the federal government since the defeat of Labor in 1996 (Peetz 1998: 84-90). This is despite some of the most important structural changes in the movement this century which the ACTU negotiated with the federal government when Labor was in power (1983–1996). A series of Prices and Incomes Accords policed wage restraint and a program of amalgamations designed to pool resources led to a small group of 'super unions' which negotiated with government and employer groups on macroeconomic planning.

The second phase of the Accord process also entailed a shift, with legislative support from the federal government, to Enterprise Bargaining, which was designed to counter the traditionally weak level of workplace organisation in Australian unionism. Rank-and-file members in individual workplaces, with the support of a well-resourced 'super union', would negotiate their own workplace agreements with management. But this came too late, as conservative state governments began introducing legislation to break compulsory unionism at the beginning of the 1990s, producing a collapse in union density to a level now lower than that of Canada, and at its lowest in Australia since 1911 (Peetz 1998: 26). The conservative federal government has pushed this to a highly confrontational level since 1996, most notable in the ugly clashes between waterside workers, police and security guards which broke out early in 1998. As Peetz points out, 'the legal environment is more difficult for unions than at almost any time this century', and they have not coped well (Peetz 1998: 191).

The Australian labour movement has a long, although typically discontinuous, history of involvement with cultural activity, which was particularly strong in the 1930s. Of note in terms of theatrical activity, the Workers' Art Clubs emerged from the Communist Party in the early 1930s and set up a number of agitprop troupes that performed from the repertoire of the international Workers' Theatre Movement. From this came the formation of the New Theatre League during the Popular Front period in the late 1930s. Although the New Theatre League maintained branches throughout the country, with varying levels of support, their activities waned during the Cold War freeze of the 1950s. They essentially became amateur companies producing 'progressive' plays not particularly related to immediate union concerns. Elements of the broader tradition were kept alive, most notably in Melbourne, by a group of Communist Party activists centred around George Seelaf of the Australasian Meat Industry Employees' Union. Seelaf had been part of a small group in the 1940s which offered opportunities for members of the Realist Writers' Group, including Frank Hardy and John Morrison and visual artists such as Noel Counihan and John Dyson, to syndicate short stories and cartoons to a number of union journals. He was still organising union arts festivals in workplaces around Melbourne in the 1970s and became the Victorian Trades Hall Council's first official arts officer. Seelaf was highly influential on union organisers in Melbourne, as well as labour historians like Andrew Reeves and cultural activists like Deborah Mills. Mills later became one of the architects of the funding policy initiatives that fed a revival of union-based cultural activities in the late 1970s and 1980s (Kirby 1991.1: 28).

While Seelaf's initiatives kept cultural work on the agenda of the movement, they did little to sustain a theatrical tradition, which remained buried, despite the ongoing branches of the New Theatre in Sydney and Melbourne. It was not until the community arts movement of the 1970s and 1980s and particularly the Art and Working Life Incentive Program of the Australia Council offered a real impetus for recuperation that the tradition was seriously investigated. This investigation was also inspired by a felt need for continuities by artsworkers attempting to form alliances with the labour movement after the counter-cultural experiments of the 1960s.

Community Arts and Community Theatre

The community arts movement in Australia was central to the development of labour movement theatre in the 1970s and 1980s, through the financial support of the Australia Council, the arts funding agency of the federal government. The Community Arts Committee was formed within the Council in 1973, as part of a number of structural changes following the election of the Whitlam Labor government in 1972 (Hawkins 1993). The revamped Council was structured around individual artform Boards and given a new charter which stressed 'access' and 'participation' as central objectives. 'Access' had long been seen as reasonably easy to handle; subsidy allowed the reduction of theatre ticket prices, and the support of touring allowed theatre to move beyond the metropolitan centres, although neither could be shown to have widened the socioeconomic base of theatre-going. 'Participation' in the arts was more difficult to promote, and responsibility for doing so mostly fell upon the Community Arts Committee, which operated separately from the specific artform Boards.

The Community Arts Committee sought to ameliorate a perceived social inequity in the distribution of funds, and was initially concerned to support arts activity which widened the audience base. In the mid-1970s, when the Committee was accorded full Board status, the importance of this initiative was signalled by a decision to fund the Popular Theatre Troupe (PTT) in Brisbane, in an arrangement with the Literature Board, which picked up half of the bill. The company was funded for its ability to reach 'non-theatre audiences', by touring popular theatre pieces to rural areas and non-theatre venues including worksites. The Troupe's consequent success established some of the basic modes of operation adopted by a number of other political theatre groups. Both the PTT and another early recipient of Australia Council funding, the Australian Performing Group (APG) in Melbourne, were initially caught up in the wave of nationalist sentiment which swept the Whitlam Labor government to power in 1972, and developed modes of local documentary theatre based on the recovery of buried 'people's histories' for broad and at this point fairly undefined audiences. These two attempts to make a 'people's theatre', were largely distinguished from each other by the fact that the APG had a home base at the Pram Factory while the PTT had no space of its own and toured. While both companies produced personnel for the emerging community theatre movement, it was the PTT's touring brief which made it the more viable model for those who followed in its wake.

For the Community Arts Board, the PTT addressed the Australia Council's charter commitment to access in more successful ways than the mere reduction of ticket prices to the 'high' arts. For the emergent political theatre scene, embracing the rhetoric of community arts was a way to secure funding. Thus the Board was instrumental in constructing the community arts movement around itself. This produced a political theatre movement which sought to address non-theatregoing audiences through popular theatre performances in non-theatre venues, which included working-class audiences in the workplace. Significantly (and somewhat confusingly from a North American perspective where the term often refers to amateur little theatre), these ventures all sailed under the same flag of convenience, 'community theatre'. The early days were marked by stories of companies that rewrote grant applications replacing the term 'political' with 'community' wherever it appeared on the form.

The community arts movement in Australia and the Australia Council's charter commitment to 'participation' in the arts in particular, was initially influenced by European models. The Council for Cultural Co-operation of the Council of Europe, a forum for European government ministers with a responsibility for culture, had been exploring cultural activity as a means of community development for some years. In the early 1970s the debate shifted from the notion of the 'democratisation of culture' to a notion of 'cultural democracy'. The former, in a view of culture advocated by the Second International almost a century earlier, unsuccessfully attempted to render the high arts more accessible to the socioeconomically underprivileged, through populist art produced by professionals for the culturally 'disadvantaged'. Cultural democracy altered the base assumptions in several ways. Instead of a single culture represented by the class-conditioned tastes of a minority, the proponents of cultural democracy argued for a plurality of cultures specific to different communities; that no one culture was necessarily any 'better' than any other; that culture was a practice rather than a set of dead artefacts; and that the cause of cultural democracy was best served, not by the imposition of a dominant sense of culture defined as art but by assisting communities to enjoy, or better still make, their own culture.

This change in thinking led to the European embrace of 'socio-cultural animation', which redefined the role of the artist as a facilitator who imparted skills to specific communities to 'voice' themselves (Simpson 1978). The point of this facilitatory mode, according to Owen Kelly, one of the British community arts movement's major theorists in the 1980s, was to consolidate or even create a sense of 'community'[1] and 'to enable working people to be creative in ways that would make their creativity socially effective', because this 'would raise their morale and lead them to seek to empower themselves in other areas of their lives' (Kelly 1984: 11). Cultural activity thus served as a central component of a mode of political activism particularly amenable to (in fact directly descendent from) the libertarian, communitarian politics of the counter-culture generation which formed the core of the community arts movement both in Britain and Australia. The development of such perspectives in policy within the Australia Council since the mid-1970s, in conjunction with a burgeoning community arts movement, produced a number of community theatre companies in the 1980s.

Concurrent with this shift towards facilitatory modes of 'voicing' communities was a policy shift from aesthetic to social criteria of value. Community arts projects were increasingly seen as a means of consolidating and celebrating communities as self-directed entities able to act socially in their own interests. The task of the theatreworker was to assist communities in effecting the social advantages of a consolidated sense of community via collaborative cultural work. Hence the Australia Council's principal community arts funding arm, the Community Arts Board, was renamed the Community Cultural Development Committee in 1987. The emphasis also helped construct a practice which demanded, as a condition of the grant, a consultative process which made impossible the sometimes arrogant vanguardism of the earliest forays into popular political theatre.

Australian companies thus moved away from the process of making shows *for* particular audiences, towards a more self-consciously dialogic process of making theatre *with* the chosen community. In this way 'political' theatre companies moved away from vanguardist, agitprop-based models established in the 1960s and 1970s, and, as 'community' theatres, embraced grass-roots modes of political activism (Watt and Pitts 1991; Watt 1995). The PTT's first big success in 1975, *The White Man's Mission*, exemplifies the earlier agitprop/people's theatre model. For this show, the bleak history of race relations in Queensland was researched through documentary sources

---

1. See Watt 1991: 55-66 for an account of the political ancestry and significance of the term within the movement.

and theatricalised by Richard Fotheringham and the British theatreworker Albert Hunt for performances by a professional troupe to 'popular' audiences in a range of venues all over eastern Australia, including a cut-down worksite version. The play was researched and written entirely in-house, structured out of a wide array of popular theatre techniques, and then taken out to this broad audience with an essentially educative impetus (Capelin 1995: 181–211).

The drift towards a more consultative model is reflected in Sidetrack Theatre's *Loco*, from 1983. In this case, the play emerged from a long residency at Chullora Railway Workshop in Sydney, during which the company spent time on the factory floor, had conversations and interviews with the workers, and hosted a series of performances and discussion sessions about their work. A script using material from that experience was developed in open rehearsals where workers could comment as the performance was generated. What emerged was a social realist play with songs which reflected the life experiences of the Workshop workers. This was then performed for them and also toured to other worksites. The effect of such a process, properly conducted, is that the initial 'audience' instead of being an anonymous group being 'informed' by the play, can see itself as intimately involved in making it and, at best, as 'owning' it (Burvill 1986; *Caper 23* 1984).

Two years later, we find a process which carries consultation a large step further. In 1985 WEST Community Theatre in Melbourne was invited to make a play for SIGNAL (Special Interest Group, Nurses' Action Lobby), a Left faction of the nurses' union in Victoria, as part of a campaign to organise a state-wide strike action. What SIGNAL expected was an agitprop show which could tour worksites and union meetings. Instead WEST facilitated a project in which seventy nurses and nurse educators made and performed a play called *Vital Signs*, with WEST supplying their professional skills and a nucleus of performers. The project was thus not just *about* the need for nurses to organise, but actually *enacted* the process of community formation through collaborative cultural work in the sense intended by the cultural activism of the community arts movement (Watt and Pitts 1991: 123–124).

Art and Working Life

Between *The White Man's Mission* and *Vital Signs* came the Australia Council's most important initiative for labour movement theatre in the 1980s, the Art and Working Life Incentive Program. This was one of three incentive schemes from the Community Arts Board designed to encourage the individual artform Boards, by matching grants from the Council, to fund projects in the areas of youth arts, multicultural arts and trade union arts or, in other words, the priority areas of youth, migrants and workers, seen to have been excluded from arts funding.

The Art and Working Life Program developed from a 1982 conference at the Victorian Trades Hall Council in Melbourne, sponsored by the ACTU but fomented by the Community Arts Board. By this point, several peak union bodies had arts officers, partially and in some cases wholly funded through the Community Arts Board. The ACTU had appointed its first full-time arts officer in 1980, and this led to a number of visual arts, theatre and music projects under the aegis of community arts (See *Caper 5* 1980; *Caper 13* 1981; *Caper 19* 1983; *Caper 23* 1984). The conference was intended as a means of extending and formalising that work, and followed the ACTU's passing of an 'Arts and Creative Recreation Policy' in 1980 which asserted that unions had a 'responsibility to bring the means of personal expression and communication into the workplace and the workers' and their families' leisure hours in recreation outside the workplace'. It also expressed a concern:

> to strongly encourage art and creative recreation, from the simplified forms to the most profound and the most demanding so that daily life elevates social usefulness, egalitarian values, challenges underprivilege, promotes freedom of expression and an understanding of the variety and depth in human personality. (Cited from Burn 1982)

The conference attracted approximately 150 delegates, of whom one-third represented trade unions, while the rest were community artists or members of the new bureaucracy community arts funding had produced. Writing in the journal *Art Network*, Ian Burn, a major ideological influence on the development of the program, noted a tension between the union members and the less political artists. Clearly the initial mismatches, when artists met unionists in the 1970s, had not been completely solved by the opportunities offered by community arts funding. His summation of the conference was not optimistic:

> Overwhelmingly, the tenor of the recommendations coming out of the seminar was for *more* of this, *more* of that, *more* arts officers, *more* money, *more* etc. There was precious little that even hinted at what *ends* all this 'more' might serve. Indeed, anything which raised matters of content or the

political potential which resides in the acquisition of skills (means) of expression, if it managed to survive the workshop sessions, was eliminated or pushed into the 'too hard' basket in the final plenary session. (Burn 1982: 38)

Undaunted, Deborah Mills, the Community Arts Board project officer who initiated the program and presided over it for a number of years, drafted a report to Council in September 1982 that established the basic shape of the Art and Working Life Program. Its objectives, she wrote, should be:

1. to encourage art practice and policy which is informed by the concerns and issues affecting workers' own lives and which acknowledges working class cultural tradition and the multicultural nature of that tradition.
2. to encourage the development of opportunities for workers and their families to gain access to the arts and to enjoy opportunities for creative self-expression and participation.
3. to promote communication within the trade union movement and between trade unions, artists and arts organisations ...
4. to encourage community, trade union, private sector, local, State and Commonwealth Government support. (Mills 1986: 3)

The Australia Council embraced the proposal by instituting Art and Working Life as one of its three ongoing cross-disciplinary 'incentive funds', which Gay Hawkins, in her account of the development of the community arts project within the Australia Council, succinctly describes as 'cultural affirmative action' (Hawkins 1993: 91). Under the program, funding was to be applied for, not by artists or companies, but by individual unions or union organisations that would act as hosts for the project, in a system widely used by the Community Arts Board, and described by Tim Rowse as 'decentralised patronage' (Rowse 1985: 24). The relationship between artists and unions was clear; artists, at least on paper, were effectively employees of unions.

Explicit in Mills' report was an important new assumption in community arts policy. Her reference to a pre-existing working-class cultural tradition suggested that an inequity in funding working-class cultures needed to be redressed. In other words the problem was not the lack of a working-class cultural tradition, but the historical emphasis on funding hegemonic high culture. Consequently, the work was given a recuperative brief as artists engaged with the history of cultural activity within the unions. One direct result of that was the exhumation of the arts activities of the 1930s, reflected in a series of publications on cultural work within the movement, particularly on union banners and ceremonials (Stephen and Reeves 1985; Reeves 1988; Kirby 1991.1 and 1991.2; Goddard and Layman 1988). This in turn led to Australia Council support for a number of projects to produce new union banners (Stephen and Reeves 1985: 42–45).

Another result was an abiding concern with a somewhat unproblematised notion of working-class culture. Theatreworkers searched for theatrical manifestations of this culture or, failing that, forms appropriate to it. Theatrical traditions, though, were much harder to locate than visual arts or musical traditions. One of the first companies to tie itself closely to the labour movement via Art and Working Life funding was Junction Theatre Company in Adelaide, which developed a continuing relationship with the United Trades and Labour Council (UTLC) of South Australia (Watt 1990). Junction made the most concerted attempt to rehabilitate agitprop, but ultimately found it necessary to create a style of its own rather than adapt a pre-existing one. As a result, they produced a sequence of plays which presented issues of central concern to union organisers, like workplace restructuring or occupational health and safety, in snappy revue forms drawn from television variety shows or popular cabaret, much influenced by John McGrath's experiments with 7:84 in Britain. Others staged documentary-based local recuperations of buried working-class histories in forms borrowed from the rich stylistic heritage which Theatre Workshop had kept alive in Britain, like Death Defying Theatre's *Coal Town*, or the Gippsland Trades and Labour Council's *The Yallourn Story*, or Deckchair Theatre's *Paddy* (about Paddy Troy, a communist activist on the Fremantle docks). All of them avoided the avant-garde at all costs, and most moved uneasily between the twin poles of agitprop and social realism, in what, by the late 1980s, became an increasingly restricted stylistic palette. All were placed in situations in which a close involvement with the constituency of each project was mandatory. If the program was ostensibly concerned with introducing artists to unionists, it was at least as important in introducing unionists to artists.

One immediate effect of that introduction was to kick some of the early romanticism about a homogeneous working-class culture out of the work. Close acquaintance with union audiences led to the discovery of difference, of ethnicity and gender in particular. Even in shows designed for workplace performance in the manufacturing industry, the home base of a particular romanticised image of the male Australian worker, companies quickly discovered that they were not playing to a monolithic culture but to audiences which did not even have the English language in common. Sidetrack Theatre, for example, found it necessary in the early 1980s to make shows in three or four languages at once, which led to a search for actors of non-English-speaking backgrounds.

Hawkins has also noted that the program defined the working class not 'in terms of distinctive artefacts and rituals but in terms of shifting political and cultural interests that emerged always in relations of domination and subordination' (Hawkins 1993: 98). In other words, the program was 'sold' to the unions as having an immediate instrumentalist function: it was not merely about consolidating and celebrating unionism through the recuperation of its cultural history, it was also a means of placing artists at the disposal of the movement in campaigning for its own ends and, significantly, at no cost to the movement itself. The program was thus defined as political from its inception, and served as a politicising influence on many of the community artists attracted by the funding it offered.

By the mid-1980s, a growing body of experience had identified several recurring issues around the program. Practical and instrumentalist analyses displaced the more romantic, essentialist voices that had initiated the program as the reclamation of the lost symbolic culture of labour. A useful assessment of the state of Art and Working Life work in 1986 was provided in a report to the United Trades and Labour Council of South Australia by their Arts Officer, Kathie Muir. In it she set out to clarify the main principles of Art and Working Life performance at a time when many 'companies and organisations are reconsidering their approach to their work' (Muir 1986). Muir's report addressed seven main points, which are worth noting because they summarised her own working experience, particularly through the UTLC's relationship with Junction, of how theatre had developed under the project.

Muir first considered the 'ownership' of workplace performance, stressing that local union involvement was necessary to ensure that the play was not received by the audience as a management-supported imposition. She touched briefly on the more complex question of form, indicating a shift beyond the original recuperative brief of the program, noting that:

> the 'form' of the project doesn't automatically belong to the workers for whom it's designed. Therefore it can take a couple of performances of different sorts before the concept of theatre in workplaces is accepted.

And many projects are designed to incorporate forms such as cabaret, music or circus skills to assist in overcoming these barriers. (Muir 1986)

That said, Muir turned to the audience itself, to point out that workplaces comprise 'an extraordinary cross section of people', with various balances of gender, background, language and ethnicity. Her main argument, which followed from this, was that companies needed to have more time to develop 'new forms' for this 'non-traditional' audience:

> The conventions understood by the initiated as good drama, clever staging, and appropriate behaviour are not universally understood immediately. ... The performers, writers, designers, directors and musicians involved in such ventures need to constantly discuss and examine their work and its relevance both with their audience and other theatre workers. (Muir 1986)

Muir also emphasised that the bodies assessing Art and Working Life (AWL) performances (union arts officers, unions themselves, the Australia Council, etc) needed to understand the demanding conditions in which the work was produced. Given that most Art and Working Life projects moved from research to performance in the time that a traditional company might rehearse a pre-existing script, Muir concluded that 'there have been extraordinarily high expectations put upon theatre workers in this area by funding bodies and mainstage theatre colleagues' (Muir 1986).

Theatreworkers trying to meet those expectations while attempting to sustain the original recuperative brief of the program, had created another set of conventions with a reliance on agitprop and socialist realism. Muir approved recent developments which had a tendency to 'far more subtle, strong and sophisticated productions', moving away from the 'linear plots or domestic sub-plots seen as necessary for the basic earthing in AWL'. She also observed the increasing use of theatrical techniques, such as 'mime, circus, dance, poetry, puppetry' to 'convey wider experience'. This showed a dynamic movement developing and changing as it familiarised itself with the internal workings and make-up of the union movement, and something more than the mere creature of funding policy.

Muir wrote when financial support for theatre activity was at its height. The mid-1980s saw the emergence of new ventures like Melbourne Workers Theatre, the only Australian company to devote itself entirely (at least in its early years) to work with unions. This is largely explained by the fact that companies were able to receive 'dovetail funding' under the program from both the Community Cultural Development Committee as well as the single artform Boards, particularly the Performing Arts Board. This dovetail funding did not last, though, and an under-funded area struggled in increasingly difficult financial circumstances from the late 1980s until the Art and Working Life program was officially removed from the books in 1996.

By then, the whole community arts program within the Australia Council had shifted back towards an emphasis on artistic 'excellence', implicitly renouncing the stress on social welfare which had dominated the late 1980s. While union-based work still receives Australia Council support, it does so on the basis of judgements about the aesthetic worth of projects and their ability to attract financial support from other sources, and not because it is based within the union movement. To some extent, this is a result of a new generation of trade union arts officers, most vocally represented by Jock McQueenie, who became the Arts Officer of the Tasmanian Trades and Labour Council (TTLC) in 1993. At a 1997 conference on Community Cultural Development he raised disappointingly few hackles by suggesting that 'some of the most restrictive practices and aesthetic abominations of late 20th century Australian art have been perpetrated in the name of community'. He went on to claim:

> The sector is under-theorised and prone to anti-intellectualism and, in an age where the vast majority of our young artists, writers and performers are university-trained professionals, I would suggest that the belligerent Philistinism which characterises a lot of trades union arts practice is a serious mistake and one of the major turn-offs for young practitioners. (*Dare* 1997: 63)

His own answer to the artistic deficiencies he saw in Art and Working Life performance was a $330,000 project, funded to the tune of $70,000 by the management of a paper mill in Burnie in Tasmania, which consisted of a visual arts exhibition by young artists who had mostly left Burnie, an opera including local amateur performers facilitated by Ehos Opera (a Hobart-based avant-garde music theatre group), and a documentary film on the project which was sold to public television. The Australia Council, never shy of sending messages to its clients, indicated its approval by selecting the TTLC as a 'National Model' under a new scheme and including a long account of the project, called *Pulp*, in a book designed to publicise the work it funded (Reid 1997: 16–25). Union-based theatre work may face a new crisis of self-definition if, as is sometimes suggested in informal discussions with its Project Officers, Australia Council funding is made conditional upon the financial support of management.

What McQueenie claims to be 'most proud of about the project', though, indicates the distance policy has shifted. His pride resides in the fact that he 'worked to maintain the artistic freedom of the creative team and also did the right thing by the community', by which he seems to mean both the workers and management of the paper mill (Reid 1997: 21). He thus repudiates, and by implication so does the Community Cultural Development Fund, two central principles upon which the community arts program rested: firstly, that artsworkers are facilitators rather than autonomous agents; and secondly, that communities are defined by a commonality of interests and shared meanings rather than mere geographical proximity. The distance travelled from the recuperative and instrumentalist vision which produced the Art and Working Life program is even greater, and the adaptability union-based theatre work has displayed over the last twenty years clearly needs a different means of maintaining a genuinely oppositional practice while surviving financially.

Canada: The Popular Theatre Process

Canadian Unionism and Social Activism

In Canada, the notion of labour culture—in the widest sense of the term—has been less institutionalised than in either Australia or Britain. As in the USA, class is a suppressed concept in popular culture, tainted still by the violent anti-leftism of the McCarthy era, during which leftist and communist unions were brutally purged. As James Laxer has observed, this suppression has been absorbed into the deep structures of social interaction:

> In North America, discussions of social classes are considered to be in questionable taste, indeed as surrounded by formidable taboos. It is less outré to converse graphically about kinky sex than to suggest that social classes exist, or that their existence has important consequences. (Laxer 1998: 32)

Class is further dispersed by the pervasive impact of mass media, which as Stanley Aronowitz has argued in the USA, displaces representations of the working class into 'upwardly mobile' consumer identities required by the service economy (Aronowitz 1989: 141). The attenuation of class as a public discourse in Canada is compounded by the fact that the major political parties tend to express regional interests in which class is subsumed by more generalised rhetorical constructs of 'sectors' and 'interest groups'. Although the New Democratic Party (NDP)—which has never formed a national government but has governed in various provinces—depends on alliances with the labour movement, it does not have the same degree of formal integration with the unions that we see in the Labour Party in Britain or the Australian Labor Party. Indeed NDP governments have found themselves locked in bitter fights with a divided union movement. In 1991, the failure of the Ontario unions to agree on support for the NDP government's desperate attempts to formulate a 'social contract' to appease the business sector's obsession with deficit-cutting led to the election of a hard-right Progressive Conservative Government that quickly moved to reverse the gains labour had made under the NDP. Time and again, political analysts have noted that the NDP attracts only a small percentage of union affiliated voters.

Most but not all unions in English-speaking Canada are members of the Canadian Labour Congress (which embraces some 2 million workers out of a national population of 35 million) and its affiliated provincial labour federations. Altogether, unions organise approximately one-third of the workforce. Palmer has noted that between 1960 and 1980 union membership doubled in Canada, as a consequence of expanding public sector unions (Palmer 1992: 353). Yet while public sector unions have been at the forefront of the social union movement, the vast diversity of trades and professions they organise has mitigated class analysis. The notable exception has been postal workers who have recurrently taken the vanguard of union radicalism.

The theatrical ventures that aligned with labour in the 1970s and 1980s in Canada did so at a time when unions were wrestling with the rapid dismantling of the Fordist accords that had governed it for decades. With a long history of purging radicals from its ranks and lukewarm support for (and from) the NDP, organised labour was in a state of paralysis. The nationalist politics of the 1960s and 1970s, which saw a break-away movement from American 'international' unions (whose internationalism was perceived by many Canadians as one-way colonialism), was followed in the 1980s by a series of recessions punctuated by the North American Free Trade Agreement, which had severe repercussions on industrial employment as industries moved south to cheaper wages and lower tax burdens. At the same time, an expansionist tendency of larger unions to broaden their membership saw stiff competition as unions sought to organise workers outside their domain, with the result, for instance, that the Steelworkers began organising security guards and restaurant workers, and the Auto Workers began signing up fishery workers in Newfoundland and Starbucks coffee servers in British Colombia.[1]

By the 1990s the public sector unions (including teachers, health care workers and public servants) dominated labour relations and politics in Canada. The large public sector super-unions (such as the Canadian Union of Public Employees, and the teachers' unions) increasingly became the often reluctant vanguard of labour struggle at a time when conservative governments aligned themselves explicitly with the business sector's 'right to manage'. In the mid-1990s, the Harris government's radical cuts to the public sector in a union-busting move brought hundreds of thousands of demonstrators onto the streets of Ontario cities in the largest mass action in recent Canadian history.

The social union tendency brought activists in the public sector unions into engagement with the reformist wings of the large industrial unions, notably the Canadian Auto Workers, the United Steelworkers of America and the Communication, Energy and Paperworkers (CEP). The shift in union focus has been described by D'Arcy Martin, who has worked as a membership educator in the Steelworkers and the CEP:

> Union activists have always looked to broader social change, but the focus of daily work has been the collective bargaining contract with the employer. During the late 1970s an activist could be entirely involved with this sphere alone. The restructuring of the economy since then has shaken both the workplace and the community, and unions have been obliged to change, to merge, to reorganize internally.
>
> Unions are now involved in a great web of consultative and decision-making bodies. And when a central labour body speaks to its corresponding level of government, it is joined formally and informally by a network of church, community, and social movement organisations. (Martin 1995: 132)

A major turning point in the development of these networks was the formation of widespread alliances (such as the Ontario Social Justice Coalition and the Alberta Common Front) that came out of the failed struggle against the Free Trade Agreement with the United States in the mid-1980s. These coalitions became the meeting ground for artists and

---

1. For discussion of the widespread move by big unions into the service sector, see Thompson 1998.

union activists. The alliances that came out of that shared struggle were built on the basis of twenty years of experiential learning, in which theatreworkers had moved beyond crudely formulated notions of class engagement to develop sophisticated analyses of their role in the community of social action. When theatreworkers like Don Bouzek (founder of Ground Zero), the Company of Sirens in Toronto and Headlines Theatre in Vancouver began to hammer out ongoing projects with union activists, they did so from a position of expertise formed by their foundational role in the Canadian popular theatre movement. And as unions began to struggle to understand their own changing, increasingly diverse memberships, cultural activists provided a set of tools that helped unions work through new issues of cultural difference. The model of theatrical intervention that came out of this was one that redeployed the work of theatre artists from external propaganda to internal communication and coalition partnership.

The Popular Theatre Model

Ironically, given that radical street theatre and agitprop drew many people into political performance, the most direct influence behind the shift from radical intervention to popular theatre came not from theatre, but from film. The principles that came to define the popular theatre movement in Canada were pioneered by the National Film Board's 'Fogo Process' which used film as a technique of community animation in remote Newfoundland fishing outports. Produced as part of the Film Board's 'Challenge for Change' series in 1967–68 by Colin Low and Memorial University of Newfoundland's Extension department, the process consisted of filmed interviews with fishery workers in each of the island communities; as each community responded on film, the results were screened back in what was called a 'communication loop'. The process of participatory research on film was by its nature a process of community development. The project drew considerable attention not only because of its innovative process but because its political result—the establishment of a fishing co-op—demonstrated that cultural action could lead to material change (Evans 1991: 163–4).

The Fogo Process was a particularly well-documented if localised application of the principles of participatory research and education influenced by the ideas of Paulo Freire, which began to circulate through the activist theatre community in the mid-1970s. In his work, beginning with the foundational *Pedagogy of the Oppressed*, Freire offered a critique of traditional systems of knowledge and education which reinforced structures of social oppression. He argued that when people 'lack a critical understanding of their reality, apprehending it in fragments which they do not perceive as interacting constituent elements of the whole, they cannot truly know their reality' (Freire 1972: 95). Adult education for Freire was a process of working with communities to codify and decode representations of reality in order to identify points of possible change. His theories of activist community education, with their emphasis on participatory democracy and local knowledge, circulated through Canada via development educators and literacy workers. They provided theatre artists with a vocabulary that enabled them to theorise and reconceptualise their largely self-taught work in community animation.

As in Australia and Britain, Canadian political theatre has a long history but the discontinuities between the workers' theatre movement of the 1930s (which saw numerous troupes sponsored by Progressive Arts Clubs in all parts of English Canada, but had no comparable history in francophone Québec) were intensified by widespread cultural amnesia on the one hand, and the vicious persecution that attended the brutal anti-communism of the 1950s on the other. The contemporary movement of political theatre began with an impulse to radical intervention, coming out of the student movements of the late 1960s. The formative condition of that radicalism was the counter-culture of the American anti-war movement, and although Canada was not directly involved in Vietnam, the mass media erasure of the Canadian–American border and the arrival of thousands of American war resisters contributed to a generalised North American youth movement. One of the consequences of this was the perception among radical youth that the union movement consisted of red-necked thugs.

Canadian student consciousness of struggle had two points of origin, which by the early 1970s had become contradictory. On the one hand, the counter-culture carnivalesque resistance against the myth of the middle-class society and its mass culture representations placed student action in a wider North American cultural framework. On the other hand, and at the same time, an incipient Canadian nationalism turned towards regionalism and localism as the sites of authentic social experience. This was in English Canada inspired in large part by the popular movement for separatism in Québec, which espoused a passionate nationalism (in which the theatre played a highly visible role) and exposed a crisis of nation (usually described in terms of 'identity') in an increasingly multicultural Anglophone Canada. The reconciliation of these two imperatives—

counter-cultural revolt and sentimentalised local culture—marked the beginning of the popular theatre movement.

In Anglophone Canada, this began in 1973, when the Mummers Troupe toured Newfoundland with an agitprop-inflected 'people's history' that narrated the history of the province as a populist struggle against colonial overlords, firstly British and then Canadian (which Newfoundland had joined in 1949). The show itself represented a major shift in political consciousness. The Mummers Troupe had been formed by Chris Brookes, a Newfoundlander whose theatrical and political education had taken place in the United States, and who had returned to his home with the idea of doing radical counter-culture puppet theatre, influenced by his exposure to Bread and Puppet Theatre. The cultural polarisation of radical engaged youth and conservative working class that framed so much of the American Left didn't translate in Newfoundland, where Brookes rediscovered a working class that struggled to retain a unique popular culture tradition. His cartoon history show was a product of that rediscovery. It was influenced too by the rhetoric of national liberation emerging from Québec, where companies like La Grande Cirque Ordinaire and Théâtre Euh! toured Marxist nationalist popular histories, and where one of the best-selling books of the early 1970s was a Québécois people's history published in comic strip format.

While touring the history show, Brookes and his troupe of young, relatively inexperienced actors had two formative experiences. The first was an encounter with a fishing village that was about to be relocated to make room for a new national park. The troupe spent several weeks with the villagers to create an intervention performance that melded documentary, agitprop and clowning. Brookes later published an article on the intervention (which he referred to as 'useful theatre') in *This Magazine*, a journal founded by a collective of radical teachers (Brookes 1974). The article had an important effect when it was read by Ross Kidd, a Canadian working in adult education in Africa. Kidd began using similar techniques in Botswana, and in the ensuing years became a principal organiser and teacher of popular theatre in the Third World, working extensively in Africa, the Philippines and Bangladesh (Kidd 1979, 1981, 1984, 1985). That work in turn had a reciprocal influence on developments in Canada when Kidd returned in the late 1970s and, with money raised from international development agencies, began forging connections between Canadian groups and companies in the developing world.

Agitprop in Newfoundland: the Mummers Troupe's 1972 *Newfoundland Night*.
(Photo: Chris Brookes)

The second opportune encounter for the Mummers in the summer of 1973 came out of a performance in Buchans, a mining town in the geographic centre of Newfoundland, where workers had undergone a series of long, unsuccessful strikes against the American multinational ASARCO. The Mummers performed during the final stages of a six-month strike, and over beer with union members worked out a proposal to return in the next summer to create a community documentary. That project marked the first major alliance between a union and a theatre company in anglo Canada, and while it was a success, it also exposed deep contradictions and limitations. Despite the successful linkage between activist artists and local union militancy, it failed to develop a methodology that could use that linkage as an instrument of political intervention. In Buchans the performance was a statement of community intervention and research but beyond that its effect was almost entirely sentimental. Sentimentalism, which the unions responded to most strongly, was an inadequate political technique.

The theatrical template of the community documentary that the Mummers used in Buchans was similar in form to countless others across Canada in the early 1970s which, following the example of Theatre Passe

Muraille's *The Farm Show*, expressed a romanticised desire to recuperate regional culture. In the summer of 1972 director Paul Thompson and a group of actors stayed in a borrowed farmhouse near Clinton, Ontario. Out of their conversations with local farmers, the cast improvised a documentary play, first performed in an auction barn to a farm audience, that combined spoken actuality and exuberant story-telling theatricality. The collage structure of the play was modelled on a community concert; as one actor warns the audience, 'the show kind of bounces along one way or another and then it *stops*' (Thompson 1975: 19)[1] The structure worked for the audience, and it provided a method by which localist shows could be researched, improvised and strung together in the space of a few weeks. This sentimentalisation of local culture by actors armed with tape recorders in quest of authenticity is a familiar postcolonial tactic; it was comparable to similar ventures in Australia, Scotland and the southern United States, although in Canada it was contextualised in a decolonising nation-building enterprise fostered by the Liberal government of Pierre Trudeau.

For middle-class Canadian theatreworkers raised in a basically American popular culture, issues of region, localism, nation and class were confused into an analysis that saw the conflict not as one between classes but between local populism and foreign (i.e. American) domination. This was true as well of the Mummers in Buchans, despite their enthusiastic embrace of union militancy. Class was a concept that was understandable only through the personalised experiences of the workers they came to know; class solidarity was something to be expressed by wearing ripped jeans, faded shirts and work boots.

In the Mummers and numerous other similar groups that followed, engaged theatreworkers came to a new understanding of politics through the often painful attempts to develop collective structures and working methods. With the advances of feminism in the 1970s, gender issues became a political arena in which artists began to understand issues of class in terms of hegemony and difference. This naturally exposed contradictions in the self-defined conditions in which artists worked, with the result that emerging class consciousness frequently turned inwards, especially as the founding generation of radical artists found themselves in the role of employers. As theatre artists constructed working relationships with

---

1. For analysis of the collective theatre movement in Canada see Bessai 1992 and Filewod 1987.

labour, their penetration into the edges of the theatrical profession also positioned them as the radical margin in an industry structured around hierarchal lines of power and creativity. One of the recurring problems was that radical theatreworkers were usually non-unionised, because the troupes they created did not fit the industrial template that Actors' Equity recognised, and, funded as they were (when they were funded) on small project grants, they could rarely pay more than a small stipend. For their part, actors could not acquire a union card without apprenticing with an Equity company. The net result of this was a situation in which the theatres that wanted to work with unions were vulnerable to criticism that they imposed working conditions less favourable to actors than mainstream unionised theatres.

This led to some occasional conflicts, when hostile elements (in arts councils, the mainstream theatre and indeed in unions) used the non-union status of labour-engaged companies to undermine their work. Again, the Mummers Troupe provided the notable example when it accepted an invitation from the Steelworkers to tour the Buchans show, *Company Town*, to their mining locals in Ontario and Manitoba. Actors Equity—which had refused the Mummers' request for a lower-salary 'alternative theatre' contract—threatened to complain to the Steelworkers; as a result the tour was cancelled, and union members lost the chance to see the only theatre troupe in the country that had undertaken to work with them.

In most radical groups, recurring debates about working conditions, decentred power and collectivity taught that political struggle was part of daily life, rather than the periodic eruption of high drama in demonstrations and strikes. The popular theatre model that emerged from this gradual alignment with ongoing social action was well in place by the late 1970s, by which time companies across Canada had forged links with a wide spectrum of activist groups, including unions and social development agencies.

The popular theatre method was articulated, and the phrase entered currency, in 1981, when Kam Theatre, a left-wing collective in Thunder Bay, sponsored Bread & Circuses: A Festival of Canadian Theatre. The companies attending the festival were small, politically engaged, and for the most part collective in their approach to playwriting. The performances followed a week long workshop, organised by Ross Kidd (then back in Canada to pursue a PhD on popular theatre at the Ontario Institute for Studies in Education, the think-tank of Freirean theory) with financial support from the development agency CUSO. The workshop brought together a dozen Canadians from a range of companies (including the Mummers, Catalyst Theatre, Great Canadian Theatre Company and Headlines) to exchange skills with popular theatreworkers from seven African and Caribbean nations. During the festival, some of the workshop participants drew up a proposal for a formal association. Previous attempts to organise such an association had run into an insurmountable inability to define a common ground and purpose. In 1981 this obstacle was overcome by the acceptance of the term 'popular theatre'. By introducing the term, Ross Kidd gave the workshop participants an instrument that enabled them to define their commonality clearly and which relocated the defining criteria for political theatre to the active collaboration with a community in the process of struggle. On this basis, the participants in the festival founded the Canadian Popular Theatre Alliance (CPTA) and formulated a statement of principles:

a) We share a common belief that theatre is a means and not an end. We are theatres that work to effect social change....
b) We see our task as an ongoing process in which art is actively involved in the changing nature of the communities in which we live and work.
c) We particularly attempt to seek out, develop and serve audiences whose social reality is not normally reflected on the Canadian stage.
d) Therefore our artistic practice grows out of a social rather than private definition of the individual.

Therefore there is a fundamental difference of purpose, priorities and aesthetics which separates us from the dominant theatre ideology in Canada today. (Filewod 1992)

The CPTA continued as a loose network of companies and individuals which came together for biennial festivals for the next decade to explore what these principles actually activated. The various methods they shared all foregrounded the role of the theatre and performance as a process of facilitating community activism. The language of analysis derived from Franz Fanon, Freire and later Augusto Boal, with their emphasis on participatory community-based animation (Boal 1979, 1992, 1995). The movement embraced dozens of companies operating in very different performance idioms. A few were engaged primarily with labour, but most were defined by particular community affinities, working with immigrants, First Nations and women's groups. What they had in common was the deployment of theatre as (in the words of the CPTA manifesto) a 'tool for social change'.

The fundamental realisation for the movement was that the sponsoring agencies had the deep investment and knowledge in the struggle, and that the theatres were there to achieve goals defined by them. One of the most innovative popular theatres in Canada in the 1980s in this regard was Catalyst Theatre in Edmonton, which was sponsored by the Alberta Alcohol and Drug Abuse Commission, doing Freirean work that was very like the work Boal was doing in France at the same time.[1]

Artists in the Workplace

For the most part, these developments went unnoticed by unions, despite occasional tactical ventures (such as Great Canadian Theatre Company in Ottawa, which mounted a series of agitprops for public service unions in the late 1970s). As late as 1981, the year the CPTA was founded, the Ontario Federation of Labour's policy book made no mention at all of the arts or culture. It was when union activists began meeting popular theatreworkers in the new coalitions of the social justice movement that more strategic forms of cooperation became possible. Like popular theatreworkers, many union educators had been exposed to Freire, which meant that they met theatre artists with a shared set of political assumptions.

Union educators were however only one, relatively marginal, segment of the labour movement, and they rarely had control of budgets large enough to sponsor theatrical work on their own. Many of the collaborations between unions and artists happened on the common ground of public protest, with the result that, as in Australia and Britain, Canadian theatre artists became proficient at agitprop processional performances designed to catch the media gaze at public events. One of the first major breakthroughs in the labour-arts alliance came about in 1986, through the work of a small group of activists in the labour community in Toronto who initiated Mayworks, an annual festival of labour and culture proposed by Catherine McLeod on the

---

1. Boal's Theatre of the Oppressed techniques were introduced to anglo Canada by a Québécois troupe, Théâtre Parminou, at the CPTA's first festival, hosted by Catalyst Theatre in Edmonton in 1983. By the early 1980s Canadian popular theatre was ripe for Boal, and in some cases, as with Catalyst, had developed forms that were virtually identical to forum theatre, and a vocabulary that has now been supplanted by Boal. Theatre of the Oppressed, particularly Forum Theatre, became popular across Canada, not because it introduced new ideas but because it legitimised Canadian practices in an international discourse.

model of Glasgow's Mayfest. Mayworks was initially a project of the Art and Communication Committee of the Canadian Labour Congress, and emerged from an arts and labour conference at the Toronto Steelworkers hall in 1983. Mayworks was also the first push in the movement that established the short-lived Artists in the Workplace (AWP) program in the Ontario Arts Council in 1988. In its first funding year, the AWP program funded four theatre projects: a musical about plant closures based on the Goodyear plant shutdown in Etobicoke, produced with the Rubberworkers' Union (Palmer 1994); a revival of the Company of Sirens' *The Working People's Picture Show*, sponsored by the North Bay and District Labour Council; a script workshop of a play about daycare workers in Ottawa by Arthur Milner, with fifteen members of the Canadian Union of Public Employees; and the production of a draft script by postal workers in Peterborough called, appropriately enough, *Post Script*. Compared to the Australian experience, the actual amount of subsidy involved was miniscule, ranging from $4,000 to $9,000.

The movement towards culture within the labour movement, and the corresponding movement of cultural activists towards labour, established a field of engagement with two main imperatives: the recognition of organised labour as a legitimising, indeed normalising, site of democratic culture, and a repositioning of artists as workers in the labour community. These were both in one sense unattainable for a host of material and ideological reasons. As Julie Davis, then Secretary-Treasurer of the Ontario Federation of Labour, stated in 1994 (in a speech ghost-written by Catherine Macleod):

> If the workers' movement was as rich as the corporate community, we would be able to finance our own films, publish our own newspapers, write our own books (for children as well as adults), broadcast our own radio and television programs. If this were the case we would say we have a democratic culture. But we're not rich so we can't do it alone. ... We believe the people on the other side of the bargaining table have dominated the perception field too long. (Davis 1994: 15)

Although D'Arcy Martin had repeatedly made the point that 'unionists must begin to take artists seriously as workers' (Martin 1994: 21), the rhetoric of democratic culture effectively recognised that artists, by virtue of their professional autonomy, occupy an ambivalent social space that intersects with yet remains apart from the working class. Artists as a sector earn less than unionised workers, but have greater control over the conditions of their working life. What separates artists from workers remains, as always, the issue of power. Carole Condé, who had been instrumental in the founding of Mayworks and the AWP program, recognised this as a fundamental reality of worker–artists alliances:

> Ideally, everyone in society should be able to represent themselves. But the truth is, most people are culturally invisible. Some are able to represent themselves politically, but few have access to the means of representation.
>
> ... We share their beliefs but that shouldn't be confused with sharing the actual experiences of working class people because we don't. We work politically to open up space and access to resources which can be used by working class people to represent themselves. (Shulz 1994: 26)

A useful model of this partnership that set out to negotiate class barriers was the 1987 production of *Straight Stitching* by playwright Shirley Barrie and director Lib Spry, sponsored by the International Ladies' Garment Workers Union in Toronto. The play was intended to show that despite their various linguistic and cultural backgrounds, women in garment factories (represented in the play by immigrants from Hong Kong, Portugal, Jamaica and Québec) can overcome their differences to unite and unionise. Shirley Barrie's description of the working process is typical of what has become a conventional method of workplace dramaturgy, and effectively explains why the constant rediscovery of a participatory process leads to story-based dramatic realism:

> At the beginning we met once a week in the Union Hall, and as the women told Lib and I both hilarious and tragic stories of their lives and work, certain themes began to emerge. Most of the women were immigrants— many of whom couldn't speak English when they arrived in Canada. What this means and how it affects their lives was the subtext to many of the stories. The treatment of the newcomer, both by the Supervisors and by other workers revealed a complex situation in which fear, control and the necessity to be tough all played a part.
>
> I developed an outline—the story of a fictional character, Mei Lee, a recent immigrant from Hong Kong, who comes to work in a garment factory. The women were wonderfully helpful in exploring what would and would not happen to this character, and in setting the limits on just how far and in what way workers in their situation can make a stand. Several of the workers decided to join with the actors who were brought in, and perform in the reading of the play. (Barrie 1991: 91)

Straight Stitching was from the standpoint of labour-arts partnership a model project, but it, like many similar ventures, fell far short of meeting the second imperative in the strategic alliance of artists and workers: the need on the part of artists to be recognised as workers, who are themselves oppressed by poverty and social attitudes that dismiss them as spoiled dilettantes. As theatreworkers in Australia have also found, their encounters with shop-level unions and local officers were often more equitable than their encounters with union bureaucracies. As Martin has pointed out:

> Artists, naturally enough, apply union principles to their encounter with the trade union movement as employer. They resent being used as pawns in internal union feuds not of their making. And they are critical of union budgeting priorities which place their creative work below activities that cater to the vanity of union leaders, or to the class collaboration current within the movement. (Martin 1994: 21)

The terms of engagement with labour required that artists learn to present themselves as independent professionals who could justify and sell a service, and negotiate contracts with partners for whom bargaining was a central fact of working life. The principles of social reform remained paramount in this relationship, but in order to continue working with labour, theatre artists had to come to a new understanding of themselves as independent business contractors. As the case study of Ground Zero shows, this entailed a major reconceptualisation of theatrical organisation, both in working methods and company structure.

The United Kingdom: Class Politics and Cultural Activism

Unionism in Britain

The British trade union movement has gone from a position of immense strength in the late 1960s and early 1970s to a point of weakness today. This follows a steady decline since the so-called 'Winter of Discontent' of 1979 precipitated the election of the Thatcher Conservative government. Indeed the movement was decimated in the 1980s to the point where union density dropped well below 50% for the first time since the war. The decline was partly attributable to 'structural changes' in the organisation of work which has afflicted unionism worldwide including the decline of manufacturing employment and the shift towards service industries, the rise of part-time and casual work, the expansion of self-employment, and massive growth in unemployment (which went from one million in the mid-1970s to two million by the end of the 1970s, three million by 1982, and showed no appreciable lessening until much later in the decade). Other factors, such as the steady privatisation of public industries, and the movement into Britain of American and Japanese manufacturers with anti-union managerial strategies, were also significant (Ackers, Smith and Smith 1996: 7).

At the same time, union power was subjected to a legislative onslaught which has been particularly severe on the issue of industrial action:

> Such action must be authorized by the appropriate union body after a majority of the workers have voted in favour by postal ballot under a statutory-defined procedure, supervised by an external agency. Unions must give seven days' notice of a ballot paper, details of the result, an additional seven days' notice of the commencement of any action, and information as to its nature, including details as to which workers will be involved (in some cases giving names). Unions remain liable in law for all industrial action (including unofficial and unconstitutional action) in which any official or lay officer participates, unless this is expressly repudiated under a statutory procedure. ... Any failure on the part of a union to remain within the law entitles a range of parties—the employer, another affected company, a member, or a citizen—to apply to a court for an injunction requiring the action to cease immediately. ... Non-compliance may threaten the viability of the union itself through fines for contempt and sequestration. (Ackers, Smith and Smith 1996: 20)

This, and other, legislation has resulted in a series of major defeats for the unions: the miners' strike of 1984–5; the dispute at the Government Communication Headquarters at Cheltenham in 1984, when employees were banned from trade union membership on the grounds that it constituted a security risk; the Wapping dispute of 1985–6, when Rupert Murdoch sacked his entire print workforce and which resulted in picketing for most of 1986 culminating in a violent clash between 7,000 pickets and 1,000 police in early 1987. Such confrontations were part of an orchestrated campaign aimed at what industrial relations theorists Nick Bacon and John Storey have described as 'the fracturing of collectivism' in the British industrial scene (Bacon and Storey, 1996: 43).

In the wake of these battles, the 1980s saw the erosion of the 'closed shop' arrangements which had sustained union density through the previous decade, and of the influence unions used to wield on government ('No more beer and sandwiches at Number 10' as Thatcher put it). The union movement was increasingly unable to protect its membership from declining wages and work conditions, and its power within the Labour Party steadily decreased.

This dwindling power may be read in two significant moments, both of central importance in the development of Banner Theatre, our British case study. The first is the miners' strike of 1972, which produced one of those heroic moments of working-class solidarity from which the labour movement has always drawn sustenance, the 'Battle of Saltley Gate' in Birmingham. This was a major victory in achieving wage increases for members of the National Union of Mineworkers (NUM), and the confidence generated by its success led to a further strike in 1973 which precipitated the early removal of the Heath Conservative government the following year. The second is the miners' strike of 1984–5, a long, attritional and often violent battle with the Thatcher government in which support was gathered from sources far beyond the NUM. This action failed to halt a program of pit closures, retrenchments and erosions of conditions and led to an eventual return to work with no ground gained. The strike also effectively split the NUM in half and, through threats of sequestration of its funds, almost destroyed the union entirely.

The 1980s and 1990s then are characterised by union defeats and, consequently, a steady loss of faith in organised unionism even among members. The labour movement theatre that survived through this period in Britain thus shows a far greater resilience than that which developed under more favourable circumstances in Australia. The initial meetings between unionists and the political theatreworkers thrown up by the 1960s, though, took place over a period when the unions were at their strongest. In the 1970s unionism in Britain achieved its highest numbers, its highest level of union density (almost 59% by 1979), and its highest level of militancy (measured in terms of strike days lost) since the General Strike of 1926. The specific nature of that militancy needs to be put in context.

The early onset of the Industrial Revolution in Britain, meant that the union movement predated the development of socialist ideas in the labour movement. The movement consequently developed an institutionalised pragmatism and was centrally concerned with issues of wages and conditions, which made it, at base, a reformist organisation rather than a politically radical one. It has not, though, been tied into a corporatist framework through compulsory systems of conciliation and arbitration, like the Australian union movement. It has fought to sustain the right to voluntarist collective bargaining, most notably in a successful battle against the Conservative government's attempted introduction of an Industrial Relations Act in 1971. Industrial action has characteristically been based in specific workplaces. This led to the development of a strong grass-roots activism through locally elected shop stewards, who have organised themselves into regional or industry-based committees not formally recognised by the Trade Union Congress (TUC), the organisational centre of the movement. The focal points of union activism have thus more often than not been at a grass-roots level while union organisers and leaders have often been more focused on disciplining their members and policing wage restraint than in leading their battles. Although this had been the case since the late 1950s, it was particularly so under the Wilson and Callaghan Labour governments (1974–1979), during which the TUC entered into a Social Contract with government not unlike the Accord between the ACTU and the Labor government in Australia in the 1980s. The essential difference between the British Social Contract and the Australian Accord was that the former proved unsustainable in the face of rank-and-file industrial militancy which produced the wave of mostly unofficial, or 'wildcat', strikes during 1979's 'Winter of Discontent'.

Unions and Culture: Centre 42, the New Left and the Folk Song Revival

Raphael Samuel has characterised the emergence of British Marxism as initially an artistic rather than a conventionally political movement, and has detailed a wide array of activity which emerged under the shadow of the Second International around the turn of the century. Its principal figures were not union activists or political theorists but artists and poets like William Morris, Walter Crane and George Bernard Shaw (Samuel 1985: 3–19). Hence amateur musical and theatre groups were commonly established within the co-operative societies and socialist parties which coalesced to form the Labour Party in 1900. This interest in cultural activity is also reflected in networks like the Workers' Education Association. In the Second International perspective, 'Art' was predominantly viewed as 'high art', and seen as a humanising influence from which an exploited working class had been excluded.

Yet, even though specific unions have occasionally been associated with particular cultural traditions (the NUM with colliery brass bands in the north of England and choirs in Wales, for example), the broader labour movement has taken a more pragmatic line on its social role, marginalising cultural activity and political radicalism as a distraction from its real work. The TUC's only direct involvement in a theatrical venture was its 1934 decision to commission a play on the Tolpuddle Martyrs, *Six Men of Dorset* by Miles Malleson and Harvey Brooks, to coincide with the centenary of their trial. Despite restaging the play for a successful tour in 1937, the TUC was not interested in establishing any ongoing involvement in theatre (Davies 1987: 96–8).[1] Instead, cultural activity has mostly come from small radical groups on the fringe of the movement, like the Communist Party in the 1930s—the focal point of the agitprop theatre scene—and the associated Workers' Theatre Movement. As in Australia and Canada, this theatre scene was largely killed off by the Popular Front period in the mid-to-late 1930s. What remained was subsumed into Unity Theatre, which eventually languished in the early 1970s.

There was, however, a substantial overture when the 1960 TUC Congress passed Resolution 42, which read:

> Congress recognises the importance of the arts in the life of the community, especially now when many unions are securing a shorter working week and greater leisure for their members. It notes that the trade union movement has participated to only a small extent in the direct promotion of plays, films, music, literature and other forms of expression, including those of value to its beliefs and principles. Congress considers that much more could be done, and accordingly requests the General Council to conduct a special examination and make proposals to a future Congress to ensure a greater participation by the trade union movement in all cultural activities. (Cited in Coppieters 1975: 39)

Subsequently, a group of artists and theatreworkers formed around the playwright Arnold Wesker and established Centre 42, an organisation committed to bridging the gap between artsworkers and a potential working-class public. Writing in the *New Statesman*, Wesker delineated his vision of what the venture could initiate:

---

1. It is worthy of note that the TUC's next substantial foray into theatrical entrepreneurialism was for a revival of *Six Men of Dorset* by 7:84 England on the 150th anniversary in 1984.

You start off with a picture: orchestras tucked away in valleys, people stopping Auden in the street to thank him for their favourite poem, teenagers around the jukebox arguing about my latest play, miners flocking to their own opera house; a picture of a nation thirsting for all the riches their artists can excite them with, hungry for the greatest, the best, unable to wait for Benjamin Britten's next opera, arguing about Joan Littlewood's latest. (Cited in Hewison 1986: 18)

Clive Barker, who was closely involved in the early years of Centre 42, described it in a letter to trade unions seeking support in 1961 as no less than an attempt 'to establish a new popular culture' in Britain. An early brochure described it as the 'First Stage in a Cultural Revolution' (Cited in Coppieters 1975: 40).

These high ambitions led to the staging of six arts festivals in conjunction with the annual recruitment weeks of six interested Trades Councils in 1961 and 1962. The festivals consisted of art exhibitions, poetry readings, jazz and folk music concerts, and a theatrical triple bill with a Bernard Kops play, a ballet with music by Stravinsky, and Charles Parker's *The Maker and the Tool* (of which more later). Alan Sinfield has described this awkward mix of 'relatively political and hopefully accessible instances of high culture together with bits of current student subculture and uncertain gestures towards the creativity of working people' as 'pure new-left subculture' (Sinfield 1989: 265). This New Left offered a Marxist intellectual context for the essentially middle-class dissidence of the activist theatreworkers who approached the union movement in the late 1960s and early 1970s. This gave them a theoretical grounding in left-wing politics which was more difficult to find in Australia and Canada at the time.

The British New Left, which emerged in the mid-1950s, clustered around the Campaign for Nuclear Disarmament rather than the organised labour movement, and was more influential on student subculture than on unionists. Its seminal texts were the works of literary and cultural critics, such as Richard Hoggart's *The Uses of Literacy* and Raymond Williams' *Culture and Society*, both published in 1958, and of left-wing historians like E. P. Thompson's *The Making of the English Working Class*, published in 1963, and Eric Hobsbawm's *Labouring Men*, which appeared in 1964. Sinfield has described the intellectual ethos these and related texts gave rise to as 'left culturalism', thus indicating its characteristic concentration on the realm of culture (Sinfield 1989: 232–250). The historians began to elaborate a long narrative of working-class organisation and opposition, traceable from the Levellers of the seventeenth century through the Chartists of the nineteenth century, for example, and put class on the agenda as an oppositional 'culture' rather than a mere statistical category. At the same time, Williams began to define some of the features of that culture, while Hoggart bemoaned its destruction in the postwar years by the imperialising influence of American 'mass' culture.

'Culture' was the site of struggle for the New Left, the point where the working class, seduced by comparative affluence following the privations of the immediate postwar years, was deflected from its revolutionary purpose. The middle-class dissidents and upwardly mobile working-class artists and intellectuals who constituted the New Left saw it as their task to educate the working class through exposing its members to the best of a radical strain in the high art tradition, or to re-educate them in the lost tradition of working-class radicalism still present in uncorrupted elements of a popular culture. The former position is clearly reflected in Wesker's fairly unlikely 'picture', or in the less patronising involvement of central figures in the movement (Williams, Hoggart and Thompson most notably) in adult education labour movement organisations like the Workers' Educational Association. The latter is partially represented by the British folk song revival.

The British folk song revival followed in the footsteps of the US Communist Party–inspired folk song movement, which descended from Joe Hill in the first decade of the century through Woody Guthrie in the Depression to Pete Seeger and Alan Lomax after the war. The American movement attempted to place a traditional music and through it an oppositional, working-class cultural history in the arena of popular culture and to turn it to political ends. In Britain, an enthusiasm for American 'folk' music was initially picked up in the 1950s and manifested itself in skiffle groups—bands built round simple, cheap instruments (guitar, tea-chest bass and washboard being particularly common) with amateur, formally untrained performers singing songs like 'Rock Island Line' to essentially rhythmic accompaniment. These groups performed outside the networks of promoters and commercial venues and became part of an aura of youthful rebellion particularly associated with the huge CND (Campaign for Nuclear Disarmament) marches of the period.

Under the influence of Ewan MacColl and A.L. Lloyd, the enthusiasm for American folk music was transmuted in the early 1960s into a search for a radical tradition in British working-class popular culture in opposition to 'art music'. Lloyd states the central political principle upon which the movement rested:

> Deep at the root, there is no essential difference between folk music and art music; they are varied blossoms from the same stock, grown to serve a similar purpose, if destined for different tables. Originally they spring from the same area of man's mind; their divergence is a matter of history, of social and cultural stratification. Traditionally, art music is a diversion for the educated classes, while folk music is one of the most intimate, reassuring and embellishing possessions of the poor (and in large tracts of the world they have been robbed even of that). (Lloyd 1969: 19)

The revivalists thus opposed the European Romantic fascination with folk music in the late nineteenth and early twentieth centuries, which saw it as a national music, essentially rural and of the past. In Britain middle-class collectors like Cecil Sharp and the English Folk Dance and Song Society sought songs from a supposedly primitive, uncorrupted oral tradition, and these were picked up by art music composers like Ralph Vaughan Williams and Percy Grainger. Under the guiding hand of MacColl and Lloyd, however, the folk revival searched for the music of working people, focussing on the urban industrial proletariat rather than the romanticised peasant. They were keen to rediscover the continuity between the radicalism of British working-class culture being exhumed by the New Left historians and a contemporary working class whose radical traditions were being swamped under American mass cultural imperialism. The revival's assertion of an oppositional culture thus concentrated attention on the performance of the music and maintaining a 'traditional' style rather than collecting 'texts' for appropriation into the art music tradition.

The folk song revival is one of the more enduring, and certainly less patronising, initiatives of New Left culturalism. The huge network of folk clubs established throughout Britain in the 1960s became a common point of entry for a younger generation into the intellectual milieu of the New Left. Of particular significance for the folk song revival was the New Left assumption that the strengths of a working-class tradition could be reclaimed in opposition to mass culture by tying a history of radicalism, as revealed by the New Left historians, into a living working-class movement. As our account of Banner Theatre will show, this was to become an influence on the development of an oppositional theatre practice in the 1970s.

The New Left was also a powerful influence on the generation which came to political theatre in the late 1960s and early 1970s through its success within the higher education system. The first great institutional success was the establishment of the Birmingham Centre for Contemporary Cultural Studies (BCCCS) in 1964 (Hoggart was the inaugural director), which exerted a powerful influence over the development of Cultural Studies as a discipline in Britain, particularly after Stuart Hall took over from Hoggart. Other New Left figures, most notably Williams, Thompson and Hobsbawm, became similarly influential within the university system, and published prolifically. The New Left created an intellectual milieu the extraordinary ramifications of which were most felt at the moment of intellectual formation for theatreworkers of the 1970s. As John Saville has written, this was the period of 'an implantation of Marxism in British intellectual life' (Saville 1987: 135). Writing in 1987 he claimed that:

> [t]here are today proportionately more socialists in Britain than at any previous period, in large part the consequences of the New Left of the late 1950s and of the generation of 1968, and the bookshelves are bursting with socialist volumes, tracts and pamphlets. (Saville 1987: 135)

But, he continues, 'the social consciousness of workers in trade unions is less radical than it was in the immediate aftermath of the war', partly because of 'the unfortunate fact that theoretical rigour in Marxist terms can apparently only be achieved by many authors in a density of language comprehensible only to a few' (Saville 1987: 135). Consequently, this new intellectual Left remained 'largely, although not wholly, divorced from working people, whether organized or not' (Saville 1987:138).

Centre 42 was an attempt to make a connection between the cultural aspirations of the New Left and 'organised' working people, and its failure to do so was in some measure a result of the union movement's indifference to the sphere of culture. The venture struggled to gain TUC support from the beginning. The 'special examination' proposed in Resolution 42 resulted in a report from the TUC Education Officer in 1961 which suggested 'that it was not the business of the unions to become involved in cultural affairs' beyond urging more public support for the arts (Coppieters 1975: 46). While Centre 42 gained some support from within the movement and the Labour Party, by 1965 the TUC had dissociated itself from the venture, thus signing its death warrant.

The failure of Centre 42 was not just a result of the indifference of the TUC. It was also unable to gain Arts Council support, and struggled with its administrative inability to cope with the enormous task it had set itself. Its brief was to stage festivals on request, and it was committed to establishing a number of arts centres throughout the country. Even when this devolved to an attempt to convert the Round House in Camden, however, raising funds proved beyond its ability. As well, and most importantly for the theatre work with unionists which was to follow a few years later, Centre 42 was consistently split over the issue of appropriate aesthetic forms as the debate about 'culture' continued within the New Left. Wesker was often accused of a 'cultural imperialism' or of imposing on the working class the sort of art he thought was good for them. This attitude had the historical imprimatur of the Second International, and filled at least partially the perspectives generated within the New Left itself, but it sat uneasily with the avowedly Marxist outlook of theatreworkers like John McGrath, who quit the venture to construct his own version of a working-class popular theatre which came to fruition in 7:84.[1]

The inability of Centre 42 to engage the TUC, or even working-class audiences, served several important purposes, and taught some lessons in the ways that ambitious failure often can. The venture put the notion of working with unionists on the agenda of theatreworkers in search of working-class audiences, so that it was there to be picked up a decade later. Its failure demonstrated that working through the upper echelons of the unions was less likely to allow access to these audiences than an approach at the grass-roots level through shop stewards—Trades Councils had proved to be as out of touch with their rank and file as the TUC (Coppieters 1975: 48). The debates raised about the theatrical forms appropriate to the task raged throughout the 1970s in various left-wing publications and the pages of *Theatre Quarterly*. And, as well as offering indications of what not to do, the venture began to suggest avenues worthy of further exploration, like the series of performances developed by Charles Parker, under the general title of *The Maker and the Tool*. These combined material from taped interviews with workers in an industry selected from each of the six Centre 42 festival sites with poetry, folk song, classical music, slides, film and dance to create a documentary theatre form which mixed professional performers and local amateurs, and gestured towards a left-wing theatre tradition with its roots in the 1930s. Parker's experiments will be further discussed in the case study on Banner Theatre, the company he later helped to form, but the tradition he was partially drawing on was very much alive in the 1960s in the work of Theatre Workshop.

---

1. See Itzin 1980: 103–109 for an account of a vitriolic debate between McGrath and Wesker on the issue.

Theatre Traditions: Theatre Workshop

Theatre Workshop, brought to prominence by their highly influential 1963 production, *Oh! What a Lovely War!*, offered direct continuities with the left-wing theatre work of the 1930s. The core group (centring on MacColl and Joan Littlewood) who formed Theatre Workshop after the war, had plundered Russian, European and US left-wing experimental theatre and film, from agitprop to constructivism and documentary theatre. They developed a popular theatre style characterised by constructivist sets, anti-naturalistic staging techniques and performance styles, with an eclectic mix of song, dance, mass declamation, documentary information, slides and film and more conventionally theatrical material. Their theatre style had continuities, perhaps not entirely perceived at the time, with an indigenous popular political theatre influenced by the Russian and German experiments in 'collision montage' of Meyerhold, Eisenstein, Brecht and Piscator (Paget 1995: 41). They toured to non-theatrical spaces, played to working-class audiences and worked to break down the separation between performer and audience as part of a program to create a 'people's theatre' with its roots in both British popular performance forms like the music hall and the rich inheritance of European left-wing modernism. Theatre Workshop was thus, as Derek Paget describes it, 'the Trojan horse through which European theatre practices from the 1918–1939 period entered post-war Britain' (Paget 1995: 212). It influenced the development of a range of political theatre ventures including small-scale touring groups like 7:84 England and Scotland (McGrath 1981: 49–53).

The company was largely responsible for developing and sustaining a tradition of popular theatre based on documentary material which swept through the newly established regional repertory companies in the 1960s as a means of attracting working-class audiences. The best known was the series of local documentaries staged by Peter Cheeseman at Stoke-on-Trent, but the style was represented in occasional productions by most of these new regional companies and also in the work of the Theatre-in-Education companies which emerged at the same time. These continuities were clarified in a flurry of publishing dating from the 1970s, initiated by Ewan MacColl in 1973, which fleshed out the history of the Theatre Workshop venture in the Red Megaphones, an agitprop troupe formed in Manchester in the early 1930s (MacColl 1973, 1985, 1986, 1990; Goorney 1981; Goorney and MacColl 1986; Littlewood 1995; Paget 1990.1, 1990.2, 1995).

Theatre Workshop became a similar, if more tenuous, link to a tradition of political theatre in Australia and Canada. George Luscombe, for example, took his experience of working on documentary techniques with Littlewood in the 1950s to Canada, which placed them on the agenda for younger theatreworkers, and the work of Peter Cheeseman was certainly well known (Filewod 1987: 16–18). In Australia, Littlewood's work was widely known through *Oh! What a Lovely War!*, and influenced pioneering groups like the Popular Theatre Troupe and the Australian Performing Group, both of which developed popular theatre styles for historical plays built on documentary material.

Britain, however, offered a richer environment in the early 1970s, an environment where the meetings of theatreworkers and unionists could be thought through. The New Left had put Marxist class analysis on the agenda of a generation working their way through tertiary education in the 1960s, making culture central to that analysis. It had also initiated a new understanding of the working class as the repository of an oppositional culture, and had begun to elaborate a notion of 'people's history' which made that culture accessible and coherent, in ways it hadn't been since the 1930s. The folk song revival constructed a means of giving that culture new life and promulgating elements of it to a generation of middle-class dissidents. Ewan MacColl and the Critics' Group had shown some natural links between folk song and agitprop and popular theatre techniques in a series of revues reminiscent of 1930s Living Newspapers under the general title of the Festival of Fools at the end of the 1960s. The influence of Theatre Workshop had helped established a burgeoning, nation-wide popular theatre movement, which offered a style and an introduction to a rich tradition of left-wing theatre work. All this made the meeting between theatreworkers and a trade union movement at its most radical since the war a logical strategy, and the failure of Centre 42 had generated sufficient debate to ensure a level of sophistication about the ways in which that approach was made.

The British alternative theatre scene of the 1970s and 1980s has been much better represented on the published record than similar work in Australia and Canada and there is little need to reiterate that history in any detail here. Catherine Itzin gives an exhaustive account of the companies that emerged after 1968, many of which worked with unionists (Itzin 1980). Baz Kershaw documents the development of a broad theatre movement and explores the social, political and institutional circumstances which shaped it (Kershaw 1992). Others have accounted for the work of individual ventures (DiCenzo 1996). It is sufficient here to point to the emergence of a popular political theatre movement in parallel with a number of other developments in alternative theatre. From the beginning, there were avowedly socialist companies like CAST (Cartoon Archetypal Slogan Theatre) and the Agitprop Street Players (later to become Red Ladder) committed to performing for working-class audiences, and later groups like 7:84 and the General Will established a touring circuit to non-theatre venues for left-wing popular theatre pieces. Other companies emerged from the developing community arts movement, and consequently brought more consultative methodologies to the process of generating material. There was no funding incentive for work to be conducted with unions, so connections with them tended to be informal and at grass-roots level. As a consequence a number of companies in search of working-class audiences made connections with radical unionists as part of a broader, clearly defined set of political objectives.

Strategic Ventures

As these narratives indicate, there was no tradition within the union movements in these three countries which would 'confirm a contemporary radical practice'. Even in Britain, which had the strongest sense of continuity with 'a radical past'—supplied by the New Left, the folk song revival and the long history of Theatre Workshop—the failure of the Centre 42 venture was probably more powerful as a disincentive for the union movement then as a clue to the possibilities inherent in alliances with young radical artsworkers from outside the movement. While artsworkers were welcome to offer support on picket lines and entertainment at rallies, there was nothing in the recent histories of the union movements to suggest a role corresponding to their political ambitions.

Further, the union movements, rather than being repositories of class consciousness, were characterised by a pragmatism which reduced their sphere of activities to improving, or increasingly merely maintaining, the wages and working conditions of their members. It was a period marked by savage New Right attacks on union power and the collapse of the Fordist accords which had structured unionism as a practice in the early years of the century. Although all of them contained pockets of a more radical politics, and it was here that artsworkers found their strongest allies, visions of the unions as the point of articulation of a revolutionary working class were quickly dissipated. Work with unions in Britain, Australia and Canada entailed substantial and continuing adaptations to a harder set of political realities, which could only be clarified through continual dialogue.

In Britain, where there was at least some sense of a radical cultural tradition and a rank and file amenable to the cultural expression of radicalism, dialogue at a grass-roots level was always possible: there were at least some common points of reference and vestiges of a shared language between artsworkers and unionists. The history of Banner Theatre which follows shows one way in which those possibilities were grasped, and also how they led to clashes with the organisational levels of the movement. Banner had the advantage of operating in a milieu in which class politics, and even class consciousness, were notions with some purchase, and their entry into that milieu via folk music offered a platform from which dialogue could build. As we hope to indicate, their emergence from the performative ethos of the folk club, and their continuing commitment to the oral history interview as the basic source material for the construction of performances, has prioritised the dialogue with their constituencies upon which adaptability relies.

Radical cultural traditions were more attenuated in Australia and Canada. In Australia, work with unions was rendered financially attractive via the Art and Working Life program, which began with a recuperative brief designed to facilitate the reconstruction of a tradition into which the work could be inserted. As well, the program prioritised dialogue between artsworker and unionist by making it a condition of the grant, and by making the unionist the employer or client of the artist. In Canada, the development of a popular theatre model built round community animation allowed a sideways entry into work with unions through social development agencies and activist groups.

In all three sites, work has been inflected by developing theorisations and methodologies of community consultation as a central feature of the process of generating performances. In Britain and Australia, the source of this focus has been the European move towards community arts, which was enshrined in funding policy in Australia, via the Art and Working Life program, for work with unions. In Canada, a similar stance emerged through the Canadian Popular Theatre Alliance's application of the community development strategies of Paulo Freire to the construction of theatre in activist community contexts. The work which forms the subject of the case studies which follow has thus developed, not as the application of a programmatic or universalising notion of workers' theatre, but as an adaptive

practice in which the styles and forms of performances have been tailored to the specific circumstances of each project. As we have said before, these are not so much 'companies', in any of the accepted senses of the term, as 'strategic ventures', built out of dialogic relationships with their union partners.

Chapter Three

Banner Theatre: Performance as Political Activism

The tape recorder is the centre of the work. You have to listen to what people say, that's the crucial thing.

Dave Rogers (Cited in Beale 1997)

anner Theatre commands our attention for four reasons. Firstly, its sheer longevity has seen it ride the crest of the wave of radical unionism in Britain in the 1970s, survive the crisis of unionism and the disappearance of funding for alternative theatre in the 1980s and negotiate the turmoil of the Left in the 1990s. By examining the strategic adjustments that made this possible, we can trace a broader history of the development of activist theatre since the late 1960s. Secondly, Banner's emergence from the British folk song revival links it, via Ewan MacColl, with the workers' theatre movement of the 1930s, revealing the unique continuities of British labour movement theatre. Thirdly, Banner's beginnings as an amateur venture and its fairly regular return to that status made political activism a priority and kept the company focused on the *instrumental* value of its work. And fourthly, Banner's commitment to *listening* led to a dialogic relationship with its audiences leaving it strategically placed to carry its political project beyond the 1990s.

The venture became Banner Theatre of Actuality in Birmingham in 1973 largely inspired by Charles Parker, a BBC Documentary Features Producer and a quintessentially New Left figure. Parker was a founding member of the Birmingham and Midland Folk Centre (1965), a committee member and singer at its offshoot the Grey Cock Folk Club (1967), and also worked in adult and workers' education in the Midlands. He gathered a group around himself bringing to it a range of experiences and connections, and some methodologies for constructing performances that inform Banner's work to this day. Among his connections, and central to the formation of Parker's sense of a political theatre, was Ewan MacColl, whom he met at the BBC in the 1950s.

When they met, MacColl had a twenty-year career in political theatre behind him and was a central figure in the British folk song revival. With Peggy Seeger he set up the Critics' Group in London in the mid-1960s, a highly influential collection of singer/songwriter/performers, keen to develop the singing style and repertoire, as well as to collect material and stage performances of the rediscovered music. MacColl was, with A. L. Lloyd, a major influence on the emerging network of folk clubs like the Grey Cock, and thus their recuperation of regional folk and industrial song traditions. Some of this recuperative work is represented by Grey Cock member and local historian Roy Palmer's prolific publication of Midlands songs, particularly for use in schools. (Palmer 1971; 1972; 1973; 1974.1; 1974.2; Leach and Palmer 1978).

Although this recuperative effort was nominally aimed at the working class, it was more inclined to draw in young middle-class dissidents and upwardly mobile working-class young people (some of whom had already been radicalised by the CND marches of the late 1950s). Banner founding member Dave Rogers describes the constituency of the Grey Cock as 'a rag bag of anarchists, liberals and lefties, and lots of young people, like myself, with no firm political affiliations at all' (Rogers 1997). As elsewhere, these clubs were a common entry point for a younger generation into the ambit of the New Left intelligentsia. A 1968 brochure of the Birmingham and Midland Folk Centre, for instance, lists Parker as President and a number of 'vice presidents' including Lloyd and MacColl, New Left historian E. P. Thompson and Richard Hoggart, inaugural director of the Birmingham Centre for Contemporary Cultural Studies. The evidence suggests that only MacColl had much to do with the Folk Centre, yet the influence of Hoggart's BCCCS work, and his position in the 'Culture and Society debate', was palpable.

Parker's affiliations to the intellectual milieu of the New Left are perhaps clearest in his embrace of the folk song revival, and its assumption that folk song was the repository of the dissident working-class cultural tradition delineated by the New Left historians. The recuperation of the folk song tradition, in opposition to American 'mass' culture, particularly popular music and television (this *was* the late 1950s), was, to the revivalists, a crucial cultural/political project, and Parker, who embraced this position by the early 1960s, saw himself as a warrior in a battle for the reclamation of working-class culture through the folk tradition. This led, among other things, to the making of *Vox Pop*, a BBC radio series critiquing contemporary pop songs with Stuart Hall, who later took over at the BCCCS from Hoggart. (The analysis of mass culture did not become the defining feature of the work of the BCCCS until the 1970s and 1980s.)

Parker, MacColl and the 'Radio Ballads'

Parker and MacColl were an unlikely combination. MacColl came from a working-class background, was a self-educated 'organic intellectual' in the Gramscian sense, and had been a political activist and renegade member of the Communist Party of Great Britain since the early 1930s. Parker came from an upper middle-class background, had served as a submarine commander in the Royal Navy during the war (for which he held a DSC), and held a Cambridge Honours Degree in English Literature. When he met MacColl he was a 'BBC type' working as a Senior Radio Features producer in Birmingham and a devout Christian with little discernible commitment to radical politics beyond the embrace of some broadly left-liberal humanist causes. His passionate interest in folk music appears to have owed as much to the middle-class ethos of the English Folk Dance and Song Society (of which he was a member) as the politicised folk movement of the 1950s and 1960s. During the early 1960s he saw folk music as a means of tapping an essentially British poetic genius less corrupted than most 'high' art of the time, and closer to the spirit of Shakespeare and Chaucer. He probably thought of MacColl as a 'source' singer, an uncorrupted voice of the poetic spirit of the working class. MacColl was a lot more hard-nosed than that, and quickly led him towards a Marxist activism. As a result, Parker started teaching Workers' Education Association courses on politics and folk song, and conducted a series of experiments in political theatre before establishing Banner.

The connection between Parker and MacColl was consolidated during the making of the 'Radio Ballads', a series of experimental radio documentaries made with Peggy Seeger for the BBC. These consisted of 'actuality' (recorded interview material and sound effects), songs (some traditional but most written in the style of the emerging folk song revival) and incidental music written or arranged by Seeger. They were spliced together without narration into impressionistic montages built around a central theme. Eight were made with a group of singers and musicians (associates of MacColl's): *The Ballad of John Axon* (1958), about a recent railway accident; *Song of a Road* (1959), with road construction workers; *Singing the Fishing* (1960), on the fishing industry; *The Big Hewer* (1961), on coalmining; *The Body Blow* (1962), based on interviews with five polio victims; *On the Edge* (1963), based on interviews with adolescents; *The Fight Game* (1963), on boxing; and *The Travelling People* (1964), on gipsies in Britain.[1] These were powerful evocations of working-class experience, and particularly notable for the sheer bravado of the music, which ranged from traditional songs through jazz arrangements to original songs, some of which owed as much to MacColl's enthusiasm for the 1930s music of Hanns Eisler as to the folk tradition. Several of these have entered the repertoire of the folk song revival, and some have actually been 'collected' as part of a continuing oral tradition.

The documentaries, seen as major innovations in radio documentary technique, were enthusiastically received by the New Left and have since become legendary. The BBC, which effectively vetoed them by sacking Parker in 1972, replayed them as 'Charles Parker's Radio Ballads', following his untimely death in 1980, giving them 'classic' status. Within the folk song revival, they fuelled a performative mode in which a group of songs would be held together in performance by readings from documentary material. They also left their mark on British documentary theatre, most notably on the work of Peter Cheeseman at Stoke-on-Trent, starting with *The Jolly Potters* in 1964 (Cheeseman 1970: xi; Paget 1990: 70–71). Their influence is further evident in plays like John McGrath's *The Cheviot, the Stag and the Black, Black Oil*, and, as Derek Paget has shown, on a developing tradition of 'verbatim theatre' (in which Paget surprisingly fails to include Banner) (Paget 1987). Parker saw them in more grandiose terms than this:

> the conviction of the authors is that the Radio Ballad indicates at least the beginning of an approach to People's Art which provides the artist and the intellectual with necessary roots in the common working experience, and so allows him to give back to the people, themselves, but sharpened and typified in art; to give them 'Fuel in Stormy Weather' and not flowers on brocade. (Parker 1972)

Parker believed 'actuality' material tapped the roots of a tradition of vernacular speech 'with the pith and immediacy of Chaucer and

---

1. Six of them were released as records in the 1960s and all eight have now been released as CDs, with extensive cover notes, by Topic.

Shakespeare', which only needed to be combined with the emergent technology:

> Every community has its hi-fi buffs and super-8 cineastes and the rest, revealing an expertise which, I believe, has only to be channelled in a creative direction—and we could be in for a renaissance of Elizabethan proportions. The technology must be anchored in working-class experience, which is where the folk revival, the ballad form and vernacular speech come in, to create a genuinely popular theatre. (Parker 1974)

Parker's enthusiasm for vernacular speech was encouraged by MacColl, who claimed that it was his idea to use 'actuality' tapes for *The Ballad of John Axon* rather than to give transcriptions or rewrites of the material to actors, on the more measured grounds that it:

> captured a remarkable picture of a way of life, a picture in words charged with the special kind of vitality and excitement which derives from involvement in a work-process. ... It wasn't merely that the recorded speech had the ring of spontaneity; there was something else—the excitement of an experience relived and communicated directly without dilution of additives, living speech unglossed by author's pen or actor's voice. (MacColl, 1990: 313)

Parker embraced the use of 'actuality' material with a characteristic enthusiasm, a result of both his perception of its power and of his exploration of the possibilities thrown up by the portable tape recorder, which was, of course, new technology at the time. His experience of interviewing working-class people began to politicise him, particularly following the work on *The Big Hewer* in 1961:

> According to Ewan MacColl, prior to this he had maintained a conventional BBC attitude to the interviewees, even seeing Sam Larner and Ronnie Balls [the two central interviewees for *Singing the Fishing*] as 'characters' rather than equals. Working with coal miners changed that. Charles could not do other than regard these people as remarkable human beings, neither quaint nor in any way inferior to him despite his professional status. From the time of *The Big Hewer* to his death, Charles maintained links with the people he had met in the coalfield, cultivating close friendships with some of the most militant and regarding these relationships as among the most important in his life. (Fisher 1986: 6–7)

The centre of this new 'People's Art' was the tape recorder, which took on the function of a musical instrument in the composition of the Radio Ballads.

To generate the final tape of *Singing the Fishing*, for example, Parker placed the tape recorder in the midst of a group of singers and musicians in the recording studio. The edited interview material and sound effects were 'played' as the lead instrument in the orchestration, so the performers could respond directly to it (MacColl 1990: 318–326). This made working-class speech the centrepiece of the documentary, unmediated by the BBC 'standard English' of the conventional narrator. Parker's refusal to reinsert this mediating narrational voice became a major factor in the dispute with the BBC which led to his dismissal.

The consistent claim that Parker was the sole begetter of the Radio Ballads (a claim which Parker himself never made) has partially obscured MacColl's and Seeger's contribution (as MacColl has often been at pains to point out), and with it some of the history of the form. Clearly the form drew on MacColl's and Joan Littlewood's experiences in the 1930s when they worked on the experiments in BBC radio documentary in Manchester of Archie Harding and others (Bridson 1971: 50–71; Scannell 1986; MacColl 1990: 229–234). Harding and his co-workers introduced the montage technique into radio documentaries at the same time as MacColl and Littlewood were introducing the technique into their experimentation on popular theatre forms.

The Radio Ballads thus drew on a pre-war left-modernist fascination with montage manifested in the emergence of collage in the visual arts and in the structural techniques of Meyerhold, Brecht and Piscator in the theatre, which re-emerged in the work of Theatre Workshop. This entailed eschewing conventional character-based narrative in favour of an issue-based form that threw together disparate material for the listener to assemble. Parker's sense of the strategy is revealed in the following:

> By dispensing with conventional continuity devices of studio narrator, caption voice, dramatic vignette, and so on, the radio ballad makes something of the same imaginative demands upon its audience as does the traditional ballad (insistently drawing the listener to participate imaginatively in the action by having, himself, to work and fill out the deliberately spare and open-ended form). (Cited in Karpf 1980:14)

This appeal to 'active' listening is accompanied by a characteristic left-modernist self-reflexivity in foregrounding the process of assembly of the documentary material, which continually declares itself as 'real' by not being mediated through the voices of actors (as had mostly been the case with Harding's experiments). The listener was thus made aware of the editorial process, but not overtly directed towards the particular viewpoint of a narrational voice. While Parker was drawn to the Radio Ballads by an enthusiasm for working-class vernacular and folk song, these theatrical precursors were to influence his own experiments in documentary theatre forms.

Parker's Early Experimentation in Theatre

Parker attempted to transfer the central elements of the Radio Ballads to the stage for the Centre 42 festivals in the early 1960s. He made four multi-media documentary pieces, collectively entitled *The Maker and the Tool*, which he described as:

> an attempt to express the relationship between man and his tools with especial reference to four basic industries (concentrated in four towns, eg., Nottingham—coal; Leicester—hosiery; Haye Middx.—electronics; Bristol—docking), and originating in tape recordings taken from those engaged in the particular industries and used as the basis for the whole work, particularly for specially written songs by young singers of the folk song revival. (Parker 1963)

Drawing at least partially on MacColl's theatrical experience, Parker used slides and film footage juxtaposed with the taped interview material and songs, alongside the dance and movement which had been part of the work of Theatre of Action and Theatre Workshop. While the pieces were not an unqualified success, Baz Kershaw described them as 'the only genuine cultural innovation' of the entire Centre 42 venture (Kershaw 1992: 106), and they became a bridge for Parker between the Radio Ballads and the later experiments which led to Banner.

One of Parker's central innovations was his inclusion of local union members as performers. This distinguished *The Maker and the Tool* from much of the work of Centre 42, which was more concerned with the making of art *for* unionists and with securing support from union officials, who were already regarded with suspicion by their rank and file. This grass-roots approach became the chosen mode for Banner and other companies.

Following the collapse of Centre 42, Parker unsuccessfully attempted to continue the work, with MacColl and Seeger among others, through a group called the Leaveners. In Birmingham the strategy bit and he drew some of the amateur participants from *The Maker and the Tool* into a new group which had gathered round him at the Grey Cock Folk Club and through his various adult education courses. Parker was clearly a charismatic figure, as Rogers makes clear:

> I joined an evening class [at the Birmingham and Midland Institute] run by Charles Parker in 1968, ostensibly about folk-song, but in reality an inspiring mix of politics, singing, ballad analysis and folk theatre which, in 1968 jargon, 'blew my mind'. Week 2 of the course Parker had me singing [something he had never done before despite an interest in the folk song revival via attendance at the Grey Cock Folk Club], week 10 of the course I was performing in a political mumming play, written by Ewan MacColl, in Smallheath Park to a belligerent crowd of barracking teenagers. Two years later, I had ditched my steady job as a computer programmer, and started to follow a precarious existence as a political cultural worker. Parker changed my life, as indeed he changed many people's lives. (Rogers 1992: 21)

Rhoma Bowdler, a trainee teacher in Dance and Drama at Wolverhampton Teacher Training College in the late 1960s, attended Parker's summer school courses on the Radio Ballad as a teaching tool, and was similarly drawn into doing research and interview work on various of his BBC projects. Still others were attracted by the aura of the Grey Cock Folk Club. By 1971 Parker was running regular weekend meetings of this burgeoning group with other acquaintances from outside the folk club, at his home, Park House. Under the title of the Park House Convention, this became a regular forum set up in response to a perceived degeneration of British popular culture.

Rogers' trajectory into this activity was typical if a little more life-changing than most, and correlates with Niall MacKinnon's characterisation of the participants in the folk song revival as middle-class dissidents and upwardly mobile working-class youth (MacKinnon 1994: 44) (Rogers was the first student of his working-class school to make it to university.) Banner, in many respects, concentrated the process of politicisation typical of the late 1960s and early 1970s. Rogers moved from the protest songs of Bob Dylan and Joan Baez to British folk music and a sense of class politics. This introduced him to the intellectual ethos of the New Left, and then, via touring shows to union venues in the early days of Banner, to grass-roots political activism and the union movement.

Park House Convention was a characteristically 1960s venture, with a sense of communitarian politics and 'a tremendous feeling of buoyancy and optimism about our capacity to change the world' (Rogers interviewed by

David Watt, Birmingham, 11 September 1996). It did not, though, view itself as part of the emerging political theatre scene. In Rogers' words, the group 'felt very estranged' from what they perceived as 'arty types', who were pre-dominantly from the cosmopolitan centre, London, rather than the working-class environment of in-dustrial Birmingham (Rogers interviewed by David Watt, Birmingham, 11 September 1996). Banner was not composed of theatre-workers turning to politics, as were 7:84 and Belt and Braces, for example, or the product of student radicalism, as was General Will in Bradford or Red

Dave Rogers and Charles Parker in agitprop mode, 1974.

Ladder in London. What held Banner together was the performative ethos of the folk club.

The conventions of this ethos are worth consideration. MacKinnon saw the 'careful and conscious deconstruction of staging' in the folk clubs as the defining, and probably the most enduring, element of the British folk song revival, and writes at length on 'the fine line between anarchy and rigidity' which it entailed (MacKinnon 1994: 77–98). The revival's concern with the recuperation of an 'uncommercial' music of 'the people' led to 'an extremely self-conscious attempt to change the social dynamics of performance' (MacKinnon 1994: 25–6):

> The focus of attention was not an entity, 'the song', but a process, 'get people singing'. The aim was not to reconstruct the past from its songs and music but to change the social role of music from one where music-making was in the hands of the music industry to one where the control of music-making was restored to ordinary people. (MacKinnon 1994: 30)

The clubs were usually based in pubs, the familiar venue for popular music, often with a bar in the same room. The performance area was not a 'stage' but merely a temporarily demarcated space in a larger, single space (and sometimes not even that). There was no 'backstage' which meant the performer became a spectator who just happened to be performing at a particular time rather than a 'star turn'. This blurring of the boundaries was further reflected in the structure of the clubs. Each consisted of a group of 'resident singers', 'floor singers' and an occasional paid guest. Resident singers were experienced performers who would sing unpaid as part of a regular night's program; floor singers had less experience and sang less often; and a fledgling group of touring professionals were paid for guest spots. The 'floor singer' (best understood as a spectator who occasionally performed) in particular helped to close the gap between performer and spectator.

The acoustic nature of the music demanded a mode of listening deliberately counter to the social process of our most common listening experience, listening to amplified or recorded music. At the same time, the calculated informality of performance avoided the silent attentiveness of the concert hall, designed to foreground the performer and render the music a finished artwork. Instead of music as a commodity, an experience purchased by the passive listener, the ambience of the folk club stressed 'the face-to-face intercommunicative nature of musical performance' (MacKinnon 1994: 81). Folk club performance aspired to 'associate the performance of the music on the stage with its performance off it'. In its most logical mode, the 'session', a group of performer–spectators arranged in a circle 'performed' in turn (MacKinnon 1994: 97, 99–107).

The furore created by the advent of amplification into the folk scene, most famously in the early 1960s when Bob Dylan turned up at the Newport Folk Festival with an electric guitar, was not merely a Luddite outcry against the onward march of technology, but a response to the violation of an essential element of a performative mode:

> PA does not just raise the volume level but also redefines the nature of the performance, and is itself a powerful statement of the separation of roles of performer and audience. It restructures the power relationship. ... Because an acoustic performance can be so easily marred by intrusions of extraneous noise, from a general bustle at the bar to background chatter, this imposes a constraint upon a folk audience, one which is integral to the structuring of a musical event. (MacKinnon 1994: 120–121)

Noise, in the form of 'interjection or even occasional boisterousness', was tolerated, even encouraged, within the event, as an indication of the active involvement of the spectator, so long as it did not threaten 'the coherence of the performance' (MacKinnon 1994: 93). A folk performance thus aimed at creating a community between performer and audience through a shared understanding and acceptance of an implicit code of appropriate modes of behaviour, or 'decorum'. The performative modes generated by emerging theatre companies at this time were similar in the way they made close involvement with audiences, both within performances and surrounding them, a central component of the work.

Banner's emergence from this performative ethos helped it avoid the more patronising possibilities of 1970s agitprop. Rhoma Bowdler explains how:

> I didn't want Banner ever to be propaganda. I didn't want it to be agitprop, and the 'actuality' and the poetic in the 'actuality' always avoided that. We didn't want to go out and shout at people. ... We always wanted to say, 'Look, this is what so-and-so told us ... at that factory in the Midlands'. (interviewed by Dave Rogers, Birmingham, March 1997)

This is performance envisaged as conversation rather than explanation, and it owes more to the folk club than the theatre.

Thus, in a series of projects in the late 1960s and early 1970s, the loose group which gathered round Parker at the Grey Cock Folk Club brought a performance aesthetic of its own rather than a particular commitment to theatre. These projects were built around song and documentary material drawn from a range of sources. Two of these, *The Making of the Midlander*—a piece about the formation of the Midland working class—and *The Funny Rigs of Good and Tender Hearted Masters*—based on a group of songs which emerged from a Kidderminster carpet weavers' strike in the early nineteenth century were compiled largely by Roy Palmer. Another, particularly remembered by Banner members, was *Of One Blood*, a powerful compilation by Parker of a combination of songs and material drawn from contemporary newspaper accounts of racism in South Africa (particularly the Sharpeville killings), Rhodesia and, much closer to home, Britain. These were not so much theatrical events as ways of structuring folk club performances. Yet the contextualisation of songs within documentary material soon led to theatre, a step encouraged by group visits to London to see the political revues staged by MacColl and the Critics' Group (including Parker). The revues were annual events at the end of the 1960s under the general title of Festival of Fools, which mixed song, skits and documentary material in the manner of MacColl's earlier experiments with Theatre of Action, most notable in the Living Newspaper *Last Edition* (Goorney and MacColl 1986: 21–33).

The final stride came in 1973, when, for a few weeks, Parker was booking a room at the Birmingham and Midland Institute for folk performances.

Bowdler recalls that Parker was having trouble filling the last booking:

> and I just said to him, I said, 'Why don't we do a stage version of *The Big Hewer*?' And he looked at me and he said, 'That's a good idea. How?' I said, 'We'll ask at the Folk Club who'd be interested'. And that is exactly how Banner started. Just as daft as that. (interviewed by Dave Rogers, Birmingham, March 1997)

The following Saturday 'a rather strange collection of folk singers, drama teachers, office workers, technicians and car workers', seventeen people in all, turned up at Park House to discuss the proposal (Rogers, 1992: 21). The result was a stage adaptation, undertaken and directed by Bowdler, of the Radio Ballad which had most influenced and even politicised Parker, re-titled *Collier Laddie*. This first show, under the name of Banner Theatre of Actuality, was intended as a one-off performance.

Banner Theatre and the Miners: *Collier Laddie*

In reassembling the script of *The Big Hewer* to create *Collier Laddie*, Bowdler brought much that she had learnt at Wolverhampton College. Her knowledge ranged from the work of Brecht and Wedekind to popular theatre forms like commedia dell'arte and those of Theatre Workshop, as well as Laban dance techniques. She had already been involved in generating semi-documentary performances and had developed a stage version of one of her own Radio Ballads as a major project within her course. She was forced by circumstance to focus on the strength of the available performers, which was musical rather than acting in any conventional sense. The production established some basic elements which permeated most of Banner's subsequent work: the use of 'actuality' material, both played on tape and as source of text for performers; a central use of folk song, both traditional and written in the idiom; and slides, back-projected on a huge screen left over from *The Maker and the Tool*. The use of slides was influenced by MacColl's knowledge of the work of Piscator and the American Living Newspaper and, according to Rogers, acted in a number of ways:

> They could work as scene setters, for example with images of pit winding gear, mining villages etc; or work in contradiction to or in dialogue with the action on the stage, for example by setting graphic images of miners working against government propaganda about how easy life was now that nationalisation had removed the rapacious mine owners. (Rogers 1992: 21)

Bob Etheridge and Richard Hamilton in *Collier Laddie*, 1974.
(Photo: John Fryer)

As a device the slides contributed to making 'montage' a central principle of the work. Like the Radio Ballad from which it emerged, *Collier Laddie* foregrounded the fact that it was 'assembled' rather than 'written', using interview material drawn from the people who were its subject (even if in this case the material pre-dated the performance by over a decade), as well as from photographic images, facts and figures drawn from various sources, and songs. The grounding of the creative process in the verifiably 'authentic' owes something to MacColl, who saw the artist in the following terms:

> My ideal was the anonymous author, the anonymous song-writer, and you only achieve anonymity by becoming part of the whole. When I write a song it is important that I make the people I am writing it for believe that I know as much as they do about the milieu that they live and work in. Only then will they accept it as a true record. If they feel for one moment that it is written from outside they will suspect its validity. (MacColl 1985: 254)

Significant, at this stage in the development of the venture, was the fact that the montage had been composed and performed, not by a group of professional theatreworkers coming from outside the life-experience of its target audience, but by a group of amateurs seeking the committed insider role MacColl described. In an early handbill advertising the company (probably about 1975) this principle is laid out:

> The techniques that BANNER uses are open to all; in our audiences are men and women who know as much as (or more than!) us about tape-recorders, cameras, lighting or public-address systems; and about music, singing or dancing. By demonstrating that these skills can be brought together, to reveal themselves and their own community, BANNER hopes to challenge its audience to create their own theatre.

Two of the most important aspects of the ethos of the folk song revival are encapsulated here: the folk club emphasis on the notion of the amateur 'floor singer' to break down the gap between performer and audience; and the attempt to achieve 'authenticity' via the self-effacement of the artist in a collective editorial process. In this sense, *Collier Laddie* laid down a pattern for the company's future work.

Collier Laddie was, though, different in one important respect from later work, in that, in the words of Rogers, it was:

> a fairly light production politically. ... it focused somewhat nostalgically on comradeship and craft pride in the industry. Though the production touched on unemployment in the 1930s, the ravages of pneumoconiosis and pit disasters, it rarely exposed the causes of these afflictions and somewhat naively promoted nationalisation as a golden opportunity for the miners. The fact that we felt no need to radically rewrite the script reflected the politics of Banner at the time. We were left of centre, but were not particularly well grounded in grass roots politics. (Rogers 1992: 22)

The one-off performance was seen by an invited group of miners, many of them friends Parker had made at the time of *The Big Hewer*. This led to invitations to perform at miners' clubs and galas, and the group quickly built up connections with union activists in the National Union of Mineworkers (NUM). The nature of the relationships formed through the informality of performance was important in Banner's development of a firmer sense of politics. Essentially a group of enthusiastic amateurs, many with little knowledge of theatre, political or otherwise, and little direct connection with the union movement were thrown, by collaborative work, into sharing their different backgrounds, experiences and skills. More importantly, they were suddenly thrown into relationships with the union movement at a number of levels, from organisers planning industrial action at meetings at Ruskin College one weekend to rank-and-file miners at a Miners' Welfare in South Wales the next. Bowdler describes what was clearly an exciting experience: 'This kind of montage of stuff was hitting— you were living almost a montage ... Everything was in juxtaposition. And I was teaching Monday morning at an inner city school!' (interviewed by Dave Rogers, Birmingham, March 1997).

The easy interplay between performer and audience in the show allowed a stream of feedback, which led to rewriting over the two years it toured for weekend performances. Several new endings were written by MacColl during 1974 and 1975, to bring the show up to date with the 1972 and 1974 strikes, and taking a militant stand on the Wilson Labour government's attempts to impose a Social Contract on the union movement. The politics of the company were thus being formed through its dialogic connections with an older political militancy.

These were exciting times to be involved with such a network. The years 1973–4 marked not only a period of union militancy in Britain, but also the culmination of a left-wing push within the NUM which brought Arthur Scargill to the leadership. The NUM had been dominated for over twenty years by a right-wing faction which had acquiesced in declining wages and a campaign of pit closures, most notably under the first Wilson government of 1966–70. The success of Scargill's strategy of strike actions in 1972 and 1973 contributed to a new sense of confidence in the power of militant unionism which spread beyond the NUM, and strengthened the position of the shop stewards' networks and the radical Trades Councils. Banner's involvement with the rank and file of the NUM quickly placed its members in the midst of a broader network of militant rank-and-file union activists, often acting in opposition to the leaderships of their own unions.

From its inception, then, Banner was playing to the most militant sections of the labour movement at a time when they were testing their strength, first against the bureaucracies of their own unions, then against the Heath Conservative government, and after the Labour election victory of 1974, against the Wilson government. This process of politicisation was aided by numerous requests to sing at rallies or for street theatre performances on particular issues. The company split into a number of smaller performance groups, which allowed members to involve themselves in grass-roots activism beyond the opportunities offered by touring full-scale shows. The most notable of the quick-response, flexible performances for particular campaigns which emerged from this direct activism was a show, *The Shrewsbury 24*, (amended from a play by Broadside Mobile

Workers' Theatre, a breakaway from the Critics' Group in London) in support of three pickets arrested and imprisoned as a result of a building workers' strike. The state of politics within the specific unions where they made initial contact and operated as activists, then, was particularly formative.

The Saltley Gate Show

Banner's most successful early show, *The Saltley Gate Show*, again directed by Bowdler, indicates the politics of the group at the time. The Nechells Green Gas Works at Saltley Gate in East Birmingham held a huge deposit of coking coal which was being used as a reserve to break the 1972 miners' strike. When the NUM leadership belatedly realised the strategic importance of the Saltley Gas Works and implemented the union's developing flying picket strategy it met with little success. In a few days, legend has it, Scargill, Midlands District Secretary of the Communist Party Frank Watters, and various others associated with the Birmingham Trades Union Council managed to bring in 400 pickets, who were joined on 10 February by 10,000 Birmingham workers. As a result, the gates were closed, and Scargill delivered a victory speech from the top of a public urinal opposite the depot, in which he christened the event 'the Battle of Saltley Gate'. Within three weeks the miners' strike was over. The NUM had beaten the Heath government, as it did again in 1974, when Heath resigned, called an election, and lost. The battle has since become a legendary event in Scargill's leadership of the NUM and more generally in the recent history of working-class solidarity in Britain.

Saltley Gate marked the beginning of widespread use of the mass picket, and stood as an emblem of working-class solidarity in a period of violent confrontation between unionists and the state. It was also a major victory for the Left which was in the process of wresting control of the NUM. Given Banner's connections with the rank-and-file left of the NUM, it made eminent sense for the company to make a show in celebration of the victory. They embarked on this in 1975, as an amateur venture, with several unpaid people working full-time for the company.

The show used recorded interviews made (for an aborted book project) by Parker and some Critics' Group friends with participants in the battle, from Scargill to rank-and-file unionists. These were augmented by others undertaken by company members. Rogers was not initially convinced by the possibilities of 'actuality', however:

I couldn't understand when we first started what Charles was on about with actuality, and it wasn't until I got out and started recording some ... myself that it actually made any impact. It seemed a rather quaint idea .... (Cited in Fisher 1986: 9)

The generation of the script introduced company members to the methodology of constructing the Radio Ballads. It was a painstaking summer's work transcribing and categorising the interviews before 'writing' commenced for Rogers, his ex-wife Chris, Bowdler and Parker. Rogers describes the next phase:

> We listened to all this tape and then out of that we argued about a shape to it. ... We had this kind of loose idea about this ball game, how it starts off very gentlemanly as a game of cricket and gradually builds up till it's like ferocious pitched battles with the police and we used the game structure, sort of agitprop ... And then we worked with the 'actuality', building it ... as *Collier Laddie* had been structured. (interviewed by David Watt, Birmingham, 11 September 1996)

The result was a theatrically convincing piece in which Bowdler was able to use the developing acting abilities of the group. Like *Collier Laddie*, it combined songs, slides, transcribed interview material and newspaper quotes. It added to the mix dramatised scenes, both naturalistic and agitprop, and the elaborate sequence of games described by Rogers, which built in ferocity as the battle escalated.

Performances were planned for the venues where Banner had toured *Collier Laddie*. These were informal spaces, often including a bar, in which an interplay between performance and audience was easy and natural. With this in mind, the play opens with musicians on the performing area, a simple raised platform at one end of a hall, and actors in the audience. Actors move from the audience onto the platform one after the other with a sequence of pieces of 'actuality':

> I've never experienced owt like it in me life!
> Something was coming off; it was like a big cloud in the air.
> Wave after wave of 'em, coming over the hill.
> I'd goose pimples the size of bloody eggs!
> They come in on five main roads and they just blotted these roads out.
> It were as though everybody had just come to their senses
> (Banner Theatre 1976. 1).

The lines are distributed between the performers but do not establish the individual voices as 'characters'; they retain their status as verbatim material being repeated by actors. As the performers reach the stage the 'actuality' material gives way to dance and 'The Song of Unity', placing Saltley Gate in the context of the tradition of working-class resistance recuperated by the New Left historians. The play then goes back to trace in detail the actual production of the political moment with which it began, ending with the audience as active participants rather than passive observers.

The Jester, a narrator figure drawn from popular performance traditions like the Mummers' play common in Banner's early shows, details the beginnings of the strike in the opening sequence:

> On January the first 1972, the Conservative Government Industrial Relations Act, designed to keep pay rises down to 7 per cent, came into force. On January the ninth, the miners of Britain went on strike. Their demand was for wage increases of 35 to 45 per cent. (Banner 1976: 3)

'Actuality' pieces then describe, mining district by mining district, the organisation of the strike. The first naturalistic scene of the play, which follows, is set on a picket line and includes a rewritten version of the Welsh traditional song, 'Cosher Bailey', which sketches a history of the mining industry since nationalisation in 1947. This scene closes when a lorry driver discloses that there are thousands of lorries descending on Saltley Gas Works.

The influence of the Radio Ballads comes out in the next sequence. Verses of a haunting unaccompanied song, 'Birmingham City', written by Chris Rogers, and brought back as one of several recurring musical motifs throughout the play, are interspersed with the Jester's narration:

> SINGER: In Birmingham City at five in the morning
> The streets are deserted, the air it is chill
> A mile from the lights of the brash city centre
> The scarred face of Saltley is silent and still
>
> The towering gasholders loom high over Saltley
> And shadow the houses that cluster nearby
> The wintry moon silent vigil is keeping
> Upon the black mountain that points to the sky
>
> JESTER: Saltley Gas Works
> Whose official name is Nechells
> Part of the vast gas and coking plant

> Which covers sixty four acres
>
> And wafts the sweet perfume of its trade
> Across east Birmingham. (Banner 1976: 13)

The first agitprop scene presents the escalation of the picketing from 6–9 February as a series of games, starting as cricket, moving through all-in wrestling, and finishing as a brutal version of something like American gridiron. This is counter-pointed by slides of the picket line and broken up by a song calling in further pickets, and by 'actuality' material from the new pickets. This then gives way to a reprise of the 'Song of Unity', now cataloguing the new arrivals by name:

> Jack Cook, Tom Smith, John Forrester
> Dai Evans and Bill Payne
> Roy Hunter and John Carpenter
> To Saltley Gate they came, came,
> To Saltley Gate they came.

Music modulates to 'Birmingham City'

> I've never been to Birmingham before.
> We got lost in that concrete jungle—what do you call it—
> the Bull Ring!
> That driver couldn't have led three blind mice to a mountain
> of cheese!
> You know this is something no lads from just a pit village
> have ever experienced. This is something. Everybody
> so helpful and kindness itself.

Miners bed down.

JESTER: What a job. What a task. Two hundred miners landed in the Star Social Club for the night.

Music: instrumental intro 'Birmingham City'.

SINGER: It's six in the morning, a cold Sunday morning
The bus stops deserted, no rush to clock in
A clatter of working boots shatters the silence
In Saltley a battle's about to begin

Instrumental play out into 'We are the Champions'.

JESTER: And welcome ladies and gentlemen to this second contest in the Saltley Gate Knockout Competition... (Banner 1976: 21-22)

Street performance, Birmingham 1974, opposing labour government public
sector cuts. (from left) Pete Yates, unknown student, Richard Hamilton,
Dave Rogers, Eileen Feeley, Joan Thomas, Charles Parker.
(Photo: John Fryer)

This sequence gives a sense of the narrative speed of the play, and its ease
with presentational theatrical conventions. The storytelling mode,
concentrating on performers rather than characters, and centring on the
story of the strike rather than individuated narratives, reflects the
collectivist nature of the performance—the story is built by a group of
performers who share responsibility for the narrative. The consistent
recourse to direct audience address stresses what MacKinnon describes as
the 'intercommunicative' nature of folk club performance. The format allows
for 'digressions' where performers can quote from the local press coverage
of events, for example, or explore the problem of pneumoconiosis, as they do
late in the first act. Neither the digressions nor the use of slides to underpin
or counterpoint certain points, fracture the narrative. In fact they constitute
it, and leave the spectator with the active listening role of drawing the
connections and piecing together the montage of information.

The second half of the play follows the pattern of the first, moving from narration and 'actuality' material to naturalistic scenes as the picketing process widens to include Birmingham workers. This expands to include verbatim reportage of speeches delivered to meetings of Birmingham workers, by Scargill among others, increasingly delivered, not to huddles of other actors, but to the audience as a whole. From there the play moves, via press accounts, to the broader response in the newspapers and the parliament. The speed and smoothness of the shifts is indicated by the following sequence:

> MEDIA WOMAN: *Birmingham Post*: The Government will today be faced with an emergency debate on the situation at Saltley, unless it can give MPs a clear explanation of what is going on there...
>
> *Game disperses.*
>
> ...The application for the debate was made by Leslie Huckfield MP.
>
> HUCKFIELD: Will the Minister for Trade and Industry press for immediate closure of the Saltley Gasworks? It is being regarded by the pickets as an open act of provocation by his department, in forcing the gasworks to stay open.
>
> SUPERCOP: That is a gross distortion and wholly without foundation. A situation of this kind gives rise to all manner of difficulties. The task of the police is very complex.
>
> MEDIA WOMAN: Earlier, Mr Maudling announced the proclamation of a State of Emergency as a result of the continuing Coal Strike.
>
> STOKES: If there are not enough police available, the Government has a duty to consider the use of troops.
>
> SUPERCOP: [MAUDLING] The Government would contemplate the use of Armed Forces only if that was absolutely essential to maintain vital services.
>
> MEDIA WOMAN: *Birmingham Post*, Leader, Wednesday February 9th: In their impatience, the miners' leaders have been trapped by other Trade Union 'friends' ... Everything points to co-ordination behind the scenes. In a sense, those men have become the tools of others, who regard them as front-line troops in a battle with the Government. ... English history shows the consequences of that kind of situation.
>
> HUCKFIELD: The honourable member for Oldbury and Hales Owen, spoke about the situation of anarchy on the horizon. It has even been alleged that the NUM was in some mystical and mythical way, taking over the running of the country. But it was the executive of the Transport and General Workers Union that decided its members

should not cross picket lines. It was the executive of the National Union of Railwaymen (NUR) and of their unions that decided that their unions would support the strike. These decisions were arrived at through the democratic procedures of the unions concerned.

All exit except JESTER.

MEDIA WOMAN: If the authorities are forced, by intimidation, to close this depot, democracy will have suffered a crushing defeat. *Birmingham Post* February 9th.

JESTER: On Wednesday, the numbers of both police and pickets were the greatest so far; hundreds were becoming thousands, and still the cry was going out to South Wales and the other areas for more men.

SINGER: In Birmingham City as evening is falling
The lathes have stopped turning the presses are still
Through dense city traffic the buses are crawling
And workers are pouring from factory and mill. (Banner 1976: 55-57)

As the pace hots up, both narratively and on stage, with the speed of events mirrored in the increasing excitement of the 'actuality' descriptions of them, the audience is invited to participate by voting on a sequence of motions to join the pickets, put to union meetings in Birmingham in the day or so preceding 10 February. This reaches a crescendo, after an 'actuality' speech from a solitary miner on stage:

> I get to the corner, look up the Washwood Heath Road—and there about eight or nine abreast down the road they come. Arthur Harper at the front, you know, barrel-chested, and he's got a big banner, 'The Miners' Struggle is Our Struggle'. That's why they'd been so long, making the banner. So I thought, well that's it I'm an engineer—and I'm going in with that lot. (Banner 1976: 63)

This leads into the singing of the play's most stirring song:

> A solid wall are we
> CLOSE THE GATES, CLOSE THE GATES
> Our strength is unity
> CLOSE THE GATES!
> No power in the land can gain the upper hand

When we united stand
CLOSE THE GATES! CLOSE THE GATES!
When we united stand
CLOSE THE GATES! (Banner 1976: 63)

During the singing performers burst in from the back of the hall and move through the audience to form the mass picket, encouraging the audience to join both the chorus and the mass march onto the stage area. This apparently worked: Bowdler describes one performance, in Nottingham, 'when I'm the only one, as the director, in the audience because all the bloody audience is on the stage' (interviewed by Dave Rogers, Birmingham, March 1997).

After a few lines drawn from Scargill's speech from atop the urinal, the play returns to its opening, with a reiteration of the 'actuality' material and a reprise of the 'Song of Unity'. This is no longer an abstract concept in the community created by the performance. Some of the ambition of the show is then revealed in the final stage direction for the Jester:

> *Here he breaks across the music which trails and stops behind him as he reads relevant quotes exposing the situation in Britain today, going straight into a plea for immediate discussion stating that the performance proper is ended. Cast initiate discussion with quotes from miners and Birmingham workers etc.* (Banner 1976: 65)

The Saltley Gate Show bristles with the techniques of earlier political theatre like that of Littlewood and MacColl, for example, as well as of much of the theatre which emerged elsewhere at the same time. The presentational nature of the performance is close to the theatrical strategies of the agitprop of the 1930s, as well as the theorisations and practice of Meyerhold, Brecht, Piscator and others, as is the use of non-individuated, episodic narratives and montage techniques. These techniques may have crept into the work via the influence of MacColl and the contemporary political theatre seen by at least some of the group, but if Rogers is to be believed it was not something of which they were particularly aware.

The connections between *The Saltley Gate Show* and the performative ethos of the folk club are much clearer. The show demanded the special way of listening described by MacKinnon, with its attendant decorum of modes of participation and defined the performance, not as commodity but as a shared event. Like the folk song revival it attempted to place the contemporary world in the context of a continuing political history: Saltley Gate is celebrated as part of E. P. Thompson's postulated continuity from the Levellers and the Chartists. It also foregrounded the collectivity of its own making, from using the verbatim words of participants in the event to the collectivist techniques for conveying a non-individuated narrative. This collectivist sense is, of course, a central concern of the play: Saltley Gate is celebrated as a manifestation of solidarity. In Parker's words, the battle marked an important shift in consciousness via two developmental steps:

1. The development from pit militancy to area militancy to National militancy.
2. The development from *miner* class consciousness to *working* class consciousness (Parker, n. d.).

The amateur-ness (as opposed to amateurishness) of the performance shared another important element with the folk club ethos, reflected in an interview with Bowdler which appeared in the NUM journal at the time:

> When we go into a miners' welfare, of course we're putting on a show with music and lights and all that. But what we're also doing is showing people to themselves, and saying: look, this is your experience, these are your words, and they're beautiful and dramatic. What we do, in fact, is something you could do yourselves, much better than we can. (Bowdler 1975: 5)

Disingenuous as this may now sound, it clearly formed an important part of Banner's sense of itself and its task. Banner has maintained a connection with its amateur origins, consistently recruiting members from amongst its audiences and consultants on various projects. Significantly when the company obtained funding in 1979 and was able to pay salaries to a core of professionals, it maintained what it called the 'main group' as an amateur ensemble with a floating population. This 'main group' has been responsible for some of Banner's most important work, particularly through the women's group, which produced its first show, *Womankind*, in 1975. The interplay between amateur participants and a professional core made it particularly easy for Banner to slide into the developing community arts model where a small group of professional facilitators assisted community groups to make their own performances. The work of the core professional group, though, was to become more difficult.

Rank and File vs the Union: *Steel*

The success of *The Saltley Gate Show* on the NUM circuit established by the *Collier Laddie* tour and the predominantly agitprop-based work for specific unions tied Banner into an expanding network of left-wing activists and shop stewards particularly in the building, automotive and steel industries. Increasingly, this led to a choice for the company: 'I think we've always tried to follow a line which identifies us with the rank and file and not with the hierarchy in the union' (Dave Rogers interviewed by David Watt, Birmingham, 11 September 1996). Because Banner worked in localised industrial struggles where the conflict between the union hierarchy and the rank and file was at its most extreme, union hierarchies have often had cause to attack them for their approach.

The possibilities for these intra-union conflicts burgeoned after the election of Labour to government in 1974 and the subsequent attempts to establish a Social Contract with the TUC. Now that unions had little to do other than to police wage restraint and acquiesce to a steady decline in manufacturing industry, the gap between union leaders and their rank and file grew. There were no more great victories like Saltley Gate, and even that victory began to appear illusory. By 1979, when the Thatcher government was elected, Banner, ironically enough, had funding to form a professional nucleus for the first time mainly to make shows about industrial defeats. The most notable was *Steel*, the development of which straddled the shift from the extreme union militancy of 1978–79 and the collapse of Labour to the first year of the Thatcher government.

Steel was 'written', or at least 'assembled', by the late Pete Yates, who had been a member of the group from the time of *Collier Laddie*, and Frances Rifkin, the company's first recruit from the emerging political theatre movement and a major influence on refining their theatrical style. The project began in 1979 in Corby, a small Northhampton steel town, with street theatre work in support of ROSAC (Retention of Steelmaking at Corby). ROSAC was a community organisation established outside the ambit of the union to fight British Steel's proposed closure of the Corby Steelworks. In ways which became typical of Banner in the 1980s, and most strongly during the miners' strike of 1984–5, the company found itself closely involved with, and even part of, communities in struggle. Rifkin and Yates became active members of ROSAC, campaigning on the streets and producing agitprop performances while working on the script for the show.

Steel was a fully professional production, using four actors who also sang and played music from the folk idiom (both original and traditional). It used many of the central devices of *The Saltley Gate Show*, including taped and transcribed 'actuality' material and the two slide projection screens which were becoming a standard feature of Banner productions, although now in a more conventionally 'theatrical' style. Song remained central, and Banner still used its signature devices such as interspersing 'actuality' and brief enacted scenes between song verses. But *Steel* attempts a broader narrative sweep than *The Saltley Gate Show* and utilises a number of cunning techniques to convert 'actuality' into dialogue, while still making substantial use of monologue and direct audience address.

The play opens in the midst of the thirteen-week national steel strike, just after the 1980 announcement that the Corby Steelworks will close. It juxtaposes the present Corby struggle with its historical antecedents. Scenes constructed from 'actuality' material drawn from surviving 'Corby pioneers' are mixed with agitprop scenes (to explain the process at a managerial and governmental level) to tell how Scottish steel workers established a community in Corby after being forced there in the 1930s by closures at home. Through 'actuality'-based scenes about the current struggle in Corby the play draws parallels between the callousness of the present closure ('It's simple. You move people onto an ore field and then you move on and leave the people to take their chances') and the original displacement of the Scottish steelworkers and their families, who were somewhat facetiously told at the time that 'Nobody will be forced to go. The choice is entirely up to you' (Banner Theatre 1980). A long historical narrative in the second half of the play traces the history of the industry from nationalisation in the postwar years through the planned restructure in the 1960s, to the establishment of the ROSAC campaign. The stylistic repertoire of the play allows the details of the campaign to emerge, from ROSAC's organisation of a march to London to its preparation of a detailed document on the economic viability of the Corby Steelworks. It also, and most importantly in the context of Banner's increasingly complicated relationship with the union movement, portrays ROSAC's sense of betrayal when their union, the Iron and Steel Trades Confederation (ISTC), and particularly its leader Bill Sirs, refused to fight against the closure or even present ROSAC's documentary evidence at meetings with the British Steel Corporation. The ISTC, in response, attempted to ban the show for its membership.

Unlike *The Saltley Gate Show*, which celebrates a working-class victory, *Steel* is the story of a defeat. Banner hoped it contained lessons for communities in similar circumstances, and there were soon to be many of them. While *The Saltley Gate Show* had enacted a community reaching out towards class solidarity, *Steel* was left with the wishful thinking of one of the Corby pioneers:

Well, we put up some good fights, but the rising generation, they're going to fight harder. And it won't be just a case of turning over vans. It'll reach the stage of revolution. (Banner 1980)

The history of the labour movement through the 1980s reveals the emptiness of this hope.

Steel is emblematic of a labour movement in retreat throughout the 1980s. With manufacturing industry in decline, and unemployment rising alarmingly as a result of redundancies and closures due to the rationalisation of nationalised industries prior to privatisation, union memberships dropped steadily. Punitive industrial legislation and increasingly draconian methods of policing it led to a steady decline in the use of the strike as a union strategy, and by 1983 the number of days lost due to strikes was at its lowest since the war. By then, legislation against secondary boycotts would have rendered the 'Battle of Saltley Gate' illegal; individual picketers could have been arrested and unions ordered to pay compensation for production losses. The rationalisation of the steel industry prior to privatisation in 1988, which lay behind the Corby closure, meant *Steel* was relevant in countless communities where similar closures were on the cards, but the lessons to be learnt were not encouraging: don't expect that profitability will save an individual enterprise, don't expect the backing of your union and don't expect to win.

Increasingly, the organised union movement ceased to be the logical focus of political activism, as the Corby rank and file discovered when the ISTC failed to support them. Clearly, if Banner was to survive the 1980s it needed to regroup and rethink. Some of that rethinking is evident in Banner's use of the opportunities thrown up by funding. The company toured professional shows, ran a women's group, and facilitated amateur, community-based shows via the 'main' group working with varied communities such as young Afro-Caribbeans, Asians, vehicle builders and the North Staffs Miners' Wives Action Group (Seymour 1996: 12–15).

Miners' Support Groups and the Emergence of a New Politics

One of the 'great learning moments' of the 1980s for Rogers came from Banner's involvement in the work of the support groups thrown up by the miners' strike of 1984–5 (Dave Rogers interviewed by David Watt, Birmingham, 11 September 1996). At the time he was on leave from the company, but with Dave Dale and Kevin Hayes worked unpaid in a song group with the Birmingham Miners' Support Group. The trio performed at almost every pit in England and Wales at socials, strike meetings, fundraisers, pickets and rallies. Rogers describes the nature of the work, and the quick-response opportunities it offered:

> We did busking on street corners, performed in miners' welfares and went to miners' support groups. We would be in a situation where someone got beat up on a picket line in the morning, we'd write a song in the afternoon and perform it at a strike social in the evening, so it was a really organic relationship with the strike. (Cited in Beale 1997)

Although the miners' strike was a defeat for the NUM, Rogers thought it 'taught the left a whole load of lessons about how to organise' (interviewed by David Watt, Birmingham, 11 September 1996). Paul Mackney, President of Birmingham Trades Council at the time, indicates why:

> The support movement for the strike involved more people at a greater pitch of activity over a lengthier period than any other campaign in the history of the labour movement. It would not be an exaggeration to say that it represented the biggest civilian mobilisation in Britain since the second world war. As such it did more than sustain the strike, it also created a whole new cadre of political activists well beyond the mining communities. (Mackney 1987: 127)

The work of the support groups marked a break with conventional labour movement industrial action because it reached far beyond the confines of the union or even the TUC. New alliances and patterns of organisation proliferated as the strike went on, and Rogers saw in these a range of new radical possibilities. Increasingly, it became difficult to sustain a notion of the organised working class, male and manufacturing industry-based, as the vanguard of political change. As Rogers put it in 1992:

> The old battalions of the working class are in disarray; many of the old industries which were the backbone of the working class movement have now all but disappeared. The main areas of struggle now no longer centre on the work place. There is clearly a need for [a] unifying politics to bring together the very different and separate strands and sites of struggle that characterise the 1990s more than any recent decades. (Rogers 1992: 25–6)

The shift of sites of struggle was made particularly clear in Birmingham. One of the most spectacular confrontations between police and inner city black and Asian people in Britain in the early 1980s took place in Soho Road in Handsworth, around the corner and just up the hill from Rogers' home.

Song group performance of Kevin Hayes, Dave Rogers and Dave Dale,
Miners' Welfare Social, miners' strike 1984. (Photo: Nigel Dickinson)

As the working-class solidarity represented by the 'Battle of Saltley
Gate' fragmented through the 1980s, it was increasingly difficult to sustain
a sense of it as more than a momentary and illusory glimmer of possibility.
The assumption that there was a homogeneous working-class culture in
Britain, unified by its tenuous connections to the folk 'tradition', began to
appear at best a New Left attempt to reconstruct a history and at worst a
myth. As the sites of struggle shifted from broad class alliances in the
workplace to issues of race and gender, and single issues ranging from the
development of motorways to the presence of American Cruise missiles on
British soil, Banner's adherence to a New Left class politics dating from
the 1950s and 1960s began to seem problematic.

Banner's maintenance of a dialogic relationship with its constituencies
(a result of both its activist role and its commitment to 'actuality' material),
kept it well placed to ride some of the changes. These entailed some
unpredictable alliances. In 1996, for example, Banner offered to take a song
group to perform at a rally to mark the first anniversary of the Liverpool
dockers' strike. The dockers had never been particularly progressive on the
matter of race, London dockers having marched in support of immigration
controls singing 'Bye Bye Blackbird' and 'I'm Dreaming of a White
Christmas' in 1968. In this case, though, they cancelled their rally so as to

join a picket line at an Oxford detention centre in support of black asylum seekers. As Rogers struggled to reorganise his schedule, and to avoid a trip to Liverpool for just one gig, he arranged for the song group to perform at another Liverpool rally organised by Reclaim the Streets, a group of anti-motorway demonstrators. At the last minute he was told that the dockers had re-scheduled their rally so as to join Reclaim the Streets. As he said:

> ... interesting things are happening, which you would not have believed possible, from horny handed sons of toil going out to support black asylum seekers in detention centres in Oxford. ... You certainly wouldn't have expected them to help these kind of hippie types who are out blocking off roads and motorways and stuff like that. (interviewed by David Watt, Birmingham, 11 September 1996)

As odd as the new alliances may appear, Banner was sufficiently well known to both groups to be invited to perform at both the original rallies.

As Banner's funding dried up in the late 1980s, Rogers and Dave Dale toured as a singing duo. Among other things, they performed a two-handed concert version of *The Saltley Gate Show*, devised after requests from NUM activists, to help the campaign against pit closures in 1992–3. Aidan Jolly joined them as a musician in late 1992, indicating a new direction in their political and artistic strategies. Jolly had worked in social welfare and community arts and had some experience of union activism but most of his experience was in Amnesty International, CND and Cruisewatch (an Oxford anti-Cruise missiles group) and campaigns against the Poll Tax. As he saw it, 'for us everything was linked, and unions and CND were equally mainstream' (Email to David Watt, 22 December 1998). He had a musical background in progressive and punk rock rather than folk music, and some technical abilities in sound and visual arts. In other words, he brought an artistic and political sensibility formed in the 1980s rather than the 1970s, and assisted the company to embark on a new venture.

While not abandoning the friends made in the union movement, or any of the company's commitment to working-class concerns, Banner widened its brief in search of new constituencies, and altered some of its performative strategies in the process. In the mid-1990s they engaged in two major projects which showed those changes. *Criminal Justice* (1996) written by a newcomer to the company, Stuart Brown, on the new Criminal Justice and Public Order Act of 1994, and *Sweat Shop* (1994–5), which focused on immigrant workers, and the broad issues of ethnicity and imperialism rather than the local industrial context of work. Both projects widened the network of community activists who worked with Banner while continuing its work through union connections, particularly in the case of *Sweat Shop*, the show that put Banner back on its feet as a funded company.

Banner in the 1990s: *Sweat Shop*

The Banner song group was in constant work in support of unionists on innumerable localised industrial disputes in the early 1990s. One of these, a dispute at a small Birmingham metal finishing plant called Burnsall's, led the company into a network of similar workplaces employing Asian workers in sweat shop conditions. Jolly describes how this network became the basis for the initial research for *Sweat Shop*, and involved drawing links between a number of unrelated campaigns:

> Their experiences were very similar and we were able to carry one lot of experiences to the next lot of strikers and say 'Hey, have you seen these leaflets?' and 'Did you know that was happening?' and 'Had you thought about talking to them?' So we … went from town to town over a period of about a year and a half, communicating at grassroots level. (interviewed by David Watt, 5 September 1996)

Sweat Shop emerged from what Rogers describes as 'a typical Banner process', beginning in 1992 (interviewed by David Watt, Birmingham, 11 September 1996). Lines from the play explain the situation:

> Jimmy O'Neil was the Boss of the Burnsall's metal finishing plant, appropriately situated at 10 Downing Street, Smethwick. Jimmy O'Neil was a typical sweat shop employer. He supplied the big contractors in the motor industry—Rover, Ford and Jaguar—with parts for their automated production lines. Jimmy O'Neil ran his company in competition with a thousand other little back street enterprises operating in the murky margins of West Midland industry. Sleazy entrepreneurs moving in like rats on the rich pickings left behind when the big manufacturers moved out in the seventies and eighties. A new first world workforce with third world wages and conditions was being created in the very heart of the big cities of Birmingham, Manchester, London, Paris, Tokyo and New York. (Banner Theatre 1994)

Kevin Hayes, a long-time Banner associate, was a prime mover in setting up a support group for the strikers. With Rogers he started going to strike meetings and joined the pickets. Jolly and Dave Dale were brought in to form a song group to offer cultural as well as direct political support by performing on the picket lines. Then, according to Rogers:

> I thought, well I've got to write a bloody show about this, and then started researching around the issue, and gradually it began to dawn that you can't talk about sweat shops without talking about global sweat shops. You can't talk about global sweat shops without talking about how they're linked to trans-national corporations. You can't talk about that without talking about the New World Order. You can't talk about ... So gradually the big issues emerge from the small issues. (interviewed by David Watt, Birmingham, 11 September 1996)

Thus the initial idea for a small show steadily became 'a bit of a bold proposition' which involved over two years of interviews and research, taking photographs and gathering other visual material for slides, scrabbling for funding from a wide range of sources (remembering the company had no income at the time) and wrestling with a mass of intractable material.

Over a hundred people were interviewed for *Sweat Shop*, ranging from the Burnsall's strikers to homeworkers in the West Midlands and Leeds, Asian machinists and factory workers in Birmingham and Luton, Turkish and Kurdish workers in Hackney, workers from a Levi factory in San Antonio, Texas (who the company went to meet at a conference in Paris), representatives of Unemployed Workers' Centres and Health and Safety Advice Centres as well as members of the company's network of union activists. As the project rolled on it gathered more personnel, more resources and more material. Interviews were transcribed, as in the early days, but now on computer and categorised by keywords for easy recall and cross-referencing. Ideas for the show were then taken back to key interviewees for comment and further information was sought from organisations like the Institute for Race Relations.

The techniques employed to assemble *Sweat Shop* were close to Banner's earliest modes of theatrical composition. The material was sorted into a sequence and individual sections were drafted, workshopped and redrafted. Songs were written, some as commentary or contextualising devices, others built out of phrases and rhythm patterns from the 'actuality' material, very much in the manner of the Radio Ballads. Jolly assembled some three hundred slides, consisting of photos taken on picket lines, maps of areas central to the narratives, file photographs, cartoons and a mass of computer-enhanced 'subvertisements' (sports trainers spattered with blood etc.).

For these he drew on the work of John Heartfield, the German artist and stage designer of the 1920s who pioneered the use of collage techniques for political posters, Peter Kennard, who did a famous Turner pastiche of Cruise missiles in a Hay Wain, and John Berger:

> I had learnt a lot of techniques through being a part of the 'copy art' movement, which produced lots of quick political flyposters round the time of the Poll Tax and the Gulf War (no 1). This involved a lot of collage, and was popular because copying machines were becoming very accessible thanks to the community arts centres that were around in the late 80's (such as Bloomin' Arts in Oxford, where a photomontage artist called Al Cane produced a series of postcards around the Gulf War that I was very influenced by). (email to David Watt, 22 December 1998)

Taped material was edited and arranged, quotations from historical texts were found, and an elaborate montage of stories, songs and slides was built up. Rogers, who wrote the script and was the guiding hand in the project, brought to bear the accumulated experience of some twenty years of political theatre work.

Nonetheless, the show is different in important respects. Firstly, while *The Saltley Gate Show* and *Steel* had focused exclusively on the story of a single community, *Sweat Shop* consisted of a number of stories and only one, the Burnsall's strike in Birmingham, was drawn from a close involvement with a specific community. Secondly, it attempted a much broader sweep, historically and geographically, than earlier projects, embedding the Burnsall's strike in the context of the development of British imperialism and capitalism since the eighteenth century and in the globalisation of manufacturing industry since World War II.

Thirdly, *Sweat Shop* moved beyond the folk club performance aesthetic of the earlier shows to embrace the possibilities inherent in affordable technology, from the amplification of music (no longer folk song but a range of contemporary sounds and styles) to a more elaborate manipulation of the 'actuality' material than had been possible twenty years previously. Taped 'actuality', both speech and sound, was now played straight as well as sampled and turned into soundscapes, and interwoven with amplified music reminiscent of Peggy Seeger's sound arrangements for the Radio Ballads. Despite the advantages of technology, there were also disadvantages, deriving from the company's search for a wider constituency. Where *The Saltley Gate Show* was able to assume and celebrate 'community' in its audiences, and consequently invite them into the performance, *Sweat*

Shop had more of the atmosphere of an older agitprop show. More concerned to tell its audiences things than share experiences, the partial loss of the folk club performance ethos left audiences with less opportunity to intervene intellectually in the experience.

Finally, the show marked the company's move into the fragmented alternative theatre scene of the 1990s. Banner, like most alternative theatre companies in Britain, now operates entirely on project funding, most of it from sources ranging from local councils and philanthropic trusts to the European Union rather than arts agencies, which means that each project needs to fulfil the funding criteria of what Baz Kershaw describes as 'an incoherent range of paymasters' in an increasingly competitive 'marketplace' (Kershaw 1992: 210). The difficulties in sustaining the company economically, particularly in the two or three years before the *Sweat Shop* project gathered sufficient funding to employ anybody, meant that while older associates forced to find employment elsewhere could do some volunteer work for the show, they were not able to have a continuing involvement as the work developed. Some, like Jan Bessant and Bill Murphy, were employed in administrative capacities for Banner, yet advertised auditions were required to attract a director, Theresa Heskens, and half the cast, Paula Boulton and Helen McDonald, none of whom had worked for the company before. Under these circumstances, the company struggled to sustain a pool of like-minded practitioners, making the search for forms appropriate to the new political circumstances of the 1990s a difficult task. In addition, it faced the problem of funding the time-consuming research needed to build shows, and did so on *Sweat Shop* basically because Rogers and Jolly exploited themselves. One attempt to self-fund has been to make use of the resources gathered for particular projects and produce educational CD-ROMs for unions.

Sweat Shop attempted the huge task Rogers set for it by utilising a storytelling mode developed in workshops with Marion Oughton, a professional storyteller who had a long association with the company (she had been in *The Saltley Gate Show* twenty years earlier). The play is divided into units, each of which describes a phase in the development of British capitalism, or details the recent strategies of globalised capitalism in a range of sites, and each with its appropriate specific narrative. The four performers shared a playful linguistic mode as a narrative device which Rogers picked up from the MacColl Festival of Fools shows in the late 1960s. The first section of the play, called 'Mercantile Capital: The Bengal Story', will indicate the technique:

STORY TELLER 1 (ST 1): Many many years ago there lived a buccateering privateer by the name of John Pound Sterling. John Pound Sterling came from the islands of Great Gritbum, which were to be found just off the left hand corner of the mighty land mass of Europumpum, situated in the top bit of the wirlyworld (or the bottom bit, depending on which way you choose to look at it).

One day, while John Pound Sterling was ploughing the stormy main he chanced upon a strange looking foreign barque.

He blasted this strange vessel with cannon shot, and went on board to collect his bounty. He pilferdilfered the usual fare, bit of gold, silver, and precious stones, when he spots these bales, bales of the finest cloth he'd ever set eyes on. 'From whence cometh these fine fabrics' he said.

'From the port of Dacca sir, in the land of Bengal. For verily the weavers of Bengal are the finest weavers in the whole of the known wirlyworld'.

So John raised the Jolly Roger and set sail, 'till he finally arrived in the distant port of Dacca in the kingdom of Bengal in the land of India.

ST 3: Now John Pound Sterling was a buccateer at sea but a marketeer on the land. He trawled the highways and byways and the sideways of Bengal in search of the finest muslin, silks and cottons.

And the first time John came, he paid a fair price for the produce of the hand loom (which was a strange custom prevailing in Bengal at that time), and the second time he paid not such a fair price and the third time he paid next to nothing at all for the produce of the hand looms.

DOC. QUOTE: William Bolt's *Consideration of Affairs* 1772. The English arbitrarily decide on the price of goods. Upon the weavers refusing to take the money offered, they are tied in their girdles and flogged.

ST 2: All of this made John Pound Sterling very rich and convinced him that Gritbummers were the greatest pilfer-killers in the whole of the known wirlyworld.

DOC. QUOTE: 1764 taxation under the last Indian ruler of Bengal 800 thousand pounds. 1765 taxation under British control, one million four hundred and seventy thousand pounds.

ST 2: This was known as bringing progress to stunterdeveloped countries. 'Oh well' said John, 'every cloud has a pilfer lining'.

F/X ACTUALITY: Britain owes them—every Black person on this earth—

they owe—if you check out India, Pakistan, the West Indies, all of these places that was under this colonialism business, how come the reason England is living so large now is 'cos of all the money they went down there and robbed off all these people—it's pay back time now. (Banner 1995: 3-4)

This leads into 'The Cotton Thread Song', which is picked up and re-inflected throughout the play but, in this first version, establishes the metaphor of threads of imperial domination:

> From the burning plains of Africa
> To the Caribbean shores
> To the hungry docks of Liverpool
> The filaments of thread were drawn. (Banner 1995: 5)

The play's next section, 'Industrial Revolution: Ten Handed Machines', is another brief narrative about the Industrial Revolution in Great Gritbum. John Pound Sterling converts his mercantile capital into machinery in the textile industry, only to be confronted by the Luddite Betty Cunliffe in a monologue describing the smashing of the looms. This is followed by a brief 'documentary quote' detailing her prison sentence, and another song, 'Hidden Hands', in praise of the exploited labourer, which like 'The Cotton Thread Song', is brought back in re-inflected versions.

Brief scenes like these follow John's career, as he gathers capital and titles, through the destruction of the cotton industry in Bengal in the early nineteenth century, the slashing of wages as competition takes hold in Britain, the postwar importation of black and Asian labour, the shifting of manufacturing industry to sources of cheap labour in the third world, and the development of subcontracting, sweat shops and outwork in the deregulated labour market in Britain. Each of these narratives includes accounts of resistant action: Betty Cunliffe and the Luddites; the Bengali rebel Miah Mohsin; the emergence of unions; attempts at unionisation in Indonesia; the Burnsall's strike; unionisation and strike action against Levi Strauss in Texas. All of this is then concluded with a brief listing of similar actions taking place around the world at the time of the production.

Obviously, such a welter of material, and such a broad historical sweep, does not allow for the leisurely development of conventional dramatic narratives. Nonetheless, stories are told, and interwoven with documentary material with an impressive degree of dramatic power. Particularly notable is a scene about an Indonesian firm which subcontracts to multinational textile and footwear manufacturers. This opens with some statistics, delivered by the performers as direct audience address:

> ST 2: Java, Djakarta, Sumatra, what's it mean to you? Swaying palm trees, strange exotic fruits, or Errol Flynn buckling his swashes on the South China Sea?
>
> ST 3: Or young women working for NIKE, Reebok, Marks and Spencer's? 50 pence a day, for a 10 hour shift.
>
> ST 2: In 1991 Paul Fireman, Chief Executive Officer of Reebok International earned more than twice as much as the entire workforce in the Indonesian shoe industry. 31 million dollars. (Banner 1995: 18)

The 'Behind the Style Song' contrasts the advertising imagery with the work conditions under which the product is made:

> Buy a pair of **** trainers
> The cutting edge of shoe design
> Super gods of sporting fashion
> Take you to the finish line
> Cantana's a **** boot boy
> Michael Jordan walks on air
> Buy the shoe and get the image
> Who you are is what you wear.

Melody and rhythm change as a different singer takes over:

> Just before you take those trainers
> Take a look inside the sole
> Ten thousand Indonesian workers
> Slaving for the corporate goal
> Junta generals say 'Just Do It!'
> No strike deals with every pair
> Michael Jordan walks on workers
> Who we are is what we wear. (Banner 1995: 5)

The song is followed by more statistics:

> To pay the whole of NIKE's Indonesian workers a comfortable living wage without overtime would put 10 pence on the cost of a pair of NIKE sport shoes. The equivalent of one prime time advert on American TV. (Banner 1995: 19)

We are then carried directly into a personalised narrative:

> ST 4 : Sadissa was 19 years old when she started working for Tangra
> Industries. (Banner 1995: 19)

Sadissa's story is briefly told, the narrative being passed from performer to performer until bits of it are minimally dramatised. Narrated conversations between Sadissa and her fellow workers are turned into dialogue as performers briefly take on roles. They move from descriptions of the workplace to descriptions of the living quarters:

> ST 2: She shared a room with three other women. Nine feet by nine feet.
> The walls were bare brick with bamboo partitions, the roof was
> corrugated iron. The floor was concrete. There was no furniture, just
> a mat on the gravel to lie on. Her room mates woke her at five o'clock
> the next morning, 'Why so early?'
> ST 3: 'We've got to go down to the stand pipe to get water'.
> ST 2: 'Stand pipe?' said Sadissa.
> ST 3: 'It's a mile away, the factory has drained all the nearby water, if we
> don't move quick it'll be too late'. (Banner 1995: 20)

This shifts back to simple narration, through to a momentary dramatisation as the workers discuss strategies of organisation in a situation in which the official union, the SPSI, had 'generals and government agents on its central committee'. Dramatisation then moves back to narration:

> ST 1: On Monday the 26th of July, there were 5,000 people on the picket
> line outside Tangra Industries
> ST 2: And no one crossed the line
> ST 1: Apart that is from the union officials
> ST 2: All 19 of them
> ST 4: The workers were singing
> ST 3: The workers were chanting
> ALL: The workers were waving their banners in the air
> ST 2: They were angry
> ST 1: They were bloody angry
> ALL: And they were going to boom boom boom
> Do it!
> But not for NIKE! (Banner 1995: 21-22)

The narrative slides into a very brief catalogue of industrial action in Indonesia, and the first half of the show closes with a powerful song about

Marsinah, the notorious case of an Indonesian woman killed as a result of her involvement in organising an illegal union in Surabaya. The slides move through photographs of Indonesian workers at work and picketing, billboard advertisements, sports trainers spattered with blood and maps of Indonesia. This final slide sequence, repeated on all three screens behind the performers, is a striking image of a young Indonesian woman with her fist in the air, progressively emerging from blood to dominate the performance area. This image will return, superimposed over the slide of the globe which opened the play.

The second half of the play brings the narrative back to the Britain of 'Maggie Maggot Snatcher, the up-jumping greengrocer's daughter from the village store in Sterlingville', to examine new employment strategies, whereby workers were increasingly employed by:

> the suby sub, sub sub-con-track-trickers who worked for the suby sub sub con-track-trickers who worked for the suby sub con-track-trickers who of course all worked for John! (Banner 1995: 26)

This is followed by an account of the Burnsall's strike, done mainly through taped 'actuality' material, stressing support for the rank-and-file, and therefore distance from the union hierarchy who had ordered them back to work. The show had, fairly controversially for a union audience, signalled its intention to take such a stance by opening with a series of slides, behind the prologue song, which moved from a picture of the world, followed by maps of Europe, Britain, Birmingham and finally Smethwick (the site of the Burnsall's factory), and then by a series of slides starting with the factory itself, followed by one of an Asian worker and then a close-up of his face.

The situation was one of many generated by Thatcherist industrial relations legislation. The illegality of secondary boycotts, and legislation under the Criminal Justice Act of 1994 threatening pickets with criminal charges and unions with financial penalties for strike action, had made unions even less inclined to ratify strike action in small workplaces like Burnsall's than they had been in the years immediately following *Steel*. To talk about the Burnsall's strike meant confronting the sense of union betrayal felt by small groups of unionists across the country, and Banner chose to declare its intention to do so in these opening moments. It then left its audience waiting one and a quarter hours into a two-hour show, during which strike action was delineated as the heroic heritage of the international labour movement. The Burnsall's scene, the least 'dramatised' and most reliant on taped voices in the play, was a direct rank-and-file expression of a sense of betrayal, historically contextualised and presented by the company as one of those stories that 'so-and-so told us', which Rhoma Bowdler referred to as the defining feature of the use of 'actuality'.

From here the play changes course entirely, offering modes of activism beyond the confines of the organised labour movement, and suggesting the need for international co-ordination against internationalised capital. This sequence centres on a depiction of the formation of a campaigning organisation, Fuerza Unida (United Strength), by a group of Texan workers thrown out of work by the closure of a Levi Strauss factory in San Antonio, Texas. Fuerza Unida embraced a more performative, grass-roots politics, reminiscent of the 1960s, with members chaining themselves to the entrance doors of the Levi Strauss head office in San Francisco, and publicly confronting company executives.

In a reprise of 'The Cotton Thread Song', the metaphor refers to the possibility of internationally organised resistance:

> The cotton thread is slender
> And fine as a spider's web
> But when this thread is woven
> It's strong and firm as a river bed. (Banner 1995: 43)

The final song, a reprise of 'Hidden Hands', closes the play with an appeal for organisation and support:

> Hidden hands across the centuries
> Hidden hands so firm and strong
> Hidden hands reach out towards us
> Carry it on, carry it on. (Banner 1995: 43)

Beyond Unions? *Criminal Justice*

While *Sweat Shop* sustained and elaborated the theatrical and compositional strategies of *The Saltley Gate Show* and *Steel*, it moved beyond them in terms of political strategy. The shift which Parker described from 'miner class consciousness to working class consciousness' that could be celebrated in a communal moment at the end of *The Saltley Gate Show* two decades earlier was no longer so easily available. Banner was left with the task, not of celebrating an existing communality, but of attempting to draw connections to construct a new one based, not on the concentrated localism of *The Saltley Gate Show* or *Steel*, but on the internationalism advocated in *Sweat Shop*. As well, *Sweat Shop*, like *Steel*, called for a rejection of what the show portrayed as the cowardice of the organised labour movement in betraying its rank and file, but it moved beyond the perspective of the earlier play in calling for a different, performative politics of a type which has re-emerged in recent years in Britain.

This performative politics was particularly evident in the demonstrations against the Poll Tax which culminated in the Trafalgar Square riot of 1990, which George McKay describes as having kick-started 'an extraordinary surge of direct action in the 1990s'. He claims that:

> the sheer popularity and widespread nature of street protest and direct action emanating from single-issue campaigns is in part a response to a lack of confidence in—or even a rejection of—parliamentary democracy, a result of approaching two decades of what's effectively been one-party rule in Britain. (McKay 1996: 128)

This lack of confidence has extended to the New Labour of Tony Blair, as it drifts towards the political middle ground following its election victory in late 1996. But it also extends to the unions, decimated by the collapse of their old blue-collar areas of strength (the NUM and the TGWU—the Transport and General Workers' Union—have seen their memberships decline by 75% and 50% respectively since 1979) and weakened by industrial legislation. Apparent 'sell outs' of workers like those at Burnsall's have made unions less than the focal point of political resistance for the emerging exponents of 'direct action politics'.

The discovery, or rediscovery, of a sort of theatricalised direct action, like that of Fuerza Unida or the Timex strikers in Dundee (who got around anti-picketing legislation by staging mass factory gates parties), which form part of the proffered ways forward at the end of *Sweat Shop*, is being duplicated in an increasing number of single-issue campaigns. McKay's account of this explosion of dissidence, *Senseless Acts of Beauty*, ranges from the peace camps inspired by the women's camp at Greenham Common to protests against live animal exports, fox hunting and motorway building by what he calls 'eco-rads' (McKay 1996: 127–158). McKay attempts to draw into this ambit a range of manifestations of youth culture, from 'New Age travellers', who have embraced itinerancy and communalism, to 'ravers', who have turned a particular form of music and the dance party into a lifestyle, forming a continuity with the counter-cultural movements of the late 1960s and early 1970s.

While few of these activities were initially conceived in conventionally political terms, McKay claims they have been rendered 'political' by the Criminal Justice and Public Order Act of 1994, which has made many of them illegal:

> ... intended to clamp down on the irritations of cultures of resistance from travellers to ravers to squatters and campaigners, it's had the opposite effect, of ensuring that people are aware of their rights and continue to use them and to interrogate the limits of the Act on the land and in the courts ... one effect of the Act has been instantly to unite previously disparate single-issue protests together. (McKay 1996: 169)

These protests have been given a new focus of attention, the Act itself, as a manifestation of authoritarianism. The inclusion of almost every conceivable explicit act of dissidence, from trade union picketing to squatting in trees to block motorway building, as well as implicit acts of dissidence like 'rave' parties or embracing an itinerant lifestyle, has started to draw surprising alliances like those between the Liverpool dockers, black asylum seekers and Reclaim the Streets.

Sweat Shop does not specifically embrace this new movement, but it indicates a move in that direction. The show played to Banner's old union constituency; bookings were secured through union activists, Trades Councils and shop stewards for performances in the same sorts of spaces and to the same sorts of audiences as had been the company's staple in the 1980s. But it also attracted a new audience of black and Asian workers, women's groups and anti-racism activists. Banner's next show, *Criminal Justice*, though, found audiences among the groups McKay details, placing them squarely within the new political dissidence of direct action. Most notable has been Banner's embrace by the Exodus Collective, a group of black and white young people in Luton who have moved from staging free outdoor dance parties to renovating derelict buildings as communal housing and creating 'an impressive, self-reliant, politically conscious party scene and community' with a network that includes groups all over Britain and into Europe (McKay: 124–6).

This almost takes the history of the company full circle, back to the single-issue campaigns of the counter-cultures which produced the guerilla theatre scene of the late 1960s. If McKay is right, and the counter-cultural movements of the 1960s live on in this new politics of direct action and 'DIY culture', Banner once again stands, as did so many in the early 1970s, between the organised union movement and a proliferating, energetic and

David Dale, Dave Rogers and Paula Boulton, *Criminal Justice* 1996.
(Photo: Kevin Hayes)

anarchic dissidence. Back then, the choice for many was to move into the arena of working-class politics through the union movement, which separated their work from the broader context of the counter-culture. Banner's recent discoveries, made through the careful listening entailed by commitment to 'actuality' material, may serve the purpose of drawing links between the radical elements of the union movement and this new dissidence more effectively than was possible in the 1970s. Rogers talks of a new political environment in which there are:

> central core workers who are more privileged in terms of having ... protected salaries ... You've got this sweat shop area of temporary, part-time, 'black' employment. ... You've got this mass of unemployed people, and you've got youth coming through this and finding new ways to exist in it, and challenging the whole basis of left thinking. They're coming from a different direction to the organised working class but interested in making connections. (interviewed by David Watt, Birmingham, 11 September 1996)

Criminal Justice was an attempt to draw some of those connections.

Like *Sweat Shop*, *Criminal Justice* had its origins in the experience of political activism. Rogers describes his response to attending the 1994 rally against the Criminal Justice Bill.

> I thought it was bloody amazing. There were all these people on the top of bus shelters pogoing up and down. They just took over the streets. It was so exciting to see all these young people involved and a new energy around. I thought this has got to be significant, we've got to do a show about this. (Cited in Beale 1997)

The result was a show not unlike *Sweat Shop* in form, consisting of a sequence of episodes detailing aspects of the Criminal Justice Act and 'actuality'-based accounts of responses to them. It carries its audience through a catalogue of single-issue campaigns including that of the Exodus Collective against the Luton police, a harrowing account of the four-day interrogation of Irishwoman Annette McNulty under the Prevention of Terrorism Act, and 'The Siege of Claremont Road', in which 700 police, 300 private security guards and 400 bailiffs took four days to remove a group of anti-motorway protesters from houses planned for demolition in London. Company members were moving into areas well beyond their accustomed modes of political action, with some initial scepticism. Rogers, for example, claims 'I was very ambiguous, quite dismissive about those kind of politics'. Still, he found the animal rights protesters he interviewed 'in a lot of ways the most politically sophisticated, in terms of understanding how the state works. They've got a much better analysis than a lot of people on the left in the trade union movement' (Cited in Beale 1997).

Paula Boulton, who joined the company for *Sweat Shop* and stayed for *Criminal Justice*, actually embodies the split between traditional labour movement politics and DIY activism. She grew up in a politically active working-class family in Corby, the site of *Steel*, but her activism had been in the peace movement rather than the labour movement. For her, the former offers 'energy' and 'empowerment', while the latter offers a 'mass solidarity' born of shared experience in the workplace. As Rogers admits, '[we] haven't got the sort of class consciousness that can organise 10,000 people immediately any more' (Cited in Beale 1997). Boulton explains why:

> How do you get it if you have a youth culture who don't understand jobs, who've not had jobs because of mass unemployment. If you're never going to get a job you'll never understand the community and solidarity of working with the same bunch of people year in, year out. (Cited in Beale 1997)

Her dual experience of political activism means that she moves easily between the two environments: 'When we're up in Eccles or in the Working Men's Club in Salford then that part of me is to the fore and I can talk that language. But I love this play because there's so much of the other part of me in it' (Cited in Beale 1997). Rogers sees the possibility of dialogue, a basis for a 'cross-over' from both sides in this. In the article from which these remarks are cited, journalist Sam Beale describes the occasions for a cross-over which performances of *Criminal Justice* initiated:

> Heated after-show debates between those fighting to protect their jobs and the ardent jobless, have allowed trade unionists and the likes of road protesters to debate the issues which separate them, to hear about each other's strengths and victories and have the potential to dispel a little of the fear and ignorance which are the enemies of political change. (Beale 1997)

The hierarchies of the British trade union movement are unlikely to bridge the gap. Banner's involvement within several networks of political activism, combined with their commitment to listening and use of the tape recorder, offers a real possibility of making those connections. Their energies are increasingly devoted to attempts to effect a synthesis which could assist the union movement to find a constituency without which it is unlikely to survive. Their forays into new territory like *Criminal Justice* run in parallel with more traditionally union-based work (reflected in their 1999 song group tour of a show called *Sticking to the Union*). In 1991, Rogers said of Banner: 'We choose our audiences deliberately, on the basis that if you want to push out capitalism, you need to support those who do the pushing' (Rogers 1991: 4). The company's present work indicates a widening perception of who's doing the pushing, and consequently an attempt to reach a number of new audiences in shows which create occasions for dialogue, not just between company and audience, but between members of audiences who are probably as suspicious of each other as were union audiences and hippies some twenty-five years earlier. Banner's accumulated experience in the intervening years leaves them well placed to be making the introductions.

Chapter Four

Melbourne Workers Theatre: The Meat in the Sandwich

I'll never forget, when we walked into the worksite, there was a feeling of resonance there, that this was going to be a place where you could make theatre...
Steve Payne (interviewed by Alan Filewod, St Kilda, 20 July 1995)

For the first five years after its founding in 1987, Melbourne Workers Theatre (MWT) was based in a temporary pre-fab shed beside the tracks at the Jolimont Train Maintenance Depot, operated by the Metropolitan Transit Authority (Metrail) just outside the central business district of Melbourne. Working and rehearsing in the midst of a busy train yard, the company defined itself in terms of an ongoing relationship with the railway workers, who (to quote an MWT brochure) 'acted as advisors, supporters, critics, and, most importantly, personal and political allies' (MWT 1990:1). MWT promoted its identity in terms of this close relationship, and frequently described itself as Australia's only theatre based in the workplace, 'bringing working class theatre to the working class' (MWT 1989:1). Early photos of the company show actors wearing industrial gear (overalls, safety boots, hardhats) and loving it. For the first two years especially, MWT enjoyed a seemingly ideal arrangement for a labour-engaged theatre: a continuing, funded, reciprocal relationship with a trade union shop committee and a workplace audience.

Writing about MWT's first two seasons in *New Theatre Quarterly*, David Watt observed that the company had reached a level of 'theatrical maturity' that 'should allow them to play a significant role in interesting times' (Watt 1990.1: 173). This promise, he wrote, depended on continuing union support, and a commitment within the union movement to democracy. Given these two conditions, MWT should 'continue the consolidation of a *functional* theatre grounded in the political realities of the trade union movement'.

By the mid-1990s, the consolidation that Watt had looked for had largely collapsed, along with the broader hope for a democratising renewal within the union movement. Having survived roller-coaster funding, MWT found that its identity as a workers' theatre—which had seemed so clear when the company was founded—had been substantially renegotiated. MWT was no less committed to the idea of theatre in the workplace for working audiences, but the valences of those defining terms had changed. No longer resident at Jolimont (which had been closed by the Ministry of Transport in 1993), but working in a small suite of offices in the old North Melbourne Town Hall, the theatre found that its union affiliations had largely dried up. In 1992, a year before the move from Jolimont, a contract worker hired by the company to revive union support found that in addition to union reluctance to recommit financial support, there 'appeared to be pre-conceived negative ideas about MWT's past role in the union movement' (MWT 1992.3: 2).

In its original moment, MWT expressed a purity of purpose (which another of the founders, Patricia Cornelius, with somewhat critical hindsight referred to as 'workerite') (interviewed by Alan Filewod, Melbourne, 24 July 1995). Its iconography (performing in red sweaters against a large banner proclaiming the company's name and purpose) recalled the classic agitprop troupes of the 1930s. But the company found (to be precise, the women of the company found) that worker identification could not be signified simply by hard hats and safety boots; that even at Jolimont there was no such thing as a homogenous, monolithic working-class identity.

MWT's history is produced by two intersecting struggles that determined the company's field of possibilities. In the first, MWT found itself as what co-founder Steve Payne has called 'the meat in the sandwich' at Jolimont when loyalty to shop-floor research and the rank-and-file point of view put it into conflict with union factions whose support was critical to the company's future (interviewed by Alan Filewod, St Kilda, 20 July 1995). At the same time, the vision of that future was contested within the company as different ideological positions clarified through the artistic work. The more this process intensified, the broader the definition of 'worker' became, moving away from the iconographies of solidarity, towards a critical stance that intervened in trade union self-identification by reinforcing alliance with cultural pluralism.

An expanding definition of 'worker' enabled the company to survive its dependence on union allegiance when Jolimont closed. The company justified its move away from shop-floor performance by resituating its authority in a consultative process of research with communities defined by a particular problem under investigation. But although the company moved from a trade union model of working-class experience to a larger, functional 'working experience' model, it maintained a fundamental allegiance to the socialist principle that the working class was the economic foundation of industrial society. It accepted the traditional divisions of proletarian worker and middle-class professional—categories which had already begun to break down in the Australian trade union movement.

If class issues seemed simple in 1987, eight years later they were much less so, both because of rapid changes in Australian unionism and the troupe's political experiences. As Patricia Cornelius mused, 'what class you are ... all that stuff has become a bit muddied. The poverty level's growing higher all the time ... it's difficult to talk about' (interviewed by Alan Filewod, Melbourne, 24 July 1995). The company's attempt to define itself in class terms encountered unexpected complexities, of class formation, gender and ethnicity, which exposed the inadequacy of the 1987 vision. MWT's subsequent history has been to maintain its political mission while recognising hybridity during a period of increasing right-wing antagonism to the union movement and cultural democracy.

The narrative of origins in a political theatre company like MWT are complex because of the ways in which historical participation in a collective is transformed into cultural capital. Political theatres are usually founded by groups rather than individuals, but those groups usually fracture and change over the years because of personal and ideological differences. As a result, the ownership of the history of the company is held in conflict between the ideological imperative of consensus and personal needs for recognition. The narratives of founding are all provisional, equally true, equally conflicted, equally self-interested.

The theatre's official history, as printed in its self-published pamphlet, was written by Michael White, who left the company after its first year. Its gloss narrates a cheerful progression from idealism to solidarity that is worth quoting in full:

> ...Imagine if you can,
> two actors sitting in a kitchen in down town St. Kilda. Over numerous cups of coffee they begin to plot a major assault on the theatre scene in Australia.

Why?... Simple. Because most of what they see is shit; boring, passionless and irrelevant. The two actors, Michael White and Steve Payne, wanted to make theatre for and about the working class, as it was the only class who could fight and win the battle for socialism. Soon Steve and Michael are joined by a third actor, Patricia Cornelius.

'What we should be doing', they thought, 'is a play about the recent attacks on the trade union movement like SEQUEB, the Mudginberri meatworkers, the Dollars Sweets dispute, the deregistration of the BLF'. Then came the question that was to be the core of the project:

'WHAT DOES IT MEAN TO BE A TRADE UNIONIST AT THIS PARTICULAR TIME AND UNDER THESE PARTICULAR ATTACKS?'

...an office at Trades Hall

We have discussions with the Australian Council of Trade Unions Arts Officer Steve Cassidy and the Victorian Trades Hall Council Arts Officer Fiona Moore about how we might go about setting up a theatre company that has strong links with the trade union and labour movement. They tell us there are already some unions who have sponsored arts activities for their members, and point us in the direction of the Australian Railways Union, the Waterside Workers Federation and in particular the Combined Unions Shop Committee (CUSC) at the Jolimont Train Maintenance Depot.

The Jolimont Shop Committee had just finished sponsoring an ART AND WORKING LIFE PROJECT with two visual artists, so they have a history of supporting projects; perhaps they would come at a theatre company in residence for 18 weeks. A project description is drawn up ready for our meeting with the CUSC.

...at the Jolimont Train Maintenance Depot

Jolimont is a symbol of the deliberate running down of the public transport industry by successive governments. The three of us are met by members of the CUSC (The unions represented are the Australia Railways Union, the Amalgamated Metal Workers Union and the Electrical Trades Union).

We put our proposition to them that they be our sponsor for the 18 week project. Within moments it seems we are being whisked around the factory on a guided tour and at the same time being shown places where we might have an office and a rehearsal space. (MWT 1990:4)

In a similar tone, Steve Payne later told a Melbourne newspaper that 'To my knowledge it is the first fully professional theatre company who has aligned itself with the labour movement' (Sutton 1987).

A somewhat less nostalgic remembrance is offered in a sidebar in the MWT pamphlet by one of the shop committee members, who writes:

> When it was first suggested to the CUSC that we have a theatre group in residence about three years ago, we discussed it at length and decided to take the idea up.
>
> As a shop committee, we agreed to the idea, then took it to a mass meeting where it was endorsed. The management was approached and they agreed. An approximate date was given for the start of the venture, but as with all things in government departments, since it wasn't supposed to start immediately, nothing occurred for quite some time.
>
> The next thing we knew was that the group were coming in a month. Then everything seemed to be happening at once. With the support of all members of the shop, and with a lot of effort from the members, we got access to a disused store and an old ATCO hut. (MWT 1990:4)

Together, these two accounts lay out the basic facts of how MWT was founded. But the difference in tone is revealing because it inadvertently points up the vast differences in perception and priority between the two partners of this new alliance. Michael White remembers a heroic, enthusiastic rush to a new venture; Jim Leslie remembers something more routine, almost procedural. As another member of the shop committee that paved the way for MWT's move into Jolimont observed, the theatre was always a low priority for the unions (Wayne Clough, interviewed by Alan Filewod, Melbourne, 1 August 1995). By definition, the union was more important to MWT than MWT was to the union.

The conditions that place theatre at the margin of union activity are the same as those that attract theatres to unions in the first place. Organised labour has traditionally claimed the cultural authority to define the working class and this means working-class theatre achieves legitimacy in front of a union audience. When companies like MWT seek to construct specific audiences, they participate in constructing the class they use to forge their own identity.

Commonly, activist workers' theatre shines in the moment of struggle because these moments create openings for intervention. Conversely, in the stable social order of the Fordist accord, the transgressive presence of theatre upsets the management-labour balance designed to systematise production and bargaining. MWT's breakthrough came when it fused the Art and Working Life methodology (see p. 48 ff. above) with the worksite militancy of the activist workers' theatre tradition. It began with the Art and Working Life model, seeking authenticity in the 'real world' of work. Yet, almost immediately, MWT concretised its understanding of the workplace by identifying the points of daily struggle. But a theatre company who seeks legitimacy through a trade union, makes itself vulnerable to that union; its opportunities for the articulation of the workplace experience will last only as long as the union thinks them useful. The unfolding issue for MWT was how to remain a legitimate working-class advocacy theatre when its original union association collapsed.

This however was an evolving analysis. Initially, according to Payne, he and White kicked around the idea of a political theatre that would take a revolutionary Marxist perspective on working-class consciousness-raising. They proposed the name, Gravediggers, from Marx's celebrated phrase, and spoke to striking building trades workers, who met them with suspicion. Fiona Moore, the Victorian Trades Hall arts officer, suggested they approach the Combined Unions Shop Committee at Jolimont. A common feature in large multi-union plants, the Shop Committee is made up of the shop stewards and delegates of several unions. In a plant like Jolimont, it was the principal site of rank-and-file union governance, responsible for monitoring work conditions, communicating with management and, when occasion arose, calling mass meetings and imposing sanctions.

To Payne, White and Patricia Cornelius (who joined them), the maintenance yards at Jolimont, with 800 workers and a vast depot infrastructure, must have seemed as solid as the labour movement itself, although they quickly found that the mood at Jolimont was uncertain. MWT began to redefine the role of political theatre in Australia just as the labour movement was about to enter its own crisis of redefinition, imposed by the Labor governments' increasingly neoconservative economic policies and the restructuring economics of transnational business. Jolimont was soon to be a casualty of this restructuring.

In 1986, when MWT forged its relationship (short lived as it was) with the Australian Railways Union, the Victorian Railways employees at Jolimont were covered by six federal awards, categorised as Drivers, Professional Officers, Salaried Officers (which included foremen and clerks), Way and Signalling Staff, Train Running, Station and Freight Grades, Metal Trades (including fitters and electricians) and Miscellaneous Grades (including truck drivers, carpenters and painters, amongst others). The theatreworkers soon found that Jolimont was the workplace of a divided and contentious rank and file. No sooner had the company established itself than it too became both the focus and the site of conflict, the 'meat in the sandwich' caught between internecine union struggles and a hostile state employer on the verge of major corporate downsizing.

The initial proposal was for an eighteen week residency that would result in two short workplace performances on the subject of unionism in the 1980s. The project was also a pilot for a long-term arrangement that would require considerable federal, state and union support. The three founders were drumming up that support from the beginning, working through the arts officers of the trades hall and the Australia Council, and expanding through ministry and union contacts. As the process of participatory research at Jolimont grew, so did the possible network of contacts. Payne recalls this as period of:

> a lot of to-ing and fro-ing, getting the details of sponsorship, getting support in place for application ... We were working on the shop floor level. We had the ok from shop committee but that doesn't mean the workforce is going to know all about us. The unions came on board quickly because it wouldn't cost anything. (interviewed by Alan Filewod, St Kilda, 20 July 1995)

Wayne Clough, one of the members of the Shop Committee at the time (and a stalwart supporter of the theatre in its post-Jolimont phase) remembers that management's initial hostility to the MWT proposal was helpful:' it took some persuasion, but basically, there was no cost to workers and management was against it ... so why not?'

Union support locked into place easily, so long as it didn't actually cost anything. Wider union support came more slowly, as this letter from Trades Hall in May 1987 reveals:

> The Victorian Trades Hall Council is unable at this stage to offer its endorsement to the Melbourne Workers Theatre application for assistance as an on-going theatre company, as the group is still only in pre-production stages of its project and we would need to see a final product.
>
> However the project has the full support, as sponsors, of three of our affiliated unions—the Australian Railways Union, the Electrical Trades Union and the Waterside Workers' Federation. We have had good reports from these unions about their work, and it appears that the group has established positive relations with the unions concerned.
>
> We wish the group well in their activities, particularly as there is no

other theatre company in Melbourne which regards the union movement as its primary constituency.

P.R. Marsh, Sec (Marsh 1987)

In June the troupe's first play, *State of Defence* premiered and widespread union endorsement followed. By the end of that first season, the company had received letters of support from the Gippsland Trades & Labour Council, the Trades and Labor Council of Western Australia, the Federated Engine Drivers & Firemen's Association (Victorian Branch), the Electrical Trades Union of Australia (VB), Electrical Trades Union of Australia, NSW Branch, the Electrical Trades Union of Queensland, Royal Australian Nursing Federation (ACT), the Hospital Employees' Federation of Australia, the Amalgamated Metal Workers' Union, the Waterside Workers' Federation of Australia (Melbourne), the Technical Teachers' Union of Victoria, the Federated Miscellaneous Workers' Union of Australia, the Australian Tramway and Motor Omnibus Employees' Association, and the crew of the ferry *Abel Tasman*.

This wave of support was important in offsetting the hostility the company met in the Victorian government; the state Ministry of the Arts had initially rejected the company's funding proposal, and union pressure was needed to secure Ministry of Transport permission to continue the Jolimont residency beyond the original eighteen weeks. This letter, from the Secretary of the Waterside Workers' Federation, is typical of the lobbying effort:

> Mr F. Beet of Metrail has written to the Melbourne Workers Theatre Group, copy enclosed, requesting them to vacate the premises at the Train Maintenance yard.
>
> On behalf of the above Group, we request you, as Minister for Transport, to assist these wonderful young people to remain at the Maintenance Depot, until they are able to secure a permanent residence for their performances. (Cumberlidge 1987)

The company's skill in marshalling union support was instrumental in securing a funding track through the Art and Working Life (AWL) incentive fund the following year. In 1987, the company was awarded $5,000 by the Victorian Ministry of the Arts and $51,000 from the Australia Council; in the next year those grants increased to $17,000 and $64,000 respectively. In overall terms, MWT's revenues increased rapidly when it secured ongoing Australia Council funding in 1991 with $90,000 from its Performing Arts Board and Community Cultural Development Committee (CCDC), which when added to state, municipal, union and performance revenues gave the company a global budget of over $180,000. By 1994 this figure had escalated to a peak of $275,000. This is a modest figure for a professional theatre company, but by any standards, and especially those that governed comparable projects in Britain and Canada, it was a phenomenal achievement. In a very short period the gravediggers of capital had become a funded, supported workplace theatre. The formation of a working ensemble was not quite so simple.

An Ensemble of Workers?

As plans fell into place with the unions, Cornelius, Payne and White began the task of putting together a company for the pilot project. They became the core actors in an ensemble formed with Julie Hickson, a veteran of the Popular Theatre Troupe and a former organiser for Equity; Andrew Bovell, whose plays were just beginning to attract attention; Irine Vela, a young musician who had her first theatre gig with the project; and John Romeril, the most celebrated playwright working in community theatre, who explained his function as 'quality control ... basically that of editor cum confidant cum office boy' (Booth 1987). Romeril's presence gave the company dramaturgical expertise and an important leverage with funding bodies. With the company in place, the three actors drove to the Australia Council office in Sydney to lobby a very supportive Deborah Mills at the CCDC; as Payne later recalled, 'Art and Working Life was the flavour of the month' (interviewed by Alan Filewod, 20 July 1995).

Melbourne Workers Theatre happened at the high tide of the Art and Working Life program. It made a relatively easy transition to Performing Arts Board funding before the Community Cultural Development Committee (CCDC) was downgraded from quasi-autonomous board status to a committee whose funding decisions were subject to a politicised approval process. For a brief moment, when Melbourne Workers Theatre and the CCDC formed a funding partnership enabled by active union support, Art and Working Life was an open field of possibility. To say that MWT was brought into being by the Art and Working Life policy would be unfair to the extraordinary initiative of the theatre's founders, but the program made it possible for the company to survive beyond its initial project. At the same time, the MWT initiative was opportune for the Art and Working Life program, which needed a pilot project.

Payne's recollection of the company's founding is tinged with pride in the accomplishment of forging a relationship between a working ensemble and a shop-based union. He envisioned the relationship as an alliance of workers; as he commented in the press, 'We can only say that we as a group of trade unionists are going in to work with them as a group of trade unionists, with that interaction we are going to make a piece of theatre and we will make it together but we will be performing it' (Sutton 1987).

But as the company began to assemble, other views came into play. A new company must form structures. For a start, a continuing ensemble has to negotiate between the personal investments, both ideological and proprietary, of its members. As political theatre collectives around the world have discovered, every addition to the collective expands the range of contestation, and produces a need to revisit principles. Consequently, they invariably remain in a state of internal crisis. MWT's response, not an uncommon one, was to form a core collective that hired contract workers as needed. Secondly, the acquisition of funding forces companies to invent management structures which attempt to sustain the original vision within the demands of arts bureaucracies. Within five years, when MWT was moving out of Jolimont, the original democratic ensemble had become a legal corporation with a ten page constitution.

Despite the pressures, Payne in particular continued to fight for the principle of an ensemble. This proved increasingly difficult to maintain as immersion in the workplace uncovered the need to bring in other voices in order to reflect more accurately what Cornelius refers to as 'the Australian face', which despite popular imagery, is many different faces.

But in the autumn of 1987, the ensemble that came together saw a fairly clear road ahead of them. The project called for three phases—research, rehearsal and performance—of six weeks each. At the commencement of the project in March, the group held a brainstorming session, the notes from which survive in the company's file cabinets. The sessions dealt with four major topics: the ensemble, purpose, actors and direction. Because the notes (written in block letters on flip-chart newsprint sheets) record the points of consensus, they provide a template by which the subsequent history of the company can be measured.

Many of these points will be familiar to anyone who has worked in a political collective. The ensemble committed itself to applying its ideological principles in its own operating structures. This would be 'a collaborative ensemble with specified functions', paying 'at least' award minimum for actors, consciously anti-sexist and anti-racist. In the optimism of the moment—an optimism generated by solidarity, excitement and the pleasure of a successful beginning—the group recognised the need to maintain 'structures for debate & dissention' [sic].

The spirit of optimism may also have been produced by the excitement of writing a new chapter in Art and Working Life. The discussion of political purpose captured an ambitious (in retrospect, perhaps grandiose) sense of the historical moment. The discussion identified three related points of 'mutual interest' between artists and the union movement:

i)   artist-as-unionist relationship with other unionists;
ii)   concern with stories and issues from the working class viewpoint;
iii) bringing trade unionists into a relationship with theatre.

As well as articulating this instrumentalist position, the discussion positioned the company in the project of recuperating and celebrating working-class culture. This project, which preoccupied so much of the AWL movement in Australia, defined the union movement as the site and sustaining medium of distinct cultural traditions and values, of particular modes of representation, and an historical tradition of struggle.

There is an unavoidable ambivalence here, because the artist is both a constituent participant in the tradition of working-class culture, with the insights and tools to voice it, and an outsider who must learn from it in order to express it. Hence, companies like MWT seek modes and signifiers that authenticate them as 'real' workers. Workplace regulations at Jolimont that required safety boots and hard hats in the yards worked to their advantage, by investing them with the markers of the 'real' world of work; at the same time, they effectively camouflaged the no less real markers of the work of theatre.

The formative meeting also hammered out agreement on the company's operating aesthetic. Actors would participate fully in the research process; scripts would avoid 'simple solutions'; the company would 'search out other performers & other forms of performance', 'incorporate nuances of language heard & seen in the workplace', work with a 'broad variety of styles & genres' and 'give music as central a role as acting'. Throughout all of the changes the company would undergo over the next decade, these principles remained fundamentally intact. As Patricia Cornelius later summarised them:

> We wanted to avoid at all costs the sloganistic, agitprop that usually only results in caricature. We set our minds to solving the problems of making

an overtly political theatre from plays which were complex, layered in meaning, that revealed contradictions and conflict. A theatre that used a number of forms, and music in an integral and exciting way. (interviewed by Alan Filewod, Melbourne, 24 July 1995)

The deeper principles had to do with the basic definition of working-class culture. Reflecting on these early sessions years later, Cornelius identified the fundamental problem:

> We knew that no union movement was a revolutionary movement. There was nowhere artistically interesting in just supporting the union movement. How interesting is that? There is still contention about that ... We knew it had to be about workers, in a workplace... But how many plays can we do about a workplace and why? Workers live, workers go out, go to the pictures, live at home. It's not a departure, not a betrayal to look at another perspective of working people not on a job. Art and Working Life meant that it had to be on the job. That's bullshit—working class doesn't mean just working. (interviewed by Alan Filewod, Melbourne, 24 July 1995)

Cornelius was inclined to this view from very early in the process; as a woman entering the male bastion of the Jolimont depot she would either have to discount her own experience and participate in a male-defined concept of work, or attempt to define a space for women in a workplace where women were confined to low echelon support and clerical jobs somewhat removed from the romanticised and rather masculinist view of the 'worker'. The heavy industry ethos of Jolimont which had attracted the new company, at the same time exposed a crisis of gender. In the pilot project, this crisis remained contained, and in *State of Defence* Cornelius played the role of a woman machinist to a mostly male workplace audience in a shop which in fact had no women in heavy industry jobs. In the company's subsequent work, the issue of women's experience would change the nature of the ensemble, and affect profoundly the meaning of 'worker' in the company's name.

Entering Jolimont

As the main suburban train depot, Jolimont was a key workplace in the rail industry, and in Steve Payne's words, 'the jewel in the union crown':

> I'll never forget, when we walked into the worksite, there was a feeling of resonance there, that this was going to be a place where you could make

theatre, it was very inspiring. Inspiring in its decrepitude, really. Huge building with big cranes, trams being lifted ... very dark and dirty. (interviewed by Alan Filewod, St Kilda, 20 July 1995)

Having perceived the workplace in these theatricalised images, the company found the real world of the workers themselves to be much less exotic. Payne recalls the shop committee as 'ten blokes sitting around, with varying degrees of political consciousness, varying degrees of commitment to the shop committee, and varying degrees of English literacy' (interviewed by Alan Filewod, St Kilda, 20 July 1995).

With the basic agreement on process worked out, the company arranged to meet the workforce. They were introduced at a mass meeting, where they gave brief individual performances to what Irine Vela calls 'a curious mix of Greek, Italian and Australian workers'. Both Vela and Cornelius recall John Romeril's performance of a political poem about American imperialism. According to Vela, who had met Romeril for the first time that day:

> He unexpectedly read and sang a piece he had written. Standing on a chair, with his long and sinewy arms flapping about, he really looked and sounded like a crow. Again I thought, 'Who is this man?' It was a relief to hear a human being whose singing was worse than mine. (Vela 1993: 196)

Cornelius recalls the meeting as 'very male, lots of noisy, earthy reactions, especially to women' (interviewed by Alan Filewod, Melbourne, 24 July 1995). Romeril's performance stuck in her mind because of her initial reaction: as he stood flapping his arms, she thought that he had gone too far for the audience, that they wouldn't accept his theatricality. Their applause demonstrated to her that the workplace audience was a plural one containing diverse cultural experiences that could not be easily categorised in terms of artistic tastes. Nor, with this cultural diversity, could particular artistic forms (such as narrative realism) be considered natural. Cornelius identifies this as a major topic of early debate:

> We had a lot of debate ... not to be belittling people and believing they only like fluffy, funny stuff. People could handle complexity of story ... There was incredible snobbery about what workers could appreciate because they'd never seen theatre. (interviewed by Alan Filewod, Melbourne, 24 July 1995)

The experience of that first concert meeting seems to have shown MWT the importance of defining dramaturgical forms in terms of the audience, the opportunities provided by the performance space, and the political analysis of the issue at hand. The meeting also seems to have confirmed the importance of music in the company's artistic practice, as proposed in the constitutional brainstorm session. This was Irine Vela's first professional job, but she became one of the mainstays of MWT, working on almost every show for the next decade as musician, composer and arranger, and making a crucial—perhaps the crucial—contribution to the company's artistic identity.

Once in place, MWT became a fixture in the shop; according to Clough, the main issue was whether the workforce would accept performances in their lunch room, or whether they would perceive them as a management-sanctioned intrusion. Again Metrail's hostility to the company was useful. Clough admits that it was much harder to rally support for the continuation of the residency after the pilot project. But by that point, MWT had become part of the regular give and take between union and management, and when electricians came to unhook the MWT's wiring one night, the shop committee responded with a black ban on the shed, after which no one would touch it without union go-ahead. In their hard hats and safety boots, the troupe members blended in with the larger workforce—until they found themselves caught in shop-floor politics, an inevitable consequence of their approach. In 1986, Payne told one reporter:

> In general there are three tiers, the union management, the shop committee and then the rank and file. The rank and file will form a committee. Each week we will have working projects and, as things develop, we will try them out. What we are looking for from the workers is authenticity, so they can say, 'No mate you don't do it like that'. (Sutton 1987)

This ideal of shop-floor participation was ambitious, but it did result in the establishment of a union advisory group, which continued to function even after the company had lost most of its union affiliations. In the beginning the group consisted of allies, like Clough, who smoothed the way for the company's research process, made the introductions and, when necessary, took a stand for them.

State of Defence

Not surprisingly, the play that developed out of the pilot project was in many ways a theatrical recapitulation of the process that produced it. As the actors widened their sphere of research and shared their findings in feedback sessions, Andrew Bovell pushed them to interpret the material dramatically. In Payne's words, 'more was asked of the actors to select the points that inspired them. Sometimes it came back in poetry, sometimes in illustrative performance, sometimes in particular characters' (interviewed by Alan Filewod, St Kilda, 20 July 1995). This collaborative process survives in the text of *State of Defence*, in the gestures the actors use to authenticate their characters, in bits of business, and in the visual mime that establishes workplace routines.

As playwright, Bovell was responsible for the final shaping of the text, but he worked within collectively defined stylistic frameworks. Most importantly the play would be theatrical (that is, it would use music and anti-illusionary techniques when useful) but look for emotional depth by focusing on a few typifying characters. Cornelius explains this as a conscious decision to avoid the overtired devices of agitprop:

> We talked a lot ... before ... *State* ... we would not produce plays that had a myriad of characters played by two or three actors, we would take characterisation right through so that you got full, rich story-lines and you actually saw a progression and change in people, rather than those caricatures that pop up to accommodate certain scenes you often see in poor didactic theatre or bad agitprop. (interviewed by Alan Filewod, Melbourne, 24 July 1995)

State of Defence comprises two short plays, which together play under an hour. The first, 'Rory's Last Day', shows a typical day 'when something had to give' at Jolimont, focusing on three workers: Lee, a female machinist; Martin, a fitter; and Andreas, their shop steward. Each has a dilemma, which is expressed to peripheral characters who are either unseen or appear briefly. Lee wants to know why she hasn't been getting overtime; Martin is frustrated by the inexplicable shortages of parts he needs to do his work; and Andreas must decide whether to accept a job as a foreman and leave the union ranks. In the half-hour of the play, Lee moves towards militancy, Martin towards defeatism, and Andreas accepts the promotion. Meanwhile, the union proposes to initiate a struggle over minor adjustments in the wage scale, while ignoring rumours of massive lay-offs. Lee's attempts to intervene in a union mass meeting are defeated when she is silenced by a procedural ruling; because she doesn't know the rules of order she cannot make her case heard. The play ends when Martin's unseen co-worker Rory has a stroke—a quiet victim of workplace oppression.

The play articulates three major findings from the research process: that the workforce is ideologically and politically divided, that the union

(from left) Julie Hickson, Andrew Bovell, Jolimont worker, Irine Vela, Jolimont worker, Michael White, Linda Stoul, Patricia Cornelius and Steve Payne (centre). (Photo: Collin Bogaars)

bureaucracy is more interested in accommodation with management than with shopfloor concerns, and the ambivalence of workers like Martin and Lee who take pride in their work but resent their employer. When Andreas dons the grey dustcoat of the foreman, he crosses the line; becoming a 'crawler' who has betrayed his former workmates.

In the second play, 'The Alexander Story', these themes develop into crisis. Andreas explains the title as a reference to Alexander the Great and the Gordian knot—a parable which illustrates that complex problems sometimes invite simple solutions. Lee has replaced Andreas as shop steward, and Martin has decided to quit and become a salesman. Lee— who now knows the rules of order—unsuccessfully tries to mobilise the workers for a mass meeting to push the question of lay-offs. Andreas must invoke coercive authority when he discovers Martin sleeping on the job. In the end, Lee faces a humiliating defeat, Martin leaves the trade he loves, and Andreas stands in silent confusion, torn between his loyalty to his comrades and the demands of the migrant ethic to climb the class ladder. Lee expresses the play's final point of determined resistance:

> What are we up against? It's hard to know. It's powerful, it's big, it's bloody strong and it wants to do away with unions. And if I shut my eyes

I know it's still going to be there—it doesn't go away.

We're under its shadow.

What's left?

I'm left.
And a lot of others like me. (Bovell 1987:16)

The play's premiere on 1 June 1987 was a highly charged event. The audience of 180 sat three rows deep along both sides of the traverse of the playing space. The band, comprising two guitars and a bazouki (played by Irine Vela) occupied a small dais at one end. Behind them hung a stern banner, made in the Jolimont paintshop, reading 'Melbourne Workers Theatre'. The theatre's own performance report—the first of many in its history— provides a handwritten summary:

> The first show for the workers we have had the greatest contact with through research and in an advisory capacity.
>
> Management had given workers an extension of half an hour on their lunch time so that they were able to see the entire show. But on the Monday Management had retracted the half hour extension in reaction to some industrial problems. At the union meeting held earlier this day the workers voted to stop work for half an hour to see the entire play.
>
> The performance was received extremely well. The audience was extremely responsive and attentive.
>
> Feedback after the show was positive. Workers felt that they identified strongly with the issues of the play.
>
> A great beginning.

In fact it was an ideal beginning, launching the theatre as an expression of industrial action. The premiere of *State of Defence* was both the product and the occasion of solidarity with the union, both the argument and the proof of a productive relationship on the shop floor.

An MWT videotape of one of the Jolimont performances makes this relationship vividly clear. The show begins with the band playing warm-up music, leading to an Iraqi folk song of struggle. The three actors, wearing red jerseys under grey overalls, emerge from the audience: workers stepping from an assembly of workers. As they enter the bare playing space, they create place with their bodies and voices, shaping their respective workspaces by speaking past each other in a montage of overlapping freezes. Gesture and gaze establish the presence of other, unseen, characters.

Throughout the play, work routines signify dramatic movement. The actors move wooden crates to establish a sense of working, and the rearranged crates create smaller acting areas when needed. Actual items from the shop added an iconic authenticity. When Martin complains about his mismatching parts, he holds up the real thing; the mass meeting is established by the use of a portable loudspeaker; the actors' costumes are standard shopfloor gear. The final effect is one of naturalised research.

The authority of the research, the iconic effect of the properties and work gear, the smooth replication of the precision of work into the routine of the performance, enabled *State of Defence* to play the ambiguities of modern union life. The assurance of the performance appears to have travelled beyond the original Jolimont performance venue. Four months later, the critic for the *Canberra Times* praised the remount of the show for its skilled precision:

> Key words and phrases are repeated and at times they have a choral insistence. 'There's a man who's tired', 'Gotta fight this one'. The actors play off each other with split second timing so that the audience moves from factory floor, to mass meeting, to the manager's office with the slightest variation of tone, and with minimum props. The musical backing reinforces changes in mood and pace while songs repeat the political message. (Nugent 1987)

State of Defence was a success for the company not just in its reception by the worker audiences and critics, but because of the possibilities it opened up for further development, which accelerated its move along a funding track. The play's development confirmed personal and shopfloor alliances with Jolimont workers, who would contribute to the company's sense of identity in the years to follow. The alliances themselves opened up new dramatic possibilities. Payne recalls that:

> On Friday afternoons we had a specific time to show back material to the workers. Later in the process we were having trouble with a scene ... where the shop steward takes a woman worker to management and we couldn't get it right, so we said to them, 'we're having trouble with this scene'. ... one of the guys said, 'if she started to go like that I'd take her outside and give her a good talking to, she's undermining what you're trying to do'. Someone else said, 'management wouldn't put up with that'. So we actually allocated it: 'you be the shop steward, you be the woman, you be the management ,,, if someone does something you would/wouldn't do, just say, "stop".' That's how we worked through the scene, so by the time the play was ready we

knew it would work because they'd been so much a part of the process ... It's not like Boal because we brought our perspective to it, we didn't just do what they said. We had quite heated arguments about our perception versus their perception. It was a negotiated interpretation. (interviewed by Alan Filewod, St Kilda, 20 July 1995)

The inclusion of workers in the creative process, even on this informal basis, became a continuing principle in the company's work, although it never actually developed into a participatory, interactive method comparable to Boal's Forum Theatre. It equipped the actors to use performance in more instrumental contexts, such as when MWT was invited to perform at a course run by the Trade Unions Training Authority. The course director wrote in his report:

> After the Group performed we invited them to stay as the 'Characters' in the play and we asked the representatives to break into syndicate groups and to identify the issues of conflict facing each of these characters and then to cross examine them about their roles. This was a 'hot seat' situation which brought out all the issues shop stewards face in their job. The participants thought that the three hours that the theatre group was with us was the highlight of the course. (Pettiona 1987)

But while *State of Defence* seemed to have successfully defined an alignment with unions, both instrumentally and as representation, it also exposed a growing crisis about cultural diversity. On the one hand, the show featured an Anglo-Australian actor playing a Greek man to an audience of whom the majority came from non-English speaking backgrounds; on the other, it masculinised women's experience. The first absence was easily rectified by a collective decision to use at least one other language in each show and seek out actors from non-English speaking background. The second absence could only be resolved by moving beyond the Jolimont plant and audience that had given the theatre its newly won identity. Cornelius recalls this as 'a huge internal conflict', even after the company agreed that the second show should focus on women and work:

> Because Jolimont had 800 male workers it was obvious that wasn't the right place to be to get the research and to get the contact with the workers to write that play. So we made contact with women at a seatbelt factory way out in Broadmeadow. ...
>
> We created another Jolimont at a pub, a huge barn of an ugly fucking thing. We met with women and their husbands and sons. It was a most

fantastic experience, listening at night, over pub fare, to their feedback over what we showed them and their heat over the conflict with the union. (interviewed by Alan Filewod, Melbourne, 24 July 1995)

With the proposed title of 'Women Are Half the Workforce' the project undertook a part-time residency at the Royal Melbourne Hospital and weekly sessions with workers from the Cool Drive Seat Belt Factory. The final text, written by Patricia Cornelius under the title of *Dusting Our Knees*, focuses on three women (one Anglo, one Macedonian and one Italian, the latter played by actors who brought their own languages into the text) and an Anglo man at an unnamed meat processing plant in Footscray, a working-class Melbourne suburb. Cornelius had from the beginning been clear that she wanted to move beyond the 'tired old forms' of social realism: 'Unless you develop new ways of working, of taking material and pulling it inside out and experimenting with that, I don't care how vibrant and politically fantastic it is, it will die' (interviewed by Alan Filewod, Melbourne, 24 July 1995). With that in mind the company engaged Robin Laurie, a director with experience in non-realist performance at Circus Oz and Sidetrack.

Dusting our Knees is written in a compressed series of short, linked scenes in which a strike by women who discover they are paid less than men in the same jobs is sold out by the union. The plays also looks at the domestic tensions of childcare, sexism and financial stress which intersect with the working lives of the women, leading to a pivotal episode when one has a breakdown:

> *Breakdown is played out. Lijuana walks to the centre of the space. She stops. She slowly sinks down to her knees. Others watch her. The song finishes and she rises.*

LIJUANA: I can't really remember much.

FRAN: You were late.

GRAHAM: Her mum died in '81.

LIJUANA: Yes, I remember I was late and it was raining.

CARLA: She was expected to take her mother's place.

GRAHAM: It was pouring.

LIJUANA: My dad. Well, he's hopeless.

FRAN: The trains were running late.

LIJUANA: Yes, it was raining and I was late (Cornelius 1987: 12).

The minimalist dramatic technique, with its overlapping narrative voices, shifting presentational modes (from direct address to terse dialogue), songs and simple story-telling gestures, was not a radical departure from the mode of social realism that had framed *State of Defence*. But the rediscovery of expressionist techniques of dramatic compression allowed for efficient storytelling by condensing the narrative moments between points of emotional resonance.

The success of these techniques justified Cornelius's adamant insistence on expanding the aesthetic ground beyond 'tired old forms', because they proved ideally suited to workplace performances. *Dusting our Knees* played mainly canteens. At the Northcote Municipal Depot canteen, a critic for *New Theatre: Australia* noted the audience:

> had not seen a play before at this workplace. Most had not seen a play like it (maybe many of them would not have seen any play before). They had watched closely, with plenty of backchat, but evaluating and frequently amused. Afterwards they chatted easily with the cast, mostly about issues raised in the play. (McCaughey 1987)

State of Defence and *Dusting our Knees* defined two imperatives of MWT's subsequent work: on the one hand a commitment to the workforce of Jolimont, and on the other a program of cultural outreach. The Jolimont connection, maintained by weekly meetings with workers, a regular series of informal concerts and ongoing personal consultations, became the platform which enabled the move towards a more plural notion of working-class audiences: from 1988 until Jolimont closed in 1993, almost all the plays produced by MWT were taken out of the depot into other workplaces.

Dusting Our Knees was soon followed by a show based on some of the same research, and featuring three of the four actors. *The Ballad of Lois Ryan*, was written by Andrew Bovell with dramaturgy by John Romeril, who in the final week of rehearsal offered the key suggestion that the play should tell the story backwards. It is an episodic narrative about a textile worker whose desperate need for an identity away from the factory floor and the kids at home is denied by her husband. (As she says to him, 'at work you may be the greatest shop steward but at home you're just another boss'.) (Bovell 1990: 107) Her decision to leave her family is the focus of the play, but the frame is the report of her death in an industrial accident at her new place of work. Watt points out in his preface to the play that it 'manages to confront its predominantly male audience with a problematisation of the position of women in a conventionally male ethos while ensuring that the death of Lois is continuously seen as an "industrial" as well as "personal" issue' (Watt 1990.2: 87). Like *Dusting our Knees*, *The Ballad of Lois Ryan* toured through workplace canteens; and it was also picked up by theatres in Adelaide, Sydney and New Zealand.

The workplace performances were hampered by a creative decision that exposed an early fracture in the company's commitment to produce work suited to the industrial conditions of its audience. The first two shows had been developed in short and long versions, to cater for audiences with only half an hour for lunch. With *Lois Ryan*, the company 'decided to do only one 50–minute version', a decision 'based primarily on artistic concerns':

> We considered that the dramatic development of the characters and the plot, and the musical dynamic of the piece, had been unacceptably restricted by the format of the 20–25 minute versions we had done in the past. In order to extend the potential to affect the audience at an emotional level, we decided to allow more time for the drama to do its work. (MWT 1989: 10)

This inevitably led to problems; in 'at least four' venues the show was cancelled because workers had insufficient time to see it. It is hard not to read this explanation in retrospect as the somewhat glossed-over statement of a decision produced by conflict. The language of the justification ('allowing more time for the drama to do its work') silences a deeper discussion about working methods and the processes of making creative decisions about genre, format and the very meaning of 'dramatic development'.

One solution to the problem was to move beyond workplace venues to include a greater number of community spaces and this dovetailed with the company's approaches to minority cultures. Over the next two seasons MWT continued to expand its territory with *The Aftermath* (1989), looking at the effect of a long strike on personal friendships, and *Taxi*, 'A Political Cabaret' which consisted of stand-up scenes in front of a band and introduced Sanhol Mat, a taxi driver who had been performing in the Turkish community when he heard that MWT was looking for ethnic actors.

Both shows attempted to engage with real politics of multicultural inclusion, often to the discomfort of reviewers, such as one who wrote (astonishingly enough in a city as culturally diverse as Melbourne in the 1990s), 'It is a disconcerting experience to sit in a theatre audience and hear the people behind you speaking a language that is other than English' (Freeman 1989). Although it may have forced reviewers to confront their own cultural expectations of professional theatre, it is possible that the company's proven commitment to lived multiculturalism was as much a contributing factor to its rapid funding growth as was its union support. At the same time, this commitment to work with migrant and minority cultures, to ensure cross-cultural representation in casting and to use other languages had limits which were felt by both sides. Sanhol Mat, who performed in *The Aftermath* as well as *Taxi*, echoed the frustration experienced by immigrant actors in virtually every (ostensibly) multicultural society:

> I'm restricted to migrant roles, because of the thickness of my accent. I would like to be given other parts. An actor should do every part. But it's hard for me to do white Australian roles. (interviewed by Alan Filewod, Melbourne, 27 July 1995)

The most complex engagement with multicultural realities came in 1990 when MWT opened its long-planned Koori show, *Nidjera*. The planning began early in 1989, when the group made a commitment to a show focusing on Aboriginal issues. Recognising the problem of reinscribed colonialism, MWT asked writer Archie Weller to lead the project, and established a Koori Advisory Group to oversee it. This acknowledgment of Koori cultural authority, made possible by a loose interpretation of the company's early assertion that a project would 'meet the company's objectives of making theatre for, with and about working class people' (MWT 1989: 4), had important ramifications. As described in the Koori community paper *Koorier*,

> The Koori play will be about an everyday Koori family, their questions, ideas, problems and solutions to whatever they face.
>
> The original concept was to be Koories at work and trade unions. But because the community said that unions had done nothing for Koories and that most work Koories do is for their own people, it has changed to a more appropriate theme. (*Koorier* 1990: 27)

This expansion of the foundational notion of work enabled MWT to move beyond the boundaries of organised labour. By 1991 MWT had lost much of the enthusiastic initial support from unions, in part because the excitement of its founding had passed, and in part because of fall-out from union politics at Jolimont in 1989 while *The Aftermath* was in rehearsal.

Payne explains the political eruption in 1989 as a result of economic pressures: as the state pressured management, management pressured the unions, and workers were pressured to take redundancy packages. The fear of massive job losses (which proved all too true) may have framed the controversy, but the immediate cause was a more familiar political rivalry on the shop floor. A move to expel MWT came after there was a shift in the shop committee membership because, in the eyes of some, MWT was too closely identified with a 'radical left faction'. Wayne Clough, who as a shop steward was one of MWT's chief allies, offers the (partisan) explanation that 'the Blow-up' was a political battle with 'one particular malcontent':

> ... one former shop steward, formerly on the shop committee, hated some of the people on the shop committee and would undermine everything they do. He worked against MWT from the start. Never stopped nipping at their heels. The mood at Jolimont wasn't healthy, there had been fighting with management.
>
> He spread rumours that MWT was costing workers in overtime because of resources from MET ... like all Messiahs he got some believers. It split the shop and came within a hair's bloody breadth of getting them out. ...We tracked down MET documents that made the facts clear. The bloke kept demanding a meeting, eventually one was called; he gave a long speech and at the end, I produced the documents, someone called for a vote and that was it. (interviewed by Alan Filewod, Melbourne, 1 August 1995)

Payne's analysis was that a number of shop stewards were threatened because 'reformers' had set out to expose a 'very cosy relationship' between supervisors and shop stewards who were dealing in overtime:

> The leadership they overthrew didn't go away; it was still there lurking in the background, sniping away, not challenging ... until the pressure that began to mount started shaking the foundations, and then we became the meat in the sandwich between these two opposing forces. It was like being in a witch-hunt really, with these quite slanderous and highly inaccurate stuff starting to get circulated, that obviously had management behind it. (interviewed by Alan Filewod, St Kilda, 20 July 1995)

MWT tried to assuage the workforce by distributing a special bulletin that sought to clarify their status in Jolimont:

> Recently some workers at Jolimont have expressed concern about our presence here. It has been suggested that the facilities provided for us are, in some way, depriving workers of upgraded facilities. ...
>
> MELBOURNE WORKERS THEATRE RECEIVES NO MONEY FOR WAGES FROM METRAIL OR THE MINISTRY OF TRANSPORT. (MWT 1989.2)

The document lists funding sources, quotes ministerial memos confirming funding, and argues that:

> We are all paying members of our appropriate unions. *We are based in a workplace because we believe that it is only by working alongside other workers and getting their input and feedback that our plays will remain relevant to workers and truthful to the issues raised in the research.* [emphasis in original]

The controversy ended well enough in the short term for the company, and it is likely that the realisation that they needed to broaden their mandate paid off in increased arts council support. But the residual anger and suspicion continued to haunt MWT for years and contributed to a measurable decline in union support. One material consequence was the decision to reformulate the company's structure, replacing the five-person core group with a governing Management Committee elected by an Artistic Advisory Group (consisting of all past and present company employees), and a Union Support Group, which was designed to broaden support beyond the three Jolimont unions.

In itself, the controversy was minor, and as Clough describes, not difficult to contain. But at the same time it shattered the founding vision of artist–worker solidarity on the shop floor. That vision had already been exposed as a conceptual fiction by the realities of cultural and gender differences; the 'blow-up' exposed it as a structural fiction as well. In order to claim their space in the workplace, the company had to prove that it was not sustained by the workers. That may seem like a harsh reading, in so far as Payne repeatedly made the point that they themselves were unionised employees, but the fact remained that, unlike the Jolimont workers, the MWT members had no employee–management relationship with their funders. As self-managed workers in an environment demoralised by management relations, they occupied an ambivalent social space that led inevitably to their implication in ideological factions. By 1990, MWT could only remain in Jolimont by defining itself outside the Jolimont workforce; only by leaving could they stay. For Payne this was a crisis that led to his withdrawal from the company; for Cornelius, it was an artistic opportunity.

In 1991, with Penny McDonald taking the reins as artistic coordinator, MWT embarked on a policy of alternating workplace projects with public shows that successfully bid for mainstream audiences, and legitimised the company in Melbourne's theatre community. The first of these, *Black Cargo*, was an ambitious musical produced at Anthill Theatre, with music by Irine

Vela and text by John Romeril, adapted from John Morrison's story about waterfront union disputes over a Canadian ship crewed by scab labour. The move into a professional theatre space was necessary for the more traditional staging the show demanded. There is a somewhat defensive tone to the company's statement in a union newsletter that:

> This is a departure for us in that we normally take our shows to the workers; this time we are hoping to bring our audience to us. We hope that this will enable many more workers to see our shows than we have been in the past able to reach as well as being [sic] us to build a working class audience. (ARU Gazette 1991)

Black Cargo was a critical success—as a combination of a Romeril script and Vela's music was likely to be—and the company banked a substantial amount of artistic capital for future dealings with arts funders. Entering the professional mainstream, even on its fringes, also recognised individual needs for artistic growth. The show placed the company in a wider field of reception, and by blurring the boundaries between labour engagement and mainstream cultural production, it also placed it in a wider field of assessment.

Black Cargo was followed by another workplace show, No Fear (Korkmak Yok), which focused on 'extreme action' and union organisation, written by Cornelius and Vicki Reynolds, who died of cancer while it was in rehearsal. The show was developed with contacts in the Turkish community, many of whom had recently walked out in a bitter strike against Ford. The juxtaposition of these two shows, the English-language labour-history in the theatre, and the touring workplace–community show aimed at migrant audiences, suggests the company had not yet found a synthesis of forms that would win critical legitimacy in the domain of professional theatre and at the same time straddle cultural divides.

The following season, MWT's final year in Jolimont, repeated this template of a public performance followed by a workplace return to community roots, but with crucial differences. The first show, Daily Grind, was the most sensational show the company had yet produced, and received by far the most press coverage, because of its focus on women working in the sex trade. The second, Last Drinks, the final show to come out of the Jolimont residency, was perhaps the most effective of the workplace touring shows, and can be seen as a mournful farewell to the company's roots.

Daily Grind was the most daring of MWT's shows, and the most public;

it enjoyed a successful run at Theatreworks in St. Kilda, Melbourne's seaside suburb noted for its trendy cafes, street ambience and often seedy night life; it then toured Hobart, Sydney, Adelaide and Brisbane. More than any other, this show brought the company recognition in the wider theatre community; as Cornelius recalls, 'It turned around our peers in the theatre industry. They hated our guts, thought we shouldn't have the money, thought we were workerite idiots, no sympathy for us at all, until *Daily Grind*' (interviewed by Alan Filewod, Melbourne, 24 July 1995).

The show was written by Vicki Reynolds and performed after her death. Reynolds' career is a testament to MWT's least acknowledged but perhaps most important contribution to developing a working-class cultural practice, its trainee programs. She had answered an advertised job for a trainee writer, was hired and began working as a team member on *The Aftermath*. She undertook placements with a community theatre in Footscray and at the Hospital Employees' Federation, and worked as co-writer on *Taxi* and *No Fear (Korkmak Yok)*.

Vicki Reynolds' script was extensively reworked in rehearsal by director Lisa Dombroski and the actors (Lyn McGranger and Belinda McClory), who played the roles of two strippers who perform between shows at an erotic cinema, facing pressure from the owner to 'work hot', by incorporating sex toys into their routines. Although contained in the genre of the backstage drama, the production raised questions of gaze politics.

Daily Grind was received by critics as a frank assessment of the industrial working conditions of the sex trade, in which (as described in MWT publicity) 'women as young as twenty-five are faced with the alternative of leaving the industry or working "hot"' (MWT 1992.5: 2). Despite a sympathetic reception (which included high praise for the conventional theatrical values of writing and acting), reviewers were circumspect about the ambivalences of representation and gaze. They commended the play for its 'warmth and conviction' (Radic 1992), its sensitivity, humour, masterful direction and 'refreshing lack of gratuitousness' (Scott-Norman 1992). But for the most part they avoided the more difficult questions about the politics of voyeurism in a theatre of desire.

By contrasting the youthful, conventionally eroticised body of the younger woman with the aging body of her co-worker, the performance creates a relational frame which invites the audience to enjoy the pleasure of unaverted visual consumption. Critics pointed to the final moments of the play, in which the naked older woman stands harshly exposed in bright light, as a distancing moment in which (to quote Leonard Radic) she is 'cruelly... revealed to herself, and to her male cinema audience, as the faded beauty she now is'. The uncomfortable suggestion is that age and the competition of youth rather than industrial conditions oppress this particular worker. It was a point picked up by one angry spectator, who in a letter to a newspaper identified herself as an 'ex-stripper', and complained that, 'In fashioning a character devoid of inherent powers, a victim is created, her power denied and the message to other women is that they have no voice and so are at the mercy of their employers' (Pilkington 1992).

The play sidestepped the deeper problems of representation and agency, accepting the necessity of nudity, and in the celebrated ending de-eroticised the worker's body suggesting that the harshly lit exposed nakedness is more authentic than the erotically lit, 'softer' nudity of the strip routine. By accepting the limits of theatrical decorum, which can only suggest actions that the 'real' show would explicitly perform, the mode of representation was fixed in ambivalence. One sequence in the play used a vibrator to signify rather than enact the extremes of 'hot' stripping that the play criticises from an industrial rather than a moral stance.

Although it raised the question of industrial conditions, the play didn't quite engage with them, in part because it personalised its story in genre conventions, and in part because it maintained a line between the respectable (stripping) and the invasive (working hot), without examining the larger questions of power, control and ownership in the industry.

While *Daily Grind* was up and running, MWT was making its farewell to the dwindling workforce at Jolimont. *Last Drinks* is a moving valedictory to the company's origins, and while it was not about Jolimont as such, it is tinged with the sadness and anger of watching friends take redundancy packages and leave their place of work.

Planning started for *Last Drinks*, under the provisional title of 'Be Thankful For What You've Got' in late 1991. The company decided on a workplace show that focused on demoralised workers facing redundancy and identified its basic shape:

> Three workers in a small factory under threat of closure reflect the fear & anxieties of workers in this period of recession. The factory will close unless the workers accept a reduction [in] wages. They are in a conflict over what should be done. (MWT 1992.2)

As always, the initial vision was modified considerably through the research and workshop phases, which took place in June and July, followed by four weeks of rehearsal and six weeks of performance. The writer, Patricia

Following the sizzling success of *DAILY GRIND*,

Melbourne Workers Theatre

invites you to attend

LAST DRINKS.

IT'S GAB'S RETIREMENT PARTY

A time for fun, festivity, songs and laughter, but also questions. Why is he retiring? Is he going to find his place in the sun, or is he being pushed into miserable poverty? Secrets are revealed and accusations fly, as we discover a workplace deep in conflict.

LAST DRINKS is a story of workers coping with the pressure of workplace change and recession in the 90s; their hopes and fears, how they escape, how they survive, how they struggle.

(MWT 1992)

Cornelius expressed an early interest in exploring the possibilities of using music as more than ambient accompaniment, 'that kind of dreadful repetition of what the action just said' (interviewed by Alan Filewod, Melbourne, 24 July 1995). She floated the idea of a more integrated score, with 'music shifting you within the story' and 'more poetic use of language'. Five years of performing in workplaces had given the company confidence in their audiences' readiness to accept stylistic innovations, but the ambitious musical structure was modified substantially by the nature of the story that developed and by the unfeasibility of writing fifty minutes of scored music in a few weeks. Even so, the final profile of the show was not clear until very late in the process; in mid-August, the company reported to its Union Support Group:

The script is almost finished & the show is firming up. The form/style has changed from the original 'song-spiel' idea. The band has taken on a sort of Greek Chorus role, commenting on the action & providing details unknown to the characters. The play is still set in the private sector. (MWT 1992.3)

Research for the show began in Jolimont, which, a year before its closing, was paring down its workforce. For Cornelius this was an emotional process, but it showed her what the play had to be about:

They were the beginning of our life as a company. These workers had been vibrant helpful and excited about us being there. By this time working conditions had changed. All of them were at the end of a working life, not being appreciated, being disposed of without qualms. I remember talking to four elderly men waiting in train cars. They'd meet in the dock and sit and chat in the cars, all waiting decisions about what would happen. (interviewed by Alan Filewod, Melbourne, 24 July 1995)

The Jolimont workers provided the emotional ground for the play, but the text examined the plight of cleaners working for an unnamed corporation. During the workshop process the four actors (Laura Lattuada, Melissa Reeves, Maryanne Sam and Phil Summer) set out to develop characters by meeting with hospital cleaners and transport workers facing retrenchment. This was more than a hunt for acting models, although that was an inevitable consequence—as one actor told Reeves, 'often I get a whole character in one hit'. Nevertheless, MWT actors approached the task as political research rather than 'bring 'em back alive' character modeling. According to Melissa Reeves:

In no way am I saying that I have the right to speak on behalf of a 35 year old woman who's working as a cleaner in a factory, I'm not saying I've had that experience; I'm saying I'm an actor who has spent a while talking to those people, reading about the stuff that affects their lives, workshopping a play about it. I'm an actor, I have skills, I can sing and I can hopefully deliver a fine line. I see it very much as a job, and I'm not scared at all. If people came up to me after and said, 'you're not a bloody cleaning woman, you're way off the mark', I'd take that criticism, but I'm not frightened of it at all. I felt like I was telling a story. (interviewed by Alan Filewod, Melbourne, 31 July 1995)

Working in a room at a local hospital, the actors improvised situations and dialogue using Laban exercises to bond as a group and find character movements; Cornelius then drafted scenes and eventually a longhand script. The final phases of rehearsal (during which the script continued to evolve) and performance were directed by David Carlin, who had directed *Black Cargo* the previous year.

From the beginning, MWT had recurring discussions about appropriate dramatic forms for workplace performances. At first, these discussions focused on the relative values of 'linear' character realism and anti-illusionist theatricalist narrative, as represented respectively by *State of Defence* and *Dusting our Knees*. In retrospect, the gradations of difference between those two shows were relatively minor, but they expressed deeper principles. One of them, which the company soon moved beyond, was whether workplace audiences would accept disruptions of normative realist modes; some members of the company had initially been apprehensive about the inverted structure of *The Ballad of Lois Ryan*.

Workplace dramaturgy, regardless of its style, must take into account fundamental imperatives: the play must outline both the social problem and a response to it in a strictly limited period of time (either twenty-five or fifty minutes); the short set-up times demand minimalist staging, with the actors carrying the weight of information that could otherwise be expressed through scenery. And finally, the audience is usually small and close to the action; as one critic noted, 'Theatre in the workplace is no picnic. It can be more of a bun-fight; clattering of crockery, scraping of chairs, talking' (Herbert 1992). The play has to be written for a very particular style of acting. Melissa Reeves commented on the 'ease' with which MWT actors were able to adapt to difficult performance conditions:

> They're sort of real, they're comfortable performing quite close to people and saying asides—they haven't got glazed eyes; they're very *there* in the space, in the canteen as well as being in the play. (interviewed by Alan Filewod, Melbourne, 31 July 1995)

Taken together, these conditions impose a set of rigorous formal conventions on workplace performances which require fine crafting by the playwright. As MWT found, these conventions worked best when the limitations of the performance space are integrated into the narrative structure—hence the powerful effect of the fragmented storytelling in *Dusting our Knees*, the ballad frame of *Lois Ryan*, the cabaret staging of *Taxi*. Each of these wrote the performance space into the dramatic logic of the play.

Last Drinks set out to explore the effect of industrial change on individual workers, rather than tell the story of a particularised issue or action.

The cast of *Last Drinks* (clockwise from bottom left) Melissa Reeves, Laura Lattuada, Maryanne Sam and Phil Summer. (Photo: Clare de Bruin, Melbourne Workers Theatre)

Cornelius had to find a structure that personalised social change in the characters which the actors were developing in the workshop. She decided to ground the action in a traditional notion of plot, in which, as the publicity announced, 'secrets are revealed and accusations fly'. The play's governing idea of a farewell party came early in the process, and proved to be the key decision. It allowed an integration of character, music and workplace performance site, by including the audience as the somewhat awkward guests at a retirement party for 45-year-old Gab. This effective dramatic hook established a set of character motives highly pressurised by the need to make the party succeed, and—like all parties—placed personal conflicts in a public space governed by fragile conventions of decorum. The result was a model of workplace neoclassicism.

The superimposition of textual and performance space works particularly well in the text of *Last Drinks* because the play assumes that the workplace audience don't actually know 'their' cleaners. As Annie (played by Melissa

Reeves) says when she hands out party hats to the audience (who are seated on three sides of the space) and circulates a farewell card at the top of the play:

> Welcome everyone, welcome. Thanks for coming. It's great to see you here. It must seem a bit strange because you don't really know us, but we're your cleaners. Ok, Ok, if you've got any complaints put it in the card. I've got you all here because Gab, someone else who cleans your dirty dunnies, is retiring after 25 years. He'd sneak out if he could, leave without a word he would. Management may not give a stuff, but I thought, he doesn't leave here without a send-off. Just something nice, an occasion, some little thing I'd like for myself when I go. (Cornelius 1993: 2)

The discomfort of an audience that doesn't know the guest of honour is shared by the characters themselves who work in separate areas of the factory. Annie hasn't seen her old friend Dorothy (played by Laura Lattuada), for some time since she now cleans the management offices. Gwen (Maryanne Sam) is a trainee cleaner on her first day at work. (In performance, Gwen was played by a young Aboriginal woman, which gave the text an added but unexpressed undercurrent of racial tension.)

The naturalised ambience of the party is seemingly reinforced by the arrival of the musicians, Irine Vela and Shirley Billing. They enter singing an apparently throwaway song:

> We are the band and we will play
> At most occasions anywhere night or day
> We play weddings, barmitzvahs,
>   engagements and parties
> In lounge rooms and dance halls
>   in the city and country
> We play standards and classics
>   zorbas and tangos
> And special requests
> But we don't play fandangos (Cornelius 1993: 3)

In fact the musicians establish the play's principal non-realist convention: the use of songs and scored monologues to express private moments of reflection publicly. Just as in a Broadway musical, the songs mark points where character-based realism can expose its subtexts. *Last Drinks* moves forward by shifting between performance modes: public address to the audience 'guests', 'overheard' dialogue encounters between characters, and musically-framed introspection. On a practical level, this enabled Cornelius to compress political and emotional information; as reported to the Union Support group, the play adapted the structural principle of classic Greek drama with its public choral frame interrupted by private encounters.

The party goes off the rails as soon as it starts. Gab, the guest of honour (played by Phil Summer), enters unseen as Annie tries to coach the audience in a few shouts of 'surprise!' Gab is edgy and, when he realises the party is for him, tries to leave. The action slips between public and private modes, as the actors attempt to keep the party moving but find themselves engaged in their own interaction. As the narrative character lines converge, the private moments become more public until the play erupts in crisis. Dorothy tries to tell Annie that their jobs may be in danger because 'the new management means business'; we later find that management is pressuring workers to accept non-unionised 'enterprise contracts' that stipulate set salaries without overtime pay. The mood of the play turns bitter as Annie tries to find out why Gab is not celebrating his retirement. Her anger sparks the revelation that Gab has been fired and replaced by Gwen, who has been hired through a works program which costs the company nothing. To top it off, we discover that Dorothy has accepted an enterprise contract.

This dramatic situation establishes *Last Drinks* as a political morality play in which individual decisions map the limits and possibilities of collective action. Dorothy's decision to accept the loss of overtime rates angers Gab, who protests, 'They're pay rates that were fought for way before you or me. They're not ours to give away'. He realises that he has been sacked because management know he won't accept an erosion of rights. Annie levers his anger into a decision to get the union involved. The party for Gab's retirement ends as 'a party for his reinstatement'.

The issue of positive endings was a recurring subject of discussion for MWT, as it is for most political theatres, because of the schematic use of individuated characters to represent class positions. Naturalised characters operating in a realist frame of character motives individuate class experience, but they also articulate the political analysis of the play. The actions of the play thus have to compress the awakening of political consciousness in an unnaturally brief time, in very isolated circumstances. The optimistic ending of *Last Drinks* resolves the character conflicts, but not the political problem that created them. As the reviewer in the *Australian* noted:

Nothing is resolved at the end of the short play, and although the issues have been made clear the long-term outcome is still unknown. There is a resolve to fight back, but the feeling is one of being caught in a powerful, continuing process which is taking us to a future that looks grim. (Thomson 1992)

By satisfying the narrative expectations of the structure but leaving the political problem open, the ending of the play is at once a gesture of resistance, a deeply felt expression of solidarity, and a reminder that (in Cornelius's words) 'things mobilise amazingly speedily over incidents that you wouldn't have imagined to be the things that would have mobilised people' (interviewed by Alan Filewod, Melbourne, 24 July 1995).

Moving On

MWT moved out of Jolimont six months after *Last Drinks* into premises provided by the Melbourne City Council. The move changed the public face of the company, which reaffirmed its determination to produce and reflect working-class culture but de-emphasised workplace performances. The following season saw more artistically ambitious work, including Kate Gillick's *Deadlines*, a high-wire performance on workplace safety (with an assist from Circus Oz), a play by Melissa Reeves on the subject of unemployment, *Great Day*, and the beginning of an exchange project in Vietnam. As the company's 1993 Annual Report indicates, the implications of these changes were clear:

> Our move from Jolimont is very significant and meant a huge reappraisal of our relationship with the labour movement. The company is pleased with the continued relevance and power of the work produced in 1993. We have been able to make changes along with the changes that are occurring so rapidly in the political and industrial arena. These changes have meant a broadening of our parameters to seek out other areas where working class people may be, to perceive a broader definition of our work, to recognise that Art and Working Life embraces a changing and complex view of working class culture. (MWT 1993: 2)

The move out of Jolimont had complex implications for the company's artistic work as well, because it foregrounded the impulse for artistic development that had already led the company to explore an identity in the theatre world. From the beginning, company members recognised the need to encourage individual artistic growth, and a number of actors who worked with MWT, like Kate Gillick, went on to write plays for the company. At the same time, all of the artists who worked with the company had artistic lives outside it as well, in other political groups, in mainstream theatres, and some in other media. Their work inevitably edged MWT closer to other theatres, as they brought new skills and interests to the company, and as the company continued to expand its pool of artistic support. Once out of Jolimont, MWT had no defining home base, and public theatre performances provided the continuity that Jolimont had done previously. The company continued to emphasise community-based performance (although workplaces figured less centrally than they had done in the heyday of union affiliation), but its public face was increasingly reflected in the world of the professional theatre.

Despite declining financial support and the disappearance of the AWL program, MWT has remained committed to working-class militancy, but the terms of struggle have changed radically from the symbiotic affinity with union culture that marked its inception. This change was historically inevitable, because the moment of opportunity—the right artists meeting the right unionists—could not be sustained beyond the life of the personal alliances that made it possible. The move towards a more plural and inclusive definition of the worker—from union to labour to class—took MWT out of the ambit of the union movement, but at the same time it gave the company a solid basis, developed over six years at Jolimont, in the practice of representing working-class life. MWT's move away from the union base is neither a repudiation of its founding mission, nor a failure on the part of the unions to sustain cultural work, although both of these might be argued. More importantly, because of its formative period in the railyards, MWT grew from an attempt by politically inspired actors to align with the working class, to find itself a decade later as a company deeply grounded in working-class life, whose continued existence marks the very notion of working-class culture in all of its diversity.

Chapter Five

Ground Zero Productions: Coalitions of Resistance

'If you resist, you are my community'
Toronto playwright Hector Bunyan at a Ground Zero forum

Ground Zero Productions is a particularly clear example of why we proposed in the Introduction to relocate the emphasis from structure to practice and thus prefer the term 'strategic venture' to that of 'theatre company'. As a corporate entity, Ground Zero's history is established in countless administrative records, grant applications, payrolls, contracts, tax forms, receipts and reports. On this level, the fact of the company is clearly apparent. Yet the company is a corporate trompe l'oeil, because it is largely the work of one man, its founder Don Bouzek. In fact Ground Zero has been the institutional means for Bouzek to pursue his activist theatre work professionally, enabling him to work with professional actors and apply for available arts council funding. The history of the 'company' is thus the history of Bouzek's own artistic and political development. It is useful to think of Ground Zero not as a company in the usual sense of a supra-individual organisation but rather as the composite record of projects, collaborations and interventions undertaken by Bouzek and his creative partners over the last two decades.

Bouzek's work is grounded in a firm belief in collaboration as a political principle and artistic method. In his theatre work he has always intersected with and drawn on the theatre communities in Toronto (Anglophone Canada's cultural metropolis), and more recently in Edmonton, Alberta, but at the same time he has distanced himself from the theatrical game where artists compete for reputation in order to advance. Instead Bouzek has focused on localised, project-based collaborations with community partners, creating a model of self-sufficient political theatre with instrumental ends and developing a unique artistic method that calls attention to issues rather than to its own processes and forms.

This has not been the usual mode of Canadian political theatre practice, where the community model has been most common. The Boal-based Theatre of the Oppressed and the Colway-style Community Play as developed by Ann Jellicoe in Britain both have Canadian counterparts (Boal 1979, 1992, 1995; Jellicoe 1987). The Canadian analyses, dramaturgies and politics in this model are similar to those of comparable theatres in other English-speaking countries which have aspired to the problematic position that the practice and inner life of a theatre troupe should embody its politics. Because the Canadian system does not easily allow the practice of alternative politics in company administration, the contradictions between ideological practice and necessity invariably lead to personal and eventually artistic crisis in the company.[1] This is particularly the case for theatre collectives because personal investment in history becomes political capital.

A second and less common model of political theatre practice has proven in the long run to be more effective. This model, derived from agitprop, moves away from an emphasis on the community to tactical interventions in the social justice movement, including, but not exclusive to, trade unions. As typified by Ground Zero, this model functions within larger communities of activism, using performance, processional demonstrations and installations to realise instrumentally defined project goals.

The success of Ground Zero and a small number of similar ventures is their survival as corporate entities in the institutional sphere of the theatre industry while, at the same time, avoiding the kind of collectivist political trauma that transforms personal history into political conflict. Ground Zero has clearly defined the structural relationship of political engagement and cultural organisation so that the two do not collide in crises of ownership, affinity and authority.

Since 1982 Ground Zero has operated as a hybrid of fringe theatre and small business providing services to client groups, and initiating its own artistic projects when arts council funding permits. Like the labour movement with which it often works, it can accommodate dominant ideology even as it challenges it. This ability to function as a service-providing agency has enabled Ground Zero to legitimise its presence in the labour and other social justice movements and operate in a network of alliances

---

[1] For a case study of the way in which arts council policy fosters ideological crisis in collective structures, see Filewod 1998.

and coalitions that focus on tactical issues. Don Bouzek explains that:

> We have always worked with different methodologies and communities. It's the fluidity of moving from video to theatre, from what the Australians call 'Contemporary Performance' to Boal, that gives us a lot of the stability to survive as the conditions change. (email to Alan Filewod, 10 October 1997)

In order to manage this fluidity, Bouzek developed an administrative structure for an artist-controlled theatre to operate on an ongoing professional basis. It had to work within a partially-subsidised theatre system that marginalised political theatres. For Bouzek, this meant renegotiating the 'charity model' of theatrical organisation in Canada with its volunteer boards:

> who are ideally people with 'clout' ie. well-heeled enough to fund raise. I have great problems with this model, preventing as it does, artists from controlling their own organisations, and re-inforcing a cult of volunteerism in Canada's social policy. (Bouzek 1986)

Bouzek here refers to the fact that the Canadian public arts councils (in Ground Zero's case, these have included the Canada Council, the Ontario Arts Council and municipal arts offices) will only subsidise cultural organisations that are incorporated as public not-for-profit organisations governed by a volunteer board of directors—even though public subsidies rarely amount to more than a fraction of a company's total revenues. Time and again Canadian arts organisations have seen self-replicating boards exercising creative control by purging the founding artistic creators of the company. The cult of volunteerism that Bouzek deplores has a long history of disenfranchising artists.

As an independent production house rather than a repertoire company, Ground Zero developed a hybrid model with a volunteer board but preserving the artist's 'right to manage' (to expropriate a current phrase from anti-labour government). It has done this by breaking the cycle of dependency on public funding. Its fundamental administrative principle, reiterated annually in grant applications, is that the company does not undertake work on a given project until all financing for it is secured. While it applies for and receives grants, they are earmarked for specific, non-revenue generating projects or for infrastructural support while the bulk of the work is undertaken as commissions from sponsoring organisations in the labour and social justice movements. Ground Zero is an anomaly in

Canadian theatre because, in a system which virtually forces arts organisations to engage in deficit financing and boards penalise artists for so doing, it has never run a deficit.

Until relocating to Edmonton, Alberta, in 1997, Ground Zero operated in two venues: an office-studio in downtown Toronto, and Bouzek's home in Peterborough, 100 kilometres to the east. Each location offered particular strengths. Toronto, as the financial and cultural capital of English Canada, is the locus of large scale political action, the power base of major unions, and the site of North America's third-largest theatre community, with more than 125 theatre and dance companies. It is also perhaps the most culturally diverse 'multicultural' city in North America, with immigrant and refugee communities from virtually every nation. For Ground Zero, Toronto offered work, contacts, political networks, causes and a pool of available, politically committed performers. In contrast, Peterborough is a small university and light industry city of 70,000 on the extreme edge of the Toronto commuting orbit. Although similar to dozens of cities across Canada, it is the home of an extraordinarily active arts community, including the innovative theatre artists, such as composer–writer R. Murray Schafer, and Robert Winslow, whose Fourth Line Theatre operates on the grounds of his family farm. With a national reputation for funky self-sufficiency, Peterborough's arts community offered Bouzek a network of kindred spirits, and a place to develop localised community activism.

Ground Zero was able to exist in two places at once (and in Bouzek's mini-van on the expressway between them) because it avoided the major trap of most theatres, which struggle to maintain and fill a theatre space, employ a company of artists and technicians, and compete for audience sales. Bouzek has ensured Ground Zero's financial stability through three primary means: by operating on a project-to-project basis, by subsidising theatre work with commissions from community and labour groups for educational videos, and by selling its shows to host organisations in lieu of selling tickets—which in practice means that the company's books have never had to forecast box office revenues. For most of its history, Ground Zero has had only two full-time employees: Bouzek and an administrator (successively, Lina Chartrand, Loree Lawrence and Bob Moher, but none since 1997) with active collaboration from a wide group of actors, puppeteers, designers, musicians and visual artists who work on a project basis. Bouzek thus had the flexibility to hire the most appropriate artists (in terms of cultural background, gender, or work experience) for a given project.

In practice, Bouzek and his staff manage a highly complex budget (with such sophistication that the company's outside auditors once tried to recruit his administrator), juggling budget lines between year-round operations (including office and studio costs) and project grants from various sources. As Moher explained in his 'Administrator's Letter' attachment in the 1997 report to the arts councils:

> Central to our ability to maintain balanced budgets is the fact that our administrative mechanisms track the company's activities directly. We commit exactly the resources needed for the year's projects and available from our revenues. Accordingly, budgets fluctuate greatly from year to year—the consistent part is that we balance them. (CC 1997: 1)

With this highly personalised structure, Ground Zero has reinvented the notion of community that informs the popular theatre movement in Canada. Rather than defining community in terms of particular geography or class, it engages in a community of activism around particular issues. This entails a systematic program of outreach to allied organisations: educational offices of trade unions, community development groups, local action programs, and minority cultures (notably Filipino, Latin American and Native Indian/ First Nations groups). In effect, Ground Zero has repudiated the essentialist notions of community that have pervaded Canadian popular theatres in favour of a tactical populism that enables it to market its services.

In 1989, Bouzek organised a retreat in Peterborough with an informal coalition of Ontario popular theatreworkers to articulate a statement of principles for this model of engagement. The retreat was Bouzek's response to the effective collapse of the Canadian Popular Theatre Alliance (CPTA), which had emerged in 1981 as a network of companies and artists, and which sponsored biennial national festivals of political theatre through the 1980s. The CPTA effectively collapsed (although it continued in name) when its funding sources dried up under the conservative Mulroney government, having already fractured in a series of artistic and personal squabbles of a kind depressingly familiar to Left activists. The Ground Zero retreat aimed at clarifying principles and establishing linkages across cultural differences. Its draft statement began by endorsing the original principles of the CPTA (as outlined in Chapter 2), but beyond these proposed a further set:

1. We do theatre for, with and by specific communities who have not been given access to resources in our society.

2. We act in partnership with organisations committed to social change (and sometimes other organisations when they are undertaking projects which may assist social change.)
3. The cultural and aesthetic standards manifest in our work are shaped by those of the intended audience(s).
    Note: When we evaluate our work, the power and effectiveness of the presentation's engagement with the audience is considered in equal measure with the execution of traditional theatrical 'production values'.
4. Our work is engaged in a process of Popular Education which has its own traditions and methods of work (OAC 1993).

Of these principles, the 'partnership' clause may be the defining characteristic of Canadian popular theatre. Beginning with the Mummers Troupe in the early 1970s, the recognition that political theatres are part of the process of struggle and not its embodiment has been of prime importance. As Bouzek explains:

> How do you build a support system with a community-based organisation that allows it not to be simply a hit and run? There's got to be somebody there who leads into the thing and follows up so you're simply a piece of that whole picture. Anything we do will have community partners.
>
> As theatre people we're good at exploring an issue, crystallizing it, presenting it and moving on. And so we will move through different issues, different situations. Ours is not the long-term commitment. I'm not going to spend 25 years of my life making sure there's affordable housing. But we've worked with people who do that. Our ability is to come in, take some stories, humanize the situation, get it out there. (Bouzek 1996)

A later draft of that statement of principles, prepared by Julie Salverson and not published until 1998 (when a new initiative to restart the CPTA resulted in a newsletter), articulated the principles of collaboration even more explicitly:

> Our interaction with these communities implies a participatory process that may include:
>
> A. Development and collection of stories from individuals affected by an issue.
> B. Accountability to the participating individuals and their communities for further use of the stories in other contexts, and appropriate acknowledgment of direct sources and contribution.

C. Respect of other people's cultures.

D. A shared evaluation of the work undertaken together. This assessment of the impact of our work is often a long term process (Salverson 1998: 2).

For most popular theatres, such partnerships were formed either with large agencies that could afford to sponsor performances (such as school boards, OXFAM, the Canadian International Development Agency) or with local alliances (such as women's shelters, rights groups and churches). Until Ground Zero, no one had formed effective continuing partnerships with organised labour. Bouzek succeeded in linking with labour in part because he quickly realised that union culture was a highly pluralised network marked by very different cultures and histories which could not be accessed from the top. His initial encounters with labour in the social justice movement brought him into contact with activists at all levels of the union movement. Through these contacts Ground Zero built a credibility within unions that few other theatres have shared.

Building a Method

Although Ground Zero began with a sense of political engagement and an attitude of cultural resistance, Bouzek hadn't initially planned it as a popular theatre. Rather, it was a way for him to work in the theatre on his own terms. After graduating from the University of Alberta with a Master of Fine Arts in Directing in the mid-1970s, he founded a small 'alternative' company in his native Ottawa under the name of Penguin Productions (after a Monty Python sketch). For five years he struggled to fill a small studio space in a school basement, and battled his way through board politics that were nastier than usual because of Ottawa's pervasive climate of political intrigue. Then Bouzek relocated to Toronto:

> I knew I never wanted again to direct a building. The focus on my work in Ottawa, was in filling a theatre space with a season. It was not on actually doing each show. I feel theatre companies must look at the models of independent artists working in dance, music and the visual arts. (Bouzek 1996.2)

Bouzek drew upon his skills in media production to land work as a producer for the Development Education Centre in Toronto, and began the usual round of freelancing in the theatre, including a season as an assistant director to John Hirsch at the Stratford Shakespearean Festival in Ontario. In his foundational sequence of self-produced plays dealing with modern science, *Waves* (1984), *St George/The Dragon* (1984), *Glow Boys* (1985) and *The Fessenden Animation* (1985), Bouzek established the principles of his theatrical technique. In a preface to the unpublished text of *Waves*, he acknowledges an array of influences ranging from Laurie Anderson and David Byrne, to Robert Wilson and JoAnne Akalitis, with nods to Dada, Happenings and Grotowski and situates his work in the 'Theatre of Images', comprised of tableaux, variable time, soundscaping and 'the tension developed by the juxtaposition of carefully created and technologically sophisticated structure with more naturalistic and personal content' (Bouzek 1984, B4). *Waves* was a deeply personal exploration which structured imagistic encounters with four characters: Niels Bohr, Lady Lovelace, Reginald Fessenden (the Canadian radio pioneer who first broadcast the human voice), and Bouzek's own father Joe, an electronics technician. The text of the play (described as 'an image pool') is a collage of drawings, instructions, dialogue and monologue. This selection is typical in its movement of images:

> *A videotape of the ZX81 programme to draw random graphs begins to play. Once we have seen the programme displayed as written, it begins to run. A voiceover repeats the programme. The tape runs under the whole section, with the voiceover only audible from time to time.*
>
> *Computer graphics form a continual visual image.*
>
> *Lady Lovelace, Lord Byron's daughter, appears. She was the lover of Charles Babbage, who invented a mechanical computer in the Victorian era. She first formed the 'objection' that machines cannot overtake man's intelligence:*

The analytical engine has no pretensions whatever to originate anything. It can do whatever we know how to order it to perform. It can follow analysis; but it has no power of anticipating any analytical relations or truths. Its province is to assist us in making available what we are already acquainted with.

> *She was also an inveterate gambler, and frequently had to pawn jewelry to pay for sessions at the racetrack.*
>
> *The cast tell stories of their experiences with their parents and their feelings about having children.*
>
> *Jumping jacks of the Sandinista government replace single leaders with a collective. Their various backgrounds, from guerilla to poet, to banker, are stated. They also utter speeches.*

> *Hayley's comet is introduced as a kind of pulse tone of the past. Tableaus*
> *from the years of its passing are called up* (Bouzek 1984: C17).

The decentred narrative juxtaposing dramatic scenes with multimedia, puppetry, object manipulation and documentary reportage became Bouzek's template dramaturgical method. What was missing in *Waves*, and quickly changed the next year, was an expressed interest in the audience itself. *Waves* played at the Theatre Centre, a fringe space founded jointly by the most experimental of Toronto's 'second wave' alternative theatres in the early 1980s, and its self-selected audience were seekers of theatrical novelty.

Bouzek moved into the sphere of political action when he undertook activist work on behalf of Theatre Ontario, a non-profit support agency, to lobby against cutbacks to the Ontario Arts Council. The campaign introduced him to Catherine Macleod, then Executive Director of the Playwrights Union of Canada, who had a background in the labour movement and went on to become media officer for the Metropolitan Toronto Labour Council and one of the founders of the Toronto Mayworks festival. Through Macleod he met labour activists and, with a coalition called Performing Artists for Nuclear Disarmament, workshopped what became an imagistic documentary on American victims of radiation entitled *St George/The Dragon*. In 1984 Bouzek took the show to the Canadian Labour Congress's summer training institute in Port Elgin, Ontario, where it was integrated into a theme-based course focusing on peace issues for shop stewards and local-level activists. Bouzek found his first performance to a labour audience 'was like coming home' (Bouzek 1999: 11). This was the turning point that offered him a conjunction of constituency and mission:

> There were three important things I learned in Port Elgin. The first is what
> it is like to play for an audience that is concerned with content first—
> people afterwards talked about 'when this character said that, I disagreed'.
> A long way from the discussions about the costume concept I was used to.
> Second, connected to the above—the Labour Movement is an oral culture—
> people hear and remember things. It places more emphasis on the spoken
> word, and less on writing. Third, it was critical to set the work in a
> performance venue where the audience felt comfortable. That meant they
> took the play on their terms, and made it work all the stronger. (email to
> Alan Filewod, 10 October 1997)

St George/The Dragon led directly to Bouzek's first collaborative venture with labour, *Glow Boys*, with a text by Catherine Macleod, who drew on her family's experiences of the nuclear power industry. Many of the cast and production crew had roots in, or were related to, the power workers' community in Kincardine, Macleod's home town and site of Ontario Hydro's Bruce nuclear power station. It also brought Bouzek into working contact with Carole Condé and Karl Beveridge, who produced the slides that functioned as one of the narrative tracks of the show. Condé and Beveridge subsequently developed this approach to narrating labour culture by exploring other topics of labour history with slide sequences that used professional actors staged in a mise-en-scène. Along with Macleod, Condé and Beveridge were leaders in the labour arts revival in Ontario, and through them Bouzek began to understand the labour movement as a human community.

After several years of building networks with activist groups and artists, Bouzek had the artistic track record required to seek funding as an incorporated company. He aligned his artistic method with a commitment to popular theatre in Ground Zero's application for charitable tax status, writing, 'we meld live performers, multi-layered soundtracks, projections, video and other elements into shows designed to play spaces like convention centres or community centres at reasonable cost' (Bouzek 1986). Further, Bouzek's system enabled the company to react quickly to emerging issues while maintaining a focus on long-term projects. His applications for arts funding included a succinct definition of this process:

> We begin work on an issue by selecting a creative team which will typically involve writers, performers and musicians with a director. [This] begins a research process which will draw on written material, interviews and workshops with people directly effected [sic] by an issue. This source material will be brought together at rehearsals as scripted scenes and scenarios for improvisations. From this a first draft will be set for presentation at a reading at an appropriate community event.... Based on feedback ... revisions will be made and some staging added prior to another event. Usually after about half a dozen such sessions the script has been solidified.
>
> The script is then mounted. We rehearse for about two weeks and add the production elements [which] typically involves the collaboration of visual artists. The show is then performed a number of times at community venues in Metro and vicinity. This allows for final feedback and any necessary revisions ... Finally, the show is made available for touring as widely as possible. (GC 1992: 4)

This model produced the *Shelter* project, a series of performances and videos for the 1987 International Year of Shelter for the Homeless (IYSH) which occupied Ground Zero's energies for much of the late 1980s. First came a show about affordable housing begun in 1987 called *In the Neighbourhood of My Heart*. The research and development phase included presentations in Toronto at an official IYSH conference on homelessness, at Homes First, an alternative housing conference, and at local women's shelters and drop-in centres. The script had been developed by the creative team of Bouzek, Rhonda Payne,[1] Lina Chartrand, Voltaire de Leon and Alan Merovitz, using material generated by workshops conducted by Bouzek and Payne at an affordable housing project. The performances integrated professional actors and community members. In the following year, 1988–89, the show toured with the support of local sponsors who used it as a centrepiece for public meetings in their area. Ground Zero developed 'site specific' material with the sponsors, including Cantonese language scenes for Toronto's Chinese community.

The *Shelter* project continued into 1993 and workshops with the Housing Equity Youth (HEY) resulted in a video entitled *On the Outside*. In Bouzek's words:

> In each of about a dozen locations, we did a basic Popular Theatre workshop moving from story telling to image building. I co-partnered these sessions with social activists from HEY. So, for example, in Stop 86 [a women's shelter] when we heard a story of problems with Family Benefits cheques, I could add it to my sense of the key stories to tell, but the woman telling the story could also get immediate practical advice on solving the problem from the people working with me. These are some of the most successful workshops I've ever done. I then created a script based on some common stories, and we shot it during a week long workshop at KYTES (Kensington Youth Theatre Ensemble). This 'work tape' was then taken back to all the places we did workshops for feedback and a sense of 'permission' to use the stories. Then I worked with a mixed group of 'professionals' and KYTES

---

[1] Rhonda Payne came to Ground Zero with a long history of work in popular theatre, beginning with the Mummers Troupe in Newfoundland in the early 1970s. Later she worked as a popular theatre educator in West Africa, and became one of a handful of Canadian experts on Forum Theatre and Theatre of the Oppressed when Augusto Boal's methodologies were introduced to Canada in the early 1980s (via francophone companies in Quebec).

people to create the final tape. The resulting tape had an educational package prepared, and HEY hired a worker who took it to schools and community venues throughout Metro Toronto. (email to Alan Filewod, 10 October 1997)

Like much of his later work, the *Shelter* project led into both theatrical and video production. From the early 1990s Bouzek devoted an increasing amount of time to video work, both as a medium of political communication and as a growing revenue base for the company. The *Shelter* project was also important in locating Ground Zero's work in the activist community in Toronto. Its productive relationships in the social justice community and with organised labour meant Ground Zero was well placed to act as one of the bridges between the emerging political coalitions as Ontario politics polarised between a relatively progressive centrist-left (which split support between the Liberals and the New Democratic Party) and an increasingly hard right Progressive Conservative party. The polarisation intensified through the 1990s and led to Bouzek's most extensive union-specific projects, *Where's the Care?* (1990) and *The Business of Health* (1991). These projects provide a useful example of an effective union–theatre alliance, and clearly show how Ground Zero's political methodology produced its artistic process.

The Health Care Projects

Where's the Care?, later described by Bouzek as 'one of the most successful agitprop things we've ever done' (email to Alan Filewod, 26 October 1997), began with a chance meeting and materialised because of an unexpected election in Ontario in 1990. Late in their term of office, the centre-right Liberals decided to call a snap election, which they unexpectedly lost to the social-democrat NDP. *Where's the Care?* contributed to the substantial social justice activity that surfaced in that campaign. It is a paradigmatic example of the effective use of agitprop in alliance with labour, and it is a rare example of a production funded entirely by a union.

The subject of *Where's the Care?* was the Liberal government's downsizing of Ontario's comprehensive public health care system. All Canadian citizens have free health care paid for by a massive public payroll insurance plan and there is no private 'second tier' system. Ontario's health system was in financial trouble by the late 1980s and in 1990 the Ontario Hospital Association forecast a $52 million deficit for Ontario hospitals and reported that over 800 beds had been closed, with another 3300 shorter-term closures (OHA 1990: 1). Yet the health care system, a provincial responsibility, consumed 33% of the entire provincial budget and the government had frozen operation increases just above the rate of inflation. Public apprehension about the future of health care became a major issue in the election—principally because of a concerted effort by the unions involved.

Ground Zero's intervention began when Bouzek met Steve Eadie, a skilled maintenance worker involved in the local branch of the Canadian Union of Public Employees (CUPE) at the Toronto Hospital for Sick Children. Eadie, along with other delegates at a CUPE convention, had seen *Hitting Home* at a rally at Toronto City Hall. Clips from the show made the national news, demonstrating the tactical effectiveness of media-oriented political theatre. Eadie had some previous popular theatre experience with the Popular Theatre Alliance of Manitoba, and had already considered its possibilities. Bouzek and Eadie decided on a one-off show for Eadie's local. As Bouzek recalls:

> The show went really well. It was in a hotel meeting room, and there must have been a hundred people or so. We thought it was pretty good, but I think Steve was dreaming of 400 or something—I always thought the purpose of this stuff was the media attention, and was less sure of the slant, to put it crassly, of getting bums in seats at members' meetings. (email to Alan Filewod, 26 October 1997)

That performance (which presented a series of puppet and agitprop scenes about the effects of underfunding in one hospital) established the basis for a more planned project. When the government called its election later that summer, Eadie was treasurer of his CUPE local, and with Michael Hurley, the local president, he proposed a plan to CUPE for a travelling show that could be used to attract local media attention to the health care issue during the campaign. As Eadie remarks in Ground Zero's videotape of the project, the idea of a theatrical performance was not easy to sell:

> The first reaction was out and out fear and hatred and loathing of anybody who would bring this idea forward. ... The hatred and loathing passed in two minutes. The fear remained. What we were trying to do was set up something that people were not familiar with and had never done before.

In an unusual move, CUPE accepted the plan, and contributed most of the $15,000 budget needed for a two-week research–script development–rehearsal process and a two-week tour of major regional centres. To put that figure into context, Ground Zero's budget for a union video was normally between $20,000 and $40,000. For CUPE, the theatre event was a bargain.

Bouzek and CUPE planned to use a 15–minute performance as a media hook to get press and television coverage of CUPE's demands that the government keep 200 beds slated to be closed, open 4,000 new beds and change restraint policy. As Eadie remarked in the video (which later became an important tool in the development of *The Business of Health*), 'One of the initiatives was to use media and theatre events as the method with which we would attract public attention'. CUPE had entered into a coalition with other health care interest groups including the Ontario Public Service Employees' Union, the Service Employees' International Union, the Association of Allied Health Professionals of Ontario, the Office and Professional Employees' International Union and, in an uncommon alliance, the Ontario Medical Association. For the most part however, the project was developed through CUPE networks. The union early identified the goals of the project. As Bouzek proposed to CUPE:

> Ground Zero would create a short scenario about health care issues based on information provided by CUPE. The emphasis would be on strong visual elements, such as large scale puppets and banners. The show would be designed so as to provide sound and visual 'bites' for local media, thus providing a 'hook' for commentary by local CUPE spokespeople. The presentation would be suitable for either the street or the meeting hall. The scenario would be written to allow the statement of local concerns in each centre, while placing these in the context of a provincial campaign. The actual presentation would be performed by CUPE members in each location, supported by professional GROUND ZERO artists. (GZP: CUPE n.d.)

The project was planned as an 'internal communication system' for the union with two complementary objectives: to encourage activism by coalitions expressing local responses to the cuts, and to integrate local action with centrally distributed media releases. Eadie suggested that Ground Zero begin by talking to Charlene Avon, president of the CUPE local at St Joseph's Hospital in Peterborough. On the video, Avon explains the process from her end:

> The fact that we would have some input into it, and then we actively go out and recruit our members and the public to take part in this was the big

thing that sold us on this. I think it's fantastic, and it makes the issue really alive then.

I got busy on the phone and phoned various presidents of hospitals and homes in the area, and also other labour people in the area, made them aware of the issue and what was going to happen, seeking their support. We then went to the memberships of both hospitals in the area, as well as getting information from some of the satellite hospitals and met with Ground Zero in the cafeteria of the hospital.

For her, the value of the project was not just in its media impact, but on the effect the process had on the participants:

It was really encouraging because it made you realise that you could do this, that you could stand there, you could talk to the media, that you could say what you felt, that you knew the issue. You just needed that confidence, and I think that's where the confidence came from, somebody saying, 'hey, you can do it, and this is what it's all about, and we're here to help you. But go for it'.

Avon's response confirms the value of the project in animating union action, particularly in the Ontario Council of Hospital Unions (OCHU) locals, which organise the low-paid hospital support workers. According to Bouzek, this focus on local mobilisation was a crucial aspect:

The organisational process of getting an event to happen for a union is part of the event. In order to stage a show the executive has got to be out talking to the members, getting the members out, they've got to figure out the logistics of holding a public meeting, getting the press to it ... A number of people we talked to felt that being part of it was as important to them as anything else. We came out with a network of people who actually had to do media contact, understood it, could then do their own stuff in a local community. (Bouzek 1996)

While the show was being researched, Bouzek assembled a team of artists to bring it together quickly. The whole project had to be devised, fitted up and toured within a 40 day union campaign; in fact the tour was booked before work started on the show. Bouzek started work simultaneously with two actors (Rhonda Payne and Gwen Baillie), designers Diana and Jerrard Smith, and country musician Washboard Hank:

Essentially the piece was constructed as a storyboard of photo ops. We worked the interview material into the images and added the song to get 15

Ground Zero *Where's The Care?*, 1990. Rhonda Payne and Gwen Baillie on stage; members of the St Joseph's Hospital local of the Canadian Union of Public Employees in Petersborough hold up signs indicating bed closures. (Photo: Ground Zero Productions)

minutes. ... Steve wrote a generic speech with space for local examples to be delivered by community spokespeople in each city. (email to Alan Filewod, 26 October 1997)

Performances took place between 21 August and 4 September 1990, the day of the election, in nine cities. Performance venues varied: a shopping centre in Hamilton, a public library in Windsor, hospitals in London and Peterborough, labour halls in Thunder Bay and Toronto, and parks in Kingston and Sudbury. The show had to be quickly erected, performable in adverse conditions and able to be picked-up and moved in the event of inclement weather. This is a useful reminder how agitprop techniques are produced by necessity.

The text of *Where's the Care?* is a compact and highly effective tactical agitprop that builds on familiar conventions of Canadian popular theatre practice. These conventions derive from the community documentary movement in the 1970s, with its gestic dramaturgy based on the montage of songs, emblematic theatrical routines, and, most importantly, authenticating presentational monologues. Added to this is Bouzek's characteristic use of puppets (including hand-held masks and larger, bunraku style figures) and multimedia. The performance was typically introduced by the president of the local hosting the show. In one taped performance, at the Peterborough Labour Day picnic, the local host invited the audience to 'enjoy the skits'. In small-town Ontario the skits at church parties and school concerts are the most familiar form of theatre. It was a useful label because a skit is in effect a performance made by 'real' people within a community and not something imposed from outside.

The frame of the show is a montage of songs, photo-op agitprop moments and presentational monologues. The song is simple and catchy, so that audience members can pick it up quickly:

> Where's the care?
> Has it vanished into thin air?
> Where's the care
> All we want is our fair share.
> Where's the care? (GZP: Care 1990)[1]

The Spirit of Care is represented by an actor in a wheelchair, who identifies herself by protesting weakly [à la Monty Python], 'I'm not dead yet!'.

Along with puppets, songs and iconic business—the international language of agitprop—the show includes audiotaped sound effects. This isn't just a stylistic nicety (although it does give the performance a technically sophisticated soundscape) but a useful technique that enables under-rehearsed and nervous local members to participate in the performance. For example, two ambulance attendants (an actor and a local member) carry in a puppet on a stretcher, travelling around the audience under taped dialogue:

Sirens

AMB. ATT: We've got a cardiac case coming in.
HOSPITAL: Our cardiac units been closed, you'll have to go to Civic.
AMB ATT: Roger. Civic do you read?

---

[1] The text of *Where's the Care?* exists in several undated loose leaf computer print-outs, with numerous discrepancies, suggesting various stages of revision. All subsequent quotations are taken from the compiled text.

HOSPITAL 2: Loud and clear.

AMB ATT: We have a cardiac case now.

HOSPITAL 2: Sorry. We have no beds at present.

When they reach a hospital they put the puppet to 'bed' vertically beside a sign that says (with each word on a separate card) HEALTH CARE SYSTEM. One of the attendants remains on stage and addresses the audience in a low-key, natural delivery that undercuts the performative distinctions between professional actors and local participants:

> I'm an ambulance attendant in a small town. We're on a central dispatch system. So last week we get this call to pick up a guy who lived on Maple Street—one block away from our station. We get there in two minutes—only to find his wife frantic—she had called over an hour ago. How it took one hour for the call to get from dispatch to our station I'll never know …

He continues his story between the interruptions of iconic agitprop bits. (The 'Economist Ogre'—a two-faced hand-held puppet mask—reaches up and removes the 'CARE' card, leaving the legend 'Health System' on the backdrop; the 'Ogre' reappears as a lying politician, promising more beds and announcing closings.) The show ends with a refrain of the song, performed by actors and local members, and broken by statements of solidarity and militancy:

> We're tired of listening to broken promises. But we're not giving up. I'm wearing my button on September 4th [election day]. And I want to see everybody in this province wearing this button, everyone who works in our health care system and everybody who uses our health care system.

The audiences for the shows were not large; a room with twenty or thirty people was common. But as Bouzek insisted, the real target audience was not the local union membership but the media, which reported the performance not as an entertainment but as an expression of popular militancy. Typically, the *Sudbury Star* gave it a front-page photo (showing the wheelchairs, banner, nurses and puppet), with the caption:

> Health care workers and professional actors participate in a dramatization of what they say are inadequate health care services on Thursday at Bell Park. The event was organised by a coalition of unions which charged the provincial government with underfunding the health care system. (*Sudbury Star* 31 August 1990)

The inside story quotes local workers on the effects of cuts on local services, picking up on the regional angle. Similarly, *Northern Life* reported the show under the headline, 'Ontario's health care system in danger of "Americanization", say union members' (*Northern Life* 2 September 1990). The article never mentions Ground Zero; stating that 'the play was put on by a coalition of front-line health care providers, including nurses, doctors, ambulance attendants, technologists and hospital clerical staff'. The disappearance of the theatre company is one of the most striking indicators of the project's success.

The other indicator of course is the pick-up from the broadcast media. This is where Ground Zero's different techniques register most clearly. Most political theatre analysis stresses the value of the community experiencing the performance, projecting a romantic notion of the theatre as a human space where meaning is enhanced by the physical act of communication. But as Ground Zero discovered, an indifferent performance could still be effective propaganda. Bouzek tells of a performance in Windsor where the union locals weren't able to drum up much support:

> There were very few people there, the participation was minimal. But a CBC crew came in and shot it. We heard later from people in the community that the reporter wanted to spike it, he said, 'hey, there's no story here, nobody came'. The camera guy said, 'No, you've got pictures, you've got great visuals, do it, you've got to do the item'. The editor in the station agreed, and they ran the item. At that point the provincial feed for the Saturday night news originated out of Windsor, and so, lo and behold, we drove through Toronto and got back at 11 o'clock that night to Peterborough, turned on the TV and there was the Windsor gig. That was ultimately what it was about, that kind of media game. (email to Alan Filewod, 26 October 1997)

The media pick-ups provided a quantitative measure of the propagandist value of agitprop when it personalises large political issues. In Ground Zero's agitprop work, the media response was part of the aesthetic totality of the process. Explicitly in *Where's the Care?*, but no less so in a rally, the audience is literally part of the performance: as on-stage performers, as demonstrators and as part of a meta-performance staged for the media. In *The Business of Health*, Bouzek made this even more explicit with a videocam puppet called 'Mr Camerahead'.

This was not an easy lesson for Ground Zero's partners to learn. Bouzek recalls an incident at an outdoor rally performance, when he met a labour activist who:

> like a lot of these union folks [...] was pissed that the show went too long and attracted all the media away from the CUPE president. Unlike a lot of others, he came up the next time I saw him and apologized. He saw the media coverage, and said he realized that we'd been right. The theatre made the point visually, and gave the feeling that it wasn't just 'a Big Union' thing. (email to Alan Filewod, 26 October 1997)

The strategy of localising and personalising a major political issue may have contributed to the significant role the health care issue played in the defeat of the Liberal government. But as events showed, the newly-elected NDP was no more adept at managing the health care crisis. Its awkward attempts to grapple with the deficit alienated the labour movement—who paid the price of its defection five years later when the NDP was replaced by a hard-right conservative government that pushed the health care crisis to a new phase. In the late 1990s, when the Tories began shutting down hospitals across the province and sought to remove the right to strike in the public sector, the closing of a few thousand beds seemed like a minor problem. Ground Zero's intervention may have helped win a battle, but in the long run it was a small skirmish in a struggle that would become much larger and more complex. Bouzek himself had no romantic illusions:

> We were only part of a real campaign to get social issues—like health care—front and centre. Obviously, we didn't win the election for the NDP by doing a play. But we were a piece of that. ... What we did do was show that you could use theatre to get a provincial message out by focusing campaigns at the local level. (email to Alan Filewod, 26 October 1997)

Where's the Care? was a minor (if important) project for Ground Zero, a quick response to a pressing issue. It was only one of several concurrent projects, and it was eclipsed in the next year by *The Business of Health*, an Artists in the Workplace project sponsored by the Ontario Arts Council (OAC) and the Ontario Council of Hospital Unions (OCHU).

The Business of Health

The Business of Health exploited the successful linkages established by *Where's the Care?*, but it was a much more ambitious project in its objectives, implementation and artistic process. Also designed to work within the union, this time, instead of provoking media attention, the show attempted to reach each of the eighty union locals (covering 19,000 service providers, office workers, nursing assistants and technicians) associated with OCHU. At the time OCHU were negotiating with the Ontario Hospitals Association (with a deadline of September 1991), in order to establish a central 'blueprint' agreement to serve as the basis for local negotiations. The process was particularly difficult because, as Hurley explained to the Ontario Arts Council in the grant application, 'We do not have the right to strike. We also have a membership with a serious literacy problem' (GZP. AWP 1991). Moreover, health care cuts were eroding the unions' membership base.

OCHU saw *The Business of Health* as an organising tool. The play would be the focal point for membership meetings across the province. Hurley stressed this in the application to the OAC:

> We want every member, in every community (no matter how remote or tiny) to be visited by this tour. Regardless of their abilities to read, everyone will understand the process of bargaining and the demands themselves.

Bouzek recalls:

> Michael and Steve were really concerned that members have a say in the bargaining priorities. To this end, they actually did a member survey to get a sense where people were at. Steve, in particular, saw the theatre tour as a way of communicating the priorities to the members once they had been set at a series of regional meetings in the spring of '91. He also again saw this as a way of getting members out to meetings and engaged with the bargaining process. (email to Alan Filewod, 26 October 1997)

The objectives as Hurley described them to the OCHU local presidents were:

- to expose as many members as we can to the bargaining agenda and the campaign for job security.
- to get the message out to the media, the public and to the provincial government and the hospitals about our bargaining agenda. Getting members out to these meetings is the first step to winning job security (GZP, OCHU 1991).

The scope of the project called for a significantly larger budget than *Where's the Care?* To find that budget, Bouzek and his OCHU sponsors (again Eadie and Hurley) turned to the OAC's Artists in the Workplace Program (AWP). Since the mid-1980s this program, closely modelled on the Australian template, required that arts groups apply through union sponsors. The arts council would provide up to 75% of the cost, contingent on union funding for the remainder. In this case, AWP provided $9,000 against the approximately $25,000 development cost. CUPE provided the remainder of the costs, which eventually totalled over $100,000, through a complex formula which collated revenue from the national office, OCHU and the locals. This was Ground Zero's third AWP project; previously it had produced a video with the Communication, Energy and Paperworkers on their strike against Bell Canada (*Re:Connecting*), and had worked through the Peterborough Labour Council on *The Otonabee River Chronicles*.

With funding in place, Bouzek began work on the first phase of the project, designed to establish a network of support. In April and May 1991, he accompanied Hurley to seven Area Council meetings where he met all the local union presidents and showed two videos: one from OAC on the AWP program, and his own of *Where's the Care?*

Bouzek kept a diary of his impressions of these meetings, jotting down bits of stories, political background and character impressions. It is a fascinating record of the day-to-day work of the research process. On one leg of the tour, Bouzek and Hurley went to Stratford, Ontario, where Bouzek had once worked as an assistant director at the Stratford Festival. He recorded his sense of dislocation because of the distance he had travelled since those days:

16.05.91

Back in Stratford. Fairly weird to be here above the old Jester's Arms, and feel totally disconnected from the scene here. Took a spin through the bar and didn't recognize anyone, although I recognized the intensity of it all only too well. Carefully constructed 'interesting' images—the bald head and shades, the top hat on the woman with the long hair. People hunched over tables, engaged in conversations as if their lives depended on it—talking about the latest dramatic theory or perhaps the latest gossip, who's in and who's not.

Meanwhile I just went for a walk with Michael, trying to explain the place to him a bit. It all sounds pretty strange to a unionist. At the same time trying to bring home the dilemma of trying to work with unionists on a limited budget, like this project. (GZP, Diary)

Having established the groundwork by meeting local presidents in the summer of 1991, Bouzek moved into the focus group phase that provided the basis of the script and began work on the creative development of the text. The focus groups with union members across the province typically met for two to four hours. The unstructured discussions generated a vast number of personal stories, which were taped and transcribed. The Toronto focus group, for example, generated eighteen single-spaced pages of material. Taken as a whole, these sessions produced a comprehensive oral history of the day-to-day work of health care. The transcripts that have survived are heavily underlined and marked with cuts, indicating that the creative team had scrutinised them for stories, lines and images. One speech from the Peterborough focus group was particularly useful [text in italics was underlined by hand in the original]:

> When you lose this bit of the personal touch, when you can share with that patient that is going through an emotional crisis, that their family isn't there. Or even their family needs you to hold them. *When you lost that bit. That's when nursing becomes a business, and it's your conveyor line. It's like putting the food on the trays. Bing. bing. bing and you lose it. Is that where we're going? Do you come in to die? I don't want that to happen to me. Or anyone I love. I want someone there that's caring... This is the part that hurts.* (GZP, OCHU 1991.2)

This gave Ground Zero their title; the first title, 'The Question of Health Care', was less concrete and less grounded in personal experience. Replacing 'Question' with 'Business' gave the play a title that conveyed both a political argument and a comment on the changes in working life.

Because the show had to be compact and economical enough to manage an arduous tour across the entire province (with 32 shows scheduled over 45 days, travelling by van, train and air), Bouzek decided to keep it small. The script was written for two actors, Gwen Baillie (who had worked on *Where's the Care?*) and Thandie Mpumlwana; Bouzek provided some of the voice-overs and ran the lights and sound in full view of the audience. Jerrard Smith designed the puppets and a scaffold set that could adapt to a variety of playing spaces (including in one venue an 8' x 12' board room). Rob Fortin and Susan Newman, two Peterborough musicians who had previously worked with the labour-oriented Rehearsal in Progress Theatre in Peterborough, wrote the songs.

From the outset, Bouzek knew that personal stories would be the foundation of the script. He asked playwright Peggy Sample to help synthesise the stories into a play that would expose the human costs of the cuts, and promote union solidarity as both a personal and systemic solution. As the basic structure evolved the focus groups provided material for revisions. The show was effectively created in a two-week period leading up to a preview in Minden, and substantially revised for the tour. Bouzek and Sample had originally imagined a cabaret, combining music, scenes, monologues and theatrical forms in a narrative based on images rather than a character-based story. The original design included a motif of puppet 'germs' growing in response to cuts in the health care system, a motif which survived in the final script. In an early project description, Bouzek described the play as:

> a kind of Alice in Hospitaland, in which four health care providers travel into different 'wards' of a fantastical hospital. In each, the character sees strange visual characters and real people; she hears real stories and listens to songs ranging from light-hearted country to moving ballad.

But the union partners resisted this idea, favouring a character drama. The final text combines both, telling the story of a worker who personifies union consciousness and performed with a theatrical economy that maximises the informational values of presentational techniques, with character doubling, monologues, agitprop sequences and puppetry providing a meta-narrative. A video of the Minden preview gives a sense of this evolution. This open air performance took place in a hospital parking lot on 1 September, just over a week before the final rehearsals began. The video shows the rough structure in place, with the principal devices that anchored the final script. The songs are ready, the characters are roughed out, and the major scenic elements—notably the videocam puppet and a giant shark-head 'germ' emerging from the scaffolding—are in place. The dialogue scenes, while sketchy, indicate the overall shape of the narrative. The video also provides a useful glimpse of the performance conditions. As the traffic drives behind him, Bouzek introduces the performance followed by the local CUPE president, in hospital greens, who reminds the audience that the show is part of a province-wide campaign to protect services and jobs. The speeches lead immediately into the performance. This folding-over of meeting and performance is reinforced by the open and undisguised backstage work of technical set-up, puppet handling and voice-overs.

The performance text of *The Business of Health* consists of three integrated narratives, in a presentational style that allows for stylistic departures and montage sequences. The first level concerns the struggle of the lead character, an immigrant housekeeper named Nomvuyo, to protect her

standard of care and her job, and to convert her anti-union friend Wanda.
This plot narrative is framed by an ongoing dialogue between Nomvuyo
and Mr Camerahead, the videocam puppet who represents corporate
hospital administration, and who brings on a parade of 'Contracting Out'
puppets, over whom Nomvuyo, Wanda and the community performers finally
triumph. The third narrative track is the interpolated contextual
information added by songs, momentary characters and monologues. Each
stage of character development is expressed in terms of emblematic
theatrical action that retains the iconic effect of agitprop. The play is written
for three characters—two actors and Mr Camerahead. Both actors move in
and out of their base characters (Nomvuyo and Wanda) to animate puppets
and personify other voices as needed. Although the character story grounds
the narrative, the performance itself is grounded by the ensemble effect of
the performers as storytellers and puppet-handlers.

The process of piecing together the various routines and bits that led
Bouzek to the idea of an image cabaret can be gleaned from the several
versions of the scene order that survive on paper. The original draft lists
twenty-seven scenes and sequences, most of which survived into the final
text in shorter, cleaner forms. Some were eliminated as their theatrical
devices were adapted into the character story leaving twenty scenes in the
final prompt script. The ordering and reordering of scene sequences is a
venerable practice in Canadian collective creation, dating from Theatre
Passe Muraille and the Mummers Troupe in the early 1970s. In practice
actors, designers and writers would generate a mass of monologues and
theatricalist routines, which (usually at the last minute) were hammered
into a workable structure. It is a creative method that has become almost
intuitive for many Canadian theatreworkers, and has developed into an
efficient technique of quick, montage-based playmaking.

In the final prompt text, *The Business of Health* begins with a whispered
audio collage itemising bed closures and layoffs across the province,
followed by an ambulance siren and the taped dialogue from *Where's the
Care?* between ambulance workers and hospitals. Under this, community
performers carry an old woman puppet through the audience and onto the
set. The two actors enter under a taped introductory song:

> There were no beds ready
> She's on a stretcher against the wall
> Another frail old woman
> To see the doctor on call

No time to stop and talk to her
No time for her at all
No time for the old woman in the hall (GZP 1991:2).

The central character, Nomvuyo, reads a letter to her sister aloud, explaining her pride in landing a job as a housekeeper: 'I'll be helping to look after people, making sure everything is clean and right so they can get well'. The text, by foregrounding her immigrant status, expressed the social realities of health care, the anti-racism social justice policies of the union and the artistic policies of the theatre company. The cultural specificity of the actor, in this case a South African woman (Thandie Mpumlwana) emphasised questions of class, ethnicity and culture common to all the locals.

A 'Hospital lottery jingle' on tape follows Nomvuyo's prefatory scene. Mr Camerahead enters and introduces Nomvuyo to the lottery:

MR CAMERAHEAD: After carefully assessing your skills, aptitudes and interests, we're about to apply our state of the art ward selection process. Now which door would you like? Door number 1, door number

The Business of Health, 1991. Thandie Mpumlwana battles
Gwen Baillie as the 'germ'. (Photo: Ground Zero Productions)

2, or door number 3.

NOMVUYO: Number 1.

MR CAMERAHEAD: You'll be working in the downsizing ward. That's one of my favourites (GZP 1991: 5).

As Mr Camerahead mouths his platitudes, Nomvuyo battles the giant germ. Initially envisioned as a recurring series of episodes concerning a cartoon 'Captain Carbolize', by the time of the preview, the germ had become an elaborate routine. To quote Bouzek:

> Jerrard and I were working with the images of the germs getting bigger as the workforce shrank. So there was a series of different germs ranging from 'bean bag' size to a huge full body affair that Gwen wore. We had a kind of hockey game wherein Thandie had to use a mop to get them off stage.
>
> How many times do you have to learn to expect anything on these tours? We had worked to what we figured were minimal hall dimensions. What we hadn't planned for was performing outdoors during a October/ November Canadian tour heading north. Ever tried to play hockey with a mop and a bean bag on grass? Thandie couldn't make it work any better. So that got cut. The big germ head did remain, despite the re-scripting of the show into a 'story'. We turned it into a stylized 'dance' battle using drumming by a Caribbean percussionist for the tour. (email to Alan Filewod, 3 November 1997)

As Nomvuyo does battle, Mr Camerahead leaves her with his signature refrain:

> We're proud of the fact that we've never had lay-offs in this hospital. However, Mr Ashbury has called in sick. You'll have to work short-handed today. Just do what you can (GZP 1991: 7).

Nomvuyo continues her fight to the percussion, as the taped voice of a nursing assistant describes the effects of cutbacks in the wards. Mr Camerahead and Nomvuyo's letter to her sister punctuate the routines, establishing an ongoing frame for montage sequences:

> MR CAMERAHEAD: We believe in our employees, so we've never had layoffs in this hospital. However, as of September first, some positions will become redundant. Under the union contract, bumping will be possible.
>
> NOMVUYO: Sometimes it seems like we don't have enough time to get everything done the way they taught us, but I guess that's okay.

LUIGI: [*a one-time character played by* GWEN *behind a mask*] Goddamn hospitale. 37 years. 37 years. Suddenly I am 'redundant'. I work my ass off for that place, and do they say thanks? They offer me this 'Building Operator'. I work years to get electrician licence. It is an insult. I will quit first.

MR CAMERAHEAD: Our record is unparalleled, we've never had layoffs in this hospital. However we will not be filling any positions that become vacant.

NOMVUYO [*sings*]: My supervisor told me
>We're a little bit behind
>If you could clean just one more thing
>We know that you won't mind.
>
>The Director needs his fish tank cleaned
>The washrooms in emergency
>The walls in physiotherapy
>The plush chairs in the boardroom
>The windows in the ICU
>The ashtrays in the waiting room
>The counter in the gift shop
>The carpets down in x-ray
>And the floors in your home ward.
>
>My supervisor told me
>We're a little bit behind
>If you could clean just one more thing
>We know that you won't mind
>You know that knob on top of the flagpole...

   (GZP 1991: 9–10; Lyrics by Rob Fortin and Sue Newman)

This sequence establishes the basic recurring syntax of the text. The remainder of the play is structured around five dialogue scenes between Nomvuyo and her friend Wanda, who is bumped from her job in the laundry to the hospital kitchen. Wanda sees no point in the union; as she says to Nomvuyo, 'Look, I'm real glad you like to get involved but don't try to drag me into that, okay?'(GZP 1991: 24). She resists Nomvuyo's arguments until she is injured. When she tries to file a claim for workers' compensation Mr Camerahead threatens her job; in the end, Nomvuyo persuades her to give the union a try. This is a very familiar trope in union agitprops, because it confronts the most pressing problem experienced in rank-and-file organising. As propaganda, such conversion plots speak to both sides of the problem, encouraging uninterested workers to get involved and committed activists to keep trying.

Wanda's oppression and subsequent conversion are theatricalised by two major performance routines. In the first, Nomvuyo and Wanda, under the constant surveillance of Mr Camerahead, demonstrate the truth behind the corporate lie of efficiency:

> WANDA: [*at work*] Mrs. Jones.
>   Soup. Chicken. Brown bread. Sugar.
> NOMVUYO: Mr. Stephens.
>   Soup. Chicken. White bread. Sweet'n'low.
> MR. CAMERAHEAD: In the interests of Customer Service, we're installing a more efficient system in the Dietary Department.
>
> > *They form an assembly line.*
>
> Jones. Soup.
> Jones. Chicken.
> Jones. White bread.
> Jones. Sugar.
> Soup. Chicken. Brown bread. Sweet'n'low.
>
> > *Repeat 4x, each faster.* (GZP 1991: 14)

The assembly line routine, performed by the two actors, demonstrates the effect of reduced services on the workers. A 'contracting out' routine in contrast shows the failure of privatisation which was, in theory, supposed to offset the effect of lay-offs. The sequences follow Nomvuyo's failed attempt to involve Wanda in the union:

> NOMVUYO: It's like pulling teeth. I can't seem to find the right words to get through to her. And, as if all this wasn't bad enough, they keep contracting out work—there's a regular parade of outside people throughout the wards—consultants, tradespeople, salesmen ...
>
> > *We hear drumming. The contracting-out puppets form a parade in the Caribana style. They are a Tradesman, a Consultant, and a Salesman.* NOMVUYO *tries to do her job, but is constantly bothered by the puppets.*
>
> SALESMAN: Wanna buy some pharmaceuticals?
> TRADESMAN: [*v/o Luigi*] At our place they bring in prisoners to take out the old asbestos. Guys on 'Prison Works' plans. They got no information, no safety gear, and no choice. So they leave the asbestos

all over. The other day I go crazy—I go by Emergency, and there is patient with bad leg. He's got leg on bale of asbestos (GZP 1991: 25).

The puppets, in the form of large hand-held cut-outs, remain on stage for the rest of the performance. This sequence is brief (the first version was substantially longer) but it is one of the iconic centrepieces of the play. The puppets set up the final moments. Wanda's acceptance of the union provides narrative closure, but the visual narrative is closed with a triumphant battle against the puppets which joins performers and union:

> NOMVUYO *and* WANDA, *joined by other* OCHU *participants, restore order to the stage, removing the contracting-out puppets. They eventually reach the* OLD WOMAN (GZP 1991: 37).

Victory is marked by a final song ('It's a question of health'). The play does not end the performance, however, because the union meeting itself can be understood as a performative event in which the agenda functions as a script. The pre-production package sent to each local included a draft speech to introduce the play which wrote a part for the local organisers:

> Sisters and Brother,
> Hi! My name is ——, I work at the —— Hospital and I am the President of CUPE Local ——, which represents the workers there (GZP, OCHU 1991).

The intro speech outlines the agenda:

> Following the play we will hear from our Area's representatives on the Central Bargaining Committee, who will be outlining the bargaining priorities in the central negotiations.
> We will discuss the activities which the Central Bargaining Committee will be asking our members to help with to support the priority demands. Then we will have a general discussion. ...

The scripting of the event even extended to the media. Although the show was intended for internal union use, it received solid press coverage in the smaller regional centres (and of course very little—if any—in the large cities). Ground Zero and OCHU could script this media coverage through their press releases because small community papers, with only a few writers on staff, routinely run press releases as news stories. Many papers followed up with a story after the performance, and like *Where's the Care?*, the media treated the show as a political news item rather than entertainment.

With *Where's the Care?* media exposure provided a clear indication of the utilitarian value of the performance. It is more difficult to assess the effect of *The Business of Health*, because it was part of a larger union campaign at a time of increasing crisis for public sector unions in Ontario. The tour, as might be expected, met different responses across the province, playing one night to several hundred people, and the next to an almost empty room. In retrospect, it is the fact of the tour rather than its concrete results that marks its importance. The health care unions grew increasingly militant though the 1990s in response to a series of government actions, including the NDP's 'social contract' in 1994, which instituted public-sector rollbacks, and the more draconian cuts (in the order of billions of dollars) implemented after 1995 by the Progressive Conservatives. By 1997, the Conservative government had moved beyond closing beds to shutting down entire hospitals. In that context, *The Business of Health* can be seen as an early expression of a public sector union reaction to cuts that would very quickly intensify in the media. For Bouzek, the increased public militancy—which frequently found performative expression in demonstrations—was the real legacy of the show.

From Labour to Social Development

The Health Care projects were Bouzek's most ambitious labourcollaborations, at least until the end of the decade. But Ground Zero also worked closely with labour partners on a series of topical interventions and agitprops, such as *Hitting Home*, a 1990 production on the effects of the Goods and Services Tax. The planning began by consulting labour educators and activists in the Canadian Labour Congress (CLC), the Ontario Federation of Labour and the Metro Labour Council in Toronto. Bouzek then assembled a creative team that combined labour and independent artists from a variety of disciplines. A tour mounted in cooperation with the Ontario Coalition for Social Justice, took the performance to union locals, churches, anti-poverty groups and seniors' centres. The culminating moment for the company, and for Bouzek personally, came when the show was invited to the CLC's national convention in Montreal, where it played to a standing ovation from 2,500 delegates. This was the first time that the convention's formal agenda had included a performance.

Shows such as *Hitting Home* remained on the books as long as they secured funding. An idea of how Bouzek juggled overlapping projects with a minimal infrastructure can be gleaned by the company's operations between 1992 and 1994. A multi-year project under the omnibus title of *A Cup of Coffee* traced the international economic and cultural histories that placed a cup of coffee on a Canadian table. In 1992–93, Ground Zero toured the first of three performances from this idea. *Hijos de Maiz/ People of the Corn*, was based on a scenario by Jorge Barahona, an El Salvadoran refugee, about an artist from El Salvador who sought shelter in a refugee camp in Central America and subsequently Canada. Framing this was an imagistic, puppet-based, re-enactment of the role of coffee production in the exploitation and revolution of El Salvador's history. The production was a collaboration with an émigré Central American group which performed traditional music. One of Bouzek's main objectives with the piece was to develop a new touring circuit in the Latin American community and also via international development agencies such as OXFAM and community-based development education centres. He collaborated closely with the Vigil Network, an association of church groups who worked with local development education centres and were coordinated by the Jesuit Centre for Social Faith and Justice. In turn the Jesuit Centre was involved in the 'Sanctuary Movement' which operated an underground railway for Latin American political refugees.

In its second year, the Coffee project moved into full gear focusing on the 'sugar' and 'milk' in the cup. The second performance, *Allos*, was first read as a workshop draft in 1992 at the 'Talent over Tradition' conference hosted by Canadian Actors' Equity and the Ontario Arts Council. It was later produced by a Filipino emigré group, the Carlos Bulason Cultural Workshop. Ground Zero secured Canada Council funding for a 1993–94 tour, which began in June with a 're-examination' of Voltaire de Leon's script. The workshop developed images based on de Leon's text and material from Bulason's book on Filipino immigrants in North America. The play added puppets and masks to de Leon's narratives about the history of Filipino resistance both in the Philippines and the United States.

Allos was touring through southern Ontario in the spring of 1994 sponsored by community-based international resource centres, when Ground Zero took a third piece, *The Milky Way*, into secondary schools. Based on a draft script by Peggy Sample, the play used 'dramatic scenes, supported by shadow puppets and music, to tell parallel stories of the Cow Goddess, the General Agreement on Tariffs and Trade (GATT), and a cross-cultural romance' (GZP, OAC 1994: 9). The tour through high schools was a one-time departure from Ground Zero's usual circuit since Bouzek was reluctant to engage in the constant negotiation with school boards about appropriate material. The *Milky Way* tour got into schools via development education centres instead of through the usual bureaucracy of school board arts consultants.

The culmination of the Coffee project came in February–March 1995, when Ground Zero made a rare foray into the domain of public performance, presenting *Hijos* and *Allos* in rep at the Poor Alex Theatre, a popular fringe space in downtown Toronto. As Bouzek later wrote:

> The repertory performances of *Allos* and *Hijos Del Maiz* produced one of the most memorable days I've spent in the theatre. One Saturday I was able to watch both shows back to back and enjoy a concert by Cayuanga (a Salvadorian band with three members who participated in the creation of *Hijos.*) It felt really good to see what peoples from different cultures could create when they collaborated with mutual respect. I was also humbled by the ability of veteran Ground Zero performers Jorge Barahona and Gwen Baillie to change from black-hooded puppet manipulators to virtual stand-up comedians in a few short hours. I also sensed a palpable joy as I watched, on one hand, Jorge's commitment to the seriousness of his work and, on the other hand, his happiness as he performed a folk dance with his children. It's a feeling I've rarely had in the theatre. (GZP, OAC 1995: 1)

Despite Bouzek's pleasure with the performance, the public run was a disappointment which failed to attract the notice of the professional theatre community. Bouzek still had a stake in this community and he also seemed, at some level, to desire its artistic validation. His disappointment however was more than personal. Both de Leon and Barahona were presenting their first full-length plays. Bouzek felt that two new voices were ignored because the theatrical community marginalised Ground Zero's work as 'community' rather than 'artistic'. Although he repeatedly tried to expose this as a form of cultural censorship, Bouzek came up against the same wall the following year with *Stolen Lands*.

The *Stolen Lands* project was initiated by Steven Bush, a widely respected actor and director who had been recently purged from his position as Artistic Director of the left-nationalist Great Canadian Theatre Company in Ottawa. Bush approached Bouzek with a draft script and a plan to create a performance that looked at five hundred years of European occupation in North America as perceived by artists from different cultural backgrounds. At a week-long retreat in Spring 1994 a professional facilitator from the social justice community led the theatre group along with participants from local First Nations reserves and Trent University's Native Studies program to work though dramaturgical issues. The group used the 'Naming the Moment' process of 'conjunctional' analysis using 'Timelines' to share understandings of history.[1] *Stolen Lands* was a performative negotiation of intercultural experience and power, in which even the artistic process involved cross-cultural power sharing between Bush and co-director Monique Mojica. It was materially and conceptually ambitious with scenes from ten leading Canadian (Native and non-Native) writers, including major voices in Canadian playwriting—such as Judith Thompson, Guillermo Verdecchia and Daniel David Moses. But when it finally toured in the 1995–96 season, the show went unnoticed by most theatre critics and professionals, again because Ground Zero had almost no profile outside its activist community.

Along with these forays into the fringes of the theatrical establishment, Bouzek continued to build on the techniques of media provocation developed in the Health Care projects, looking for ways to use agitprop as a media hook at street demonstrations and rallies. Bouzek referred to these agitprop and processional events as 'streeters'. In the period framed by the Coffee project, they included 'The Puppetmaster', a 20-foot puppet of a corporate magnate, representing the Business Council on National Issues, who manipulated an effigy of conservative prime minister Brian Mulroney outside the national Progressive Conservative convention in Toronto. There was 'The M.A.S.H. Tent', an installation erected outside the Ontario provincial parliament in Toronto for a health care rally organised by CUPE in April 1992. In the 30' x 50' army hospital tent a bed enclosed by a padlocked wire cage was guarded by three huge 'body/head' figures, personifying fee-for-service billing (a doctor), a hospital administrator and the for-profit sector (a consultant), who threatened the cradle-to-grave health insurance plan so deeply valued by the Canadian public.

Similarly, in the spring of 1994, Bouzek worked with a team of artists from Peterborough to devise a parade performance for the Peterborough Social Justice Coalition Project, on the subject of the North American Free Trade Agreement. They created figures representing a Canadian farmer and industrial worker, a Mexican campesino and Maquillador [tariff-free]

---

[1] Conjunctional analysis involves pooling knowledge and perceptions of an issue (by writing on a blackboard for instance) so that a collective understanding accrues. Everyone shares what they know; out of these conjunctions comes a sense of community analysis.

Zone worker, and a corporate magnate. After May Day performances in Peterborough, Ground Zero performed in Ottawa in front of 75,000 on Parliament Hill as part of the massive national day of protest organised by the Canadian Labour Congress and the Action Canada Network.

The most complex 'streeter' was a sequence of promenade performances in Peterborough called *The Otonabee River Chronicles* in 1992. Taken together, they comprised a community pageant that narrated a people's history of Peterborough, from the perspective of working and First Nations people. It began with a series of workshops with local groups, such as the Labour Council and adult education classes to create 'timelines' into which participants could insert their own stories. A major thrust of the project was to link the Peterborough arts community (including Bouzek, Payne, designers Diana and Jerrard Smith, choreographer Patricia Johnson, and clown artist Tom Schroeder) and local labour activists to bridge the cultural gap with Native Indian artists from the nearby Curve Lake reserve. First Nations artists Rosa John and Ron Meetoos were instrumental in the process.

The workshops provided a mass of material that could be translated into visual images and parade floats. Along with puppet and processional events, the *Chronicles* included dramaturgy, with Bouzek drafting a play on Peterborough's labour history, and a play development process with young people from local reserves. The project culminated in three performances on a Labour Day weekend, with some 75 participants performing in fourteen locales:

> During the performance, the audience made their way from the banks of the Trent Canal up to the top of the hill where the Centennial Museum and Archives are located. During the journey they encountered 14 different performance sites. The events ranged from a puppet presentation in a tent to a circle dance around a corn roast. In between the major locations were 'side shows' (to use the Bread & Puppet Theatre term). In one a young girl enmeshed in an antique gear recited actual testimony of a 12 year old worker in a cotton mill of the late nineteenth century. (GZP, CC 1998)

Bouzek credits Rosa John for much of the success of the project, which he measured by the linkages it formed between First Nations and labour:

> To me the success of the show was that a former chief of the Curve Lake First Nation came up and shook the hand of the President of the Labour Council and told him, 'Thank You. This is the first time I've ever felt you

Rosa John in Ground Zero's *The Otonabee River Chronicles*, 1992. (Photo: Ground Zero Productions)

had acknowledged the contribution of my people to this community'. (email to Alan Filewod, 10 October 1997)

The *Chronicles* project was not simply a series of public presentations: it was an active program of outreach to promote a network of activism. Outreach projects were the final area of Ground Zero's activity in this period. These programs included popular theatre workshops in Peterborough, a series of workshops for the Refugee Participation Network in Toronto, monthly workshops with the Jesuit Centre for Social Faith and Justice (with their 'Naming the Moment' process), and the three-day popular theatre retreat.

Performances like *Allos*, the various 'streeters' and occasional one-off events (such as a traditional Ceilidh with labour people telling stories and sharing songs for the Canadian Labour Congress convention in Toronto in 1993) typified the kind of theatre that Bouzek openly admired, marked by solidarity, celebration and instrumental action. This represented the main thrust of Ground Zero's work, in which union-specific projects played a minor but important role.

Moving Shop

In the years following the Health Care projects Bouzek produced a series of videos, a number of one-off labour events (mostly convention shows which he describes as 'industrials for the social services') and two plays on early labour history. In all of his projects he continued an active collaboration with labour activists and councils although not on the scale of the Health Care projects. Ground Zero didn't need to restrict itself to identifiably union-specific projects to sustain its presence in the domain of labour culture. It had become part of the diversified social landscape that framed the labour movement.

By the late 1990s, Ground Zero was operating at a frantic pace, with major projects overlapping and dozens of agitprops and 'streeters' as well as a constant output of labour videos. These efforts, and the professional capital Bouzek had built with Ontario unions, were drastically affected by the changes in the political climate when the right-wing Progressive Conservatives defeated the New Democratic Party in 1995. The radical Tory 'Common Sense Revolution' (inspired by American Republicans) initiated drastic cutbacks on social and cultural programs. Not only was Ground Zero's subsidy cut by approximately one-third (as part of larger across-the-board cuts to the Ontario Arts Council), but the social justice and community development organisations that formed its market were slashed even more and demonised as 'special interest' lobbies.

In the spring of 1997, Ground Zero relocated to Alberta where Bouzek began again. There is some irony in this, in that Alberta is the heartland of Canadian right-wing fundamentalist populism and the home base of the hard-right Canadian Alliance Party that forms the official Opposition in the Canadian Parliament. But while the Alberta government's attitudes towards culture might be as hostile and draconian as Ontario's, they are mitigated somewhat by a smaller population and a culture that fosters Bouzek's kind of entrepreneurial initiative.

The flexibility of Ground Zero's structures meant the move was not particularly difficult, but it did require rebuilding links with local labour and social justice groups. Bouzek simplified the company's structure by dividing it into two. Ground Zero remained as the theatrical not-for-profit charitable arm, and a new privately owned company took on commissioned video work under the name of D.ACTIVE, and returned a percentage of its revenues to Ground Zero. Within six months of the relocation, Bouzek had worked out video projects with the Canadian Labour Congress and the Communications, Energy and Paperworkers and had worked out plans for a three-year research–workshop–production schedule for Ground Zero. In addition he planned the establishment of a 'Rapid Action Team' to create on-call agitprop, and a long-range collaboration with Banner Theatre in Birmingham on the subject of health care in Canada and Britain.

The move to Alberta opened up new directions of artistic and political growth for Bouzek and creative challenges which played to his strength at building and developing. After the first year in Edmonton, Bouzek re-established the Ground Zero pattern of multi-year project developments, focusing on two broad but intersecting issues. The first was a series of events planned around May Day, with a long-range view for a major processional event for May Day. In this Bouzek was inspired by his visit to the Darwin May Day in 1998. The 1999 May Day project established a working relationship with the Edmonton and District Labour Council, and presented a series of performances over a week, including a workshop presentation of a show about the 1919 Edmonton General Strike, written by Bouzek, and an evening of labour songs.

The second area of development continued Bouzek's quest for identity in Celtic culture, which was both a personal search for cultural roots, and an ongoing inquiry into the relationship of history, culture and political action. In his pilot application to the Alberta Foundation for the Arts, Bouzek outlined a program of four workshops: the 1919 General Strike play; 'Ogma', a retelling of Celtic myth in which Ogema, son of the god Danu, discovers the Ogham runic alphabet; 'The Alphabet', a First Nations perspective on the Ogema project in which Native artists would create 'stories from their own culture which paralleled and contrasted the Celtic story'; and '1919 First Nations', a look at 'the historical situation for the Blackfoot and Cree peoples in 1919' (GZP, AFA 1998: 5–6). These workshops were projected as development phases leading to a single final script of a show to tour in 2,000, in which Bouzek's commitments to linking labour and First Nations cultural histories through common points of resistance and activism could also examine crosspoints of spirituality. This, as Bouzek explained to the Canada Council, was a lesson he had learned from his work with artists from other cultures and which he began to understand when Rosa John, with whom he had worked in Peterborough and planned to work with again in Edmonton, said to him, 'Within my culture I can only really know you if I know you seven generations back' (GZP, CC 1998). The fusion of these narratives was predicated on the Celtic notion of the Otherworld, which enabled Bouzek to reconcile his compelling interests in the metaphysics and the materiality of culture.

This interest continued beyond the plans for the Ogma project, which by the end of 2,000 had been stalled because of funding difficulties and the pressure of more immediate work.

Metaphysics and materiality meet in the human body, as Bouzek had explored years before in *Waves*. In Edmonton, he saw the social possibilities of mythic performance when he worked with three women, Eva Colmers, Jan Henderson and Lorna Thomas on a puppet theatre/video exploration (initiated by Thomas, who asked Bouzek to direct) which retold the classical myth of Psyche in terms of the modern experience of breast cancer (GZP, CC 1999:1). Once again, the Ground Zero method of constructing community linkages gave Bouzek access to a community of local artists and institutional partners, such as the cancer clinic that sponsored the Psyche project.

Despite the relative ease with which Bouzek transferred his work to Alberta, the move set off a ripple of disturbance in the Canada Council. So established is the equation of community, culture and geography in the arts councils model of public funding that it is virtually unheard of for an arts organisation to relocate from one province to another. For Ground Zero one immediate consequence was the loss of the Canada Council operations grant. With his board, Bouzek decided not to apply for an operations grant for 1998, but an application for a project grant to fund the '1919' workshop was denied because, in the bland language of the Canada Council notice, it was 'not a priority at this time'. As Bouzek remarked, 'at least it wasn't overtly insulting'.

The move from Toronto came at a time of intensified right-wing assault on the social justice movement, and in that sense, Ground Zero moved shop when it may have been needed most. The changes in the political and economic climate however meant that the company's work had to be reconceptualised (for one thing the cuts meant that the company could no longer afford its studio), and some of the deeper reasons for the move had to do with personal changes in Bouzek's domestic life. But if the life of the theatre company was contingent on the energy and involvement of its founder, its political work and theatrical techniques were more broadly grounded. The most tangible result of Ground Zero's work over the years has been an active and continuing community of activist performers working in the theatrical idiom that Bouzek explored, through the political networks he helped to establish.

In most circumstances, a theatre company's board would respond to a director's decision to move with a 'goodbye handshake'. In Bouzek's case, his board of close allies saw no point in continuing a Toronto operation without him. Ground Zero's institutional structure was personalised to the extent that it could not continue independently of the artist who founded it. Historically this has been the major failure of many political theatres, which time and again have collapsed under the weight of ideological conflicts over personal creative authority and collective structures. But if Ground Zero has been the institutional extension of one artist's vision, it remains a productive model of how an activist artist can appropriate the entrepreneurial models of market capitalism to generate self-employment while at the same time working and enacting a radical politics of community and resistance.

Chapter Six

May Days in Darwin: The Participatory Performance Model

'We simply couldn't preserve a day when we had sixty or seventy people making a protest'.
          Rod Ellis, union official (Cited in Ingleton 1989).

The striking feature of our fourth case study is that an Australian union body, the Northern Territory Trades and Labour Council (NTTLC) in Darwin, plays the central role. Starting in the mid-1980s, when unionism was in serious decline throughout the country, the NTTLC used the Australia Council's Art and Working Life Program to employ a number of community artsworkers and reach beyond the confines of the union movement. As part of a strategy to remake itself, it devised an instrumentalist model of union arts activity by revitalising the May Day march, one of the international movement's oldest ceremonials. The NTTLC re-theatricalised the march, making it the focus of a range of community arts activities which involved hundreds of people as participants and thousands more as marchers and 'audiences'.

May Day

The 'invention' of 1 May as a significant date for the international labour movement resulted from a resolution passed by the Second International in 1889 to co-ordinate an international demonstration to support the campaign for an eight-hour day. The eight-hour day had been a central objective of the First International in 1866. The date was chosen for varied reasons, but one of the most obvious was to commemorate (somewhat tentatively) the Haymarket Incident of 1886 when an 80,000-strong march in Chicago turned into a violent clash between demonstrators and police. Eight anarchists were arrested for the murder of a policeman and four were ultimately executed following a trial so unjust it produced an international outcry.

In the northern hemisphere May Day marks the beginning of summer and is 'heavily charged with symbolism by ancient tradition' although, as Hobsbawm notes, this appears to have been more coincidental than planned (Hobsbawm, 1983: 248). This association with pre-industrial seasonal rituals helped to establish the day, adding an element of the carnivalesque with its 'repertoire of traditional forms, which included processions, races, mock battles, mock weddings, and mock executions' (Burke 1979: 199). In this way, May Day tied working-class political activism to traditional rituals of death and rebirth even though the day itself was not a central date in the ancient rites of European carnival. William Lane in a May Day editorial in the Brisbane *Worker* in 1890, attempted yoking together past rites, present activism and the impending birth of a new age of socialism:

> May Day, this is May Day, the by-gone jubilation of our forefathers for the reconquering by the bright sunshine of the bitter Northern winter, the new-born celebration of the passing of the workers' winter of discontent. In Germany, in Austria, in Belgium, in France, all through Europe, in the United Kingdom and in the great English-speaking republic across the Pacific, millions of workers are gathering at this hour to voice the demands of Labor for fair conditions of labouring. (Cited in James and Fox 1989: 753–4)

This accretion of meaning offered two choices for structuring May Day events, one carnivalesque and one confrontational. The clash between the anarchy and libidinism of carnival and the discipline required of an organised political demonstration were awkwardly held together in the emerging ceremonial. The state licensed the temporary occupation of public space and the labour movement called for discipline of its 'troops'. The result was usually a family day in which:

> the original political content of the day—the demand for an eight-hour day—inevitably dropped into the background to give way to whatever slogans attracted national labour movements in a particular year, or, more usually, to an unspecified assertion of the working-class presence. (Hobsbawm 1983: 285)

The intentions of the Second International in inaugurating the event were threefold: firstly, as an international show of strength in an emerging class conflict with the aim of recruiting new members; secondly, to help establish the class-consciousness needed for the creation of socialism by promoting a sense of the power of disciplined organisation; and thirdly, to petition the state for an eight-hour day. The centrepiece would be a procession, a 'proto-theatrical' event characteristic of the Second International (Samuel 1985: xv). Socialists and anarchists in particular, however, disputed whether May Day was a festival and holiday or a general strike; a celebration of solidarity with a reformist appeal to the state or an expression of all-out class war more like the Haymarket Incident. Sometimes this came down to whether May Day should be celebrated on the nearest Sunday or by the withdrawal of labour on 1 May.

The Second International, of course, favoured a self-policed peaceful celebration over a confrontationist demonstration and, pointedly, the 1889 resolution made no reference to the Haymarket Incident. The success of its disciplining strategy, and the broad significance of the event, varied in different countries. An eight-hour day, while partially achieved in Australia some forty years earlier, was not universally attainable. So while industrially advanced countries like Britain adopted the demand, in France, for example, the aim was modified to a more realistic ten-hour day. Despite geographical and social differences, however, the day has taken on an international significance as an 'invented tradition'.

The forms of the event are well established worldwide, despite local variations, sometimes drawing on public rituals originating in the Middle Ages. The central procession, for example, with its display of trade union banners and (at least in the early years) union-based floats, is reminiscent of the *tableaux vivant* built by individual craft guilds on which the mystery plays were performed at European religious festivals of Corpus Christi. A formal meeting, usually outdoors in a public space, with speeches and music, and in some cases theatrical performances, conventionally follows the procession. It often ends with a family picnic in a fairground atmosphere, with stalls and displays, entertainments and sporting events. In Australia the family element of the event has, in recent years, usually been truncated in favour of an essentially masculine drinking session.

In Australia May Day struggled to assert itself against the older celebrations of Eight Hour Day or Labour Day built around the craft unions which were responsible for the initial growth of Australian unionism in the nineteenth century. These dated from 1856 in Melbourne, when the first eight-hour day was gained, and were held on different dates in each state. The craft unions were not particularly radical bodies, however, since their members were skilled and therefore had a strong bargaining power in a capitalist economy. Despite the romanticising attempts of some labour historians to see them as confrontationist events, the original Labour Day rallies were conservative affairs, genteel ceremonials rather than political demonstrations. Bob James, examining these events in the Hunter Valley, NSW, has rather contentiously made a case for their origins in the rituals of Masonic lodges and friendly societies, with some important ramifications:

> The shared ancestry of masonic lodges, friendly societies and trade societies explains their common form and their common interest in preventing disorder within their own ranks, including the prohibition on talking 'politics', extolling 'unity' and standardizing membership. (James 1993: 210)

May Day was a more radical affair. May Day took over the forms of the older Labour Day celebrations—banners, floats, a picnic, sporting events, entertainments—and added some elements of its own, even a maypole in Melbourne in 1909 (Fox 1966: 12). But it was also a focal point for a Marxist-inspired revival of banner-making and a gathering point for the unemployed workers' organisations set up by the Communist Party in the early 1930s.

Members of the shearers union in the midst of a huge strike organised the first May Day march in Australia at Barcaldine in Queensland in 1891. Elsewhere in the country the earliest marches were initiatives of groups on the radical fringe of the union movement like the Melbourne Social Democratic Club or the Australian Socialist League in Sydney (Fox, 1966: 7–12). Nevertheless, it was only in the 1920s and 1930s that May Day challenged the dominance of the reformist strategies of the older craft unions and began to take on more importance as 'a declaration of militancy within an increasingly divided labour movement' (Stephen and Reeves 1985: 39). The Labour Council in Sydney, for example, did not officially authorise May Day until 1921, and Melbourne Trades Hall Council actually withdrew official support in 1932. May Day took over from Labour Day most emphatically in areas dominated by the emergent industrial unions like Newcastle and Wollongong, towns built on coalmining and steelmaking, where confrontation in the workplace felt strategically appropriate. It became the focus of militant industrial unions, the 'new unions' of predominantly unskilled workers which drew much of their inspiration from the far Left, in particular the push for One Big Union initiated by the American-based Industrial Workers of the World (the 'wobblies').

May Day, then, was associated with the radical impulse towards industrial action. In contrast, the Labor Party once it gained office, was tied to political modes of operation within the parliamentary system. Thus in Australia May Day marked the rise of militancy almost in opposition to the Labor Party. In Britain, where the Labour Party took longer to gain office and developed as an informal coalition of socialist groupings, the opposite was the case until recently (Farrell, 1981: xiii).

May Day has waned with the decline of militancy in the Australian union movement. It is no longer well attended or seriously promoted by a movement which, through the period of its Accords with successive Labor Governments (1983–1996), has been less than enthusiastically committed to the more militant aspects of its own history. Left-wing unions throughout the country, though, have attempted to maintain and enliven its traditions and funding from the Art and Working Life (AWL) program helped to rejuvenate the nineteenth century trade union banner tradition.

Yet while May Day has languished throughout Australia, it has burgeoned in Darwin. The NTTLC, with the aid of AWL funding, not only employed visual artist Deb Humphries in 1989 and 1990 to produce a number of banners but they also revived the more carnivalesque aspects of May Day with some spectacular results. The union organised a large number of unionists and groups on the fringes of the movement to participate in a series of community arts-based events which attracted local and national attention. Their success was due to the intelligent use of cultural work for union purposes, and also to the special circumstances of Darwin. At the same time, Darwin's experience shows the tensions between political demonstration and celebration, carnival and disciplined display of working-class solidarity, that are built into the structure of the event itself.

Darwin

The Northern Territory, one of the most sparsely populated areas on earth, was administratively part of the state of South Australia until 1911 and subsequently a protectorate of the Commonwealth Government until 1978, when it became a self-governing Territory. Darwin, its capital in the far north, is closer to Singapore than Sydney. For much of its history Darwin has been little more than a village sustained as an administrative centre and a strategic defence outpost, a 'frontier town' regularly ravaged by cyclones, and almost bombed out of existence during World War II.

Today Darwin is better described as a 'tropical suburbia where forty or fifty nationalities and every colour of human being under the sun live and mix' (Powell 1996: 211). Yet the town still cultivates its 'frontier town' image for strategic reasons. The Northern Territory has been ruled by successive conservative governments committed to sustaining a very high level of Commonwealth Government expenditure—in excess of 80% of revenue in the 1980s (Mewett 1988: 4–5; Taylor 1991: 22). Indeed, the development of the Territory has substantially been a public sector exercise and almost half the workforce of Darwin have jobs in public administration, defence and community services. The frontier myth helps to legitimise a policy of public spending which runs against the rhetoric of free enterprise and 'small government' characteristic of the Liberal–National coalition in the south. A further quarter of the workforce who are involved in service industries, particularly tourism, also have a vested interest in the 'frontier myth'.

Darwin now has a population of about 80,000, with an average age of 29 and the highest level of mobility in the country. Residents include travellers on the hippie trail through South East Asia and public servants on short 'term transfers', although some who came for a while have never gone away. Indeed, the huge investment in education, health and welfare services in the 1960s and 1970s brought a large number of public servants from the southern states. The town has also had several waves of immigration starting with the Chinese miners, railway workers, traders and gardeners who arrived during the latter half of the nineteenth century (when they outnumbered Europeans by seven to one) and followed by southern European labourers. Particular industries have brought their own immigrants, notably the Malays, Indonesians and Filipinos involved in pearling. The most recent arrivals are refugees from East Timor, Vietnam and Cambodia, and some skilled workers and business people from China and Hong Kong. The town was almost destroyed by Cyclone Tracy on Christmas Eve 1974, and 35,000 people had left by New Year. Most, though, returned and Darwin continues to grow.

Darwin's substantial Aboriginal population has meant the town has lived the bleak history of Australian race relations with a closeness of contact unknown in the southern states. Aborigines constitute about a quarter of the population of the Territory as a whole, and are a real presence in Darwin. This includes a floating population of fringe-dwellers on the edge of the city, 'escapers', as anthropologist Basil Sansom calls them, avoiding 'for whatever time they can manage, the authority on cattle stations or on settlements and rejecting, too, the hostels and other forms of institutional accommodation available to Aborigines in town' (Sansom 1980: 10).

Sections of the union movement have backed an emerging Aboriginal self-assertiveness in the Northern Territory through strike actions since the immediate postwar years and a series of claims to land or compensation beginning in the 1960s. The most famous was the Gurindji walk-off from Wave Hill cattle station in 1966 to protest their working and living conditions. An Aboriginal 'tent embassy' established outside Parliament House in Canberra in 1972 consolidated the move for change and the assimilationist policies of the conservative governments that had dominated Australia since the war were replaced. Aboriginal rights, particularly land rights, were recognised by the Whitlam Labor Government in the early 1970s. The Aboriginal Land Councils, which emerged in the wake of this change and became statutory authorities under the Aboriginal Land Rights (Northern Territory) Act of the Commonwealth Government in 1976, continue to mount land claims.

Two landmark rulings by the High Court of Australia—Mabo in 1992 and Wik in 1996—effectively demolished the notion that Australia was *terra nullius* when the British arrived. Despite the considerable hysteria about land claims whipped up following these decisions, Aboriginal aspirations remain a fairly abstract matter for people in the southern states. In Darwin, on the other hand, the Northern Land Council has two outstanding land claims which seek control over the development of crown land in the suburbs. This renders the issue concrete and immediate for white Australians and successive conservative Territory governments have never felt shy of 'playing the race card' in election campaigns. The fact that Darwin lives the problems of reconciliation on a daily basis has made people acutely self-conscious about the clashes between Aboriginal cultures and aspirations and the cultures of the colonisers.

The Union Movement in Darwin

Unionism in Darwin began on the wharves under the influence of the rhetoric of the Industrial Workers of the World (IWW or the 'wobblies'). It therefore had an internationalist character and campaigned for a forty-hour week, the central reason for establishing May Day. The first union was the Amalgamated Workers' Association (AWA), formed as a branch of the Queensland AWA in 1912, the year John Gilruth, the inaugural Commonwealth Government Administrator of the Northern Territory, was appointed. Gilruth quickly 'adopted the role of a Viceroy' presiding over a colonial outpost rather than that of a senior public servant (Alcorta 1984: 3). His troubled tenure began when he arrived in the middle of a wages dispute between the AWA and shipping agents. His confrontationist stance over a minor issue of work starting times immediately established his mode of handling industrial relations.

Gilruth almost succeeded in smashing the AWA in 1913, when a poorly organised and badly timed strike left it deserted by the Commonwealth Labor government and the Queensland branch of the Australian Workers' Union (AWU), to which it had been recently affiliated. The affiliation proved important, however, when Harold Nelson was elected organiser in 1914, and rebuilt the union to the status of an independent branch of the AWU and the dominant union in the Territory. His work led to the 'Darwin Rebellion', the formative moment of Darwin unionism and one of the most spectacular demonstrations of union power in Australian history (Lockwood 1968: 189–215). The 'Rebellion' commenced in December 1918 when a group of workers employed by Vestey's meatworks led a community-wide march on Government House and demanded that Gilruth answer a list of charges on his governance. A scuffle ensued when he refused and an effigy of him was burnt. Gilruth and his family were then held under siege until they were forced to depart in February 1919 after a public campaign led by the AWU. The riot, while ostensibly produced by Gilruth's decision to impose a 30% rise in the price of beer, which was only available through hotels under the control of the administration, followed a protracted battle between Gilruth and the AWU. Gilruth's acts of autocracy and maladministration dated back to his arrival in the Territory.

Following Gilruth's departure, Nelson and others established a Reform Committee, made up of a group of AWU members. This included Darwin's mayor who sent a telegram to the Commonwealth government minister responsible for the Northern Territory demanding an elected Council. The minister offered a government-appointed Advisory Council with two labour representatives nominated by the Industrial Council, the recently-established peak union body. Within a year, however, the unions had driven out the three government appointees of this Advisory Council including its Chair—the new Director of the Northern Territory—amid further accusations of corruption.

Union power abated somewhat when Nelson left to take a non-voting seat in the Commonwealth parliament in 1922. Nelson's departure followed an unsuccessful attempt to turn IWW 'One Big Union' rhetoric (which, according to historian Alan Powell, 'permeated the whole of the Territory union movement') into reality (Powell 1996: 137). The attempt to set up the North Australian Industrial Union led to bitter inter-union conflicts which were only resolved by the formation of the radical North Australian Workers Union (NAWU) later that year. The NAWU campaigned aggressively throughout the 1920s and early 1930s for hundreds of unemployed workers, some of whom had been involved in the Darwin Rebellion and others who had come seeking work from all over Australia, leading one Sydney newspaper to describe Darwin as 'Little Moscow' (Lockwood 1968: 242). The early 1930s were characterised by violent clashes between police and demonstrators carrying the Red Flag as Darwin struggled through a devastating Depression. While the union remained 'the strongest association amongst non-Aboriginal workers' until Darwin was virtually evacuated after wartime bombing (Sager 1993: 58), it was also 'a major player in institutionalising racism' and excluded Aboriginal and Chinese workers from its membership during the Depression (Mark Crossin interviewed by David Watt, Darwin, 18 July 1997). After the war a rebuilt NAWU was powerful throughout the Territory and rendered Darwin a virtual closed shop. It also fought a number of battles in support of Aboriginal workers leading up to Wave Hill in the 1960s (Mark Crossin interviewed by David Watt, Darwin, 18 July 1997).

The NAWU has maintained a high profile in Darwin, involving itself in fundraising for 'worthy causes' such as children's playgrounds, or the Leprosarium on Channel Island in Darwin harbour. In 1946, it took on the cause of Aboriginal domestic workers trucked in from compounds to clean the houses and tend the gardens of public servants, and helped them fight for the provision of a school for their children. The NAWU also established a Workers' Club in 1946, as a union meeting place, a public venue for sporting events, from boxing matches to local basketball games, and for fundraising concert performances for local artists. It maintained this central social and cultural role well into the 1980s.[1]

Darwin unionism, then, was strong and radical from the beginning, and the centrality of the maritime industry gave it an internationalist flavour. This created an environment in which May Day has typically flourished in Australia. Today, the union scene is very different. Following the heavy postwar investment of public sector funding in Darwin, the white collar

---

[1] Trevor Surplice, organiser with the AMIEU and ALMHWU and unofficial historian of the NAWU, supplied much of this information.

unions, such as the Community and Public Sector Union (CPSU) or the Australian Education Union have grown and the old blue-collar unions are in decline. The NAWU has been amalgamated into the Australian Liquor, Hospitality and Miscellaneous Workers Union, one of 21 unions affiliated to the NTTLC, which was formed in 1971. Darwin's huge percentage of public sector workers makes it an unlikely site for the militant union activism conventionally associated with blue-collar unions in industrial centres. Nevertheless, its union history contributes to a continuing radicalism. Against the national trend, union membership in the Northern Territory is actually increasing. And the NTTLC has carried on the legacy of its radical origins: its first President, Brian Manning was a former member of the Communist Party and a major campaigner for the rights of Aboriginal workers. The radical legacy is also evident in the importance placed on May Day and the union's involvement in cultural activities.

The Arts in Darwin

The Darwin arts scene in the 1980s was characterised by cross-cultural interactions developed through a community base by funding and infrastructural circumstances (Chance 1989: 11–32). Under the Country-Liberal Party's Don Dale, whose ministerial portfolio in the 1980s ranged across Health, Welfare, Sport and Recreation, Ethnic Affairs, Arts, Correctional Services, Juvenile Justice, Consumer Affairs, Childcare and Pensions, it made sense to pair arts activity and community development. Community arts activists like Barbara Pitman, who then worked for the Migrant Resource and Settlement Centre, and Maggie Sydenham, who headed the Office of the Arts, grasped the opportunity. The Northern Territory Arts Council and Brown's Mart Community Arts Project were central to the range of projects involving artsworkers in community contexts which emerged from this environment.

In the early 1980s the seven regional branches of the Arts Council not only co-ordinated tours of performing groups from outside the Territory to isolated areas but also brought in artsworkers to work with particular communities in a facilitatory mode. These included Aboriginal groups that sought to maintain traditional cultures through bodies like the Aboriginal Cultural Foundation and the Land Councils. It also encouraged community development through arts-related activity, most notably by nurturing Aboriginal rock bands like the now internationally famous Yothu Yindi. The program helped to develop a pool of community artsworkers with experience of cross-cultural work throughout the Territory. Many found a natural home at Brown's Mart, one of the longest-running and most successful community arts organisations in the country.

Brown's Mart has been central to the development of a community arts ethos in Darwin since its inception in 1972, under the directorship of Ken Conway, a pioneer of the Australian community arts movement. It has been responsible for what Ian Chance has described as 'a constant stream of one-off community arts projects, artists-in-residencies, large-scale community theatre events, celebratory or festival activities and community music programs' (Chance 1989: 26). It has nurtured Corrugated Iron Youth Theatre and the Darwin Theatre Company, both of which have combined professional theatreworkers with local amateur participants. The latter runs a season of its own productions with this professional–amateur mix. It also supports one-off projects by amateur cultural groups such as the play commissioned from community theatre writer Graham Pitts called *Death at Balibo, the Killing, by Indonesian Forces, of Five Australian T.V. Newsmen during an Attack on Balibo, East Timor, on October 16th 1975* (to give it its full and incendiary title), which created a minor diplomatic incident in 1988, after a group of Indonesian journalists took offence at the poster for the show (Burvill 1998: 234). The play, an initiative of the Timorese Association Cultural Group (the Lafaek—crocodile—Club), was brought to the company by Barbara Pitman and financially supported by the NTTLC. Community-based cross-cultural work like this has generated a broad interest in Darwin in the possibilities of community arts work.

Brown's Mart was also responsible for street processions and festival events, including a huge outdoor performance in 1988 called *Fire on the Water*, devised and directed by Neil Cameron. This spectacular multicultural event created by visual artists, musicians and performers drew thousands of people to Mindil Beach, the site of an evening market. It incorporated sculptural images erected at low tide on 30-foot poles, shadow puppets, fireworks and a steel band (Cameron 1993: 164–167). In short, Brown's Mart was instrumental in constructing the ethos from which the union movement was to remake its May Day celebrations and Cameron played a central role in its development.

May Days in Darwin

May Day has been celebrated in Darwin since the beginnings of unionism. The Northern Territory is the only Australian state or territory where it remains a gazetted public holiday, held on the first Monday in May (although in Queensland this is gazetted as Labour Day). May Days were well-attended events in the immediate postwar years. The NAWU was particularly committed to the May Day tradition, both for fundraising and to campaign on union and social issues, and at least occasionally on Aboriginal workers' rights. In 1948, for example, the NAWU proposed a May Day Queen competition, and nominated the eventual runner-up, local Aboriginal woman Jane Ah Matt, as its candidate. After six weeks of intense competition £1,600 was raised. This was divided between the Leprosarium and Children's Playground Committees. In 1951 the May Day march was led by 200 Aboriginal members who had just won an industrial campaign through the NAWU.

Interest had waned significantly by the early 1980s, however, as the then President of the NTTLC, Jamey Robertson, admitted in 1989:

> When I took over the job as Secretary in '81 May Day had really slumped down into about a hundred odd unionists walking around town with banners, a few beers at the Workers' Club, and that was basically it. (Cited in Ingleton 1989)

By this time, the May long weekend was dominated by 'On the Beach', an event organised by the Lions' Club and sponsored by local business groups. Janet Crews, Branch Secretary of the CPSU, described it as 'a beer, wet T-shirt, swill and surf event whose purpose was to celebrate the beginning of the dry season' (letter to David Watt, 24 February 1998). Mark Crossin, who has served as President and Secretary of the NTTLC, saw it as 'a piss-up on the beach' organised to undercut the significance of May Day as a labour movement event (Mark Crossin interviewed by David Watt, Darwin, 18 July 1997). Moves to cancel the holiday in the mid-1980s galvanised the NTTLC into battle over its symbolic importance. They organised a rival event which extended beyond what NTTLC Employment Liaison Officer Didge McDonald, who now administers the May Day program, described as 'a march, a speech and a piss-up' (interviewed by David Watt, Darwin, 17 July 1997). As union official Rod Ellis put it:

> We simply couldn't preserve a day when we had sixty or seventy people making a protest ... the reality is that people aren't going to be involved in that sort of thing, and we ... had to make it a fun affair as well—we had to involve families and we had to involve kids. (Cited in Ingleton 1989)

Robertson had been attempting to inject life into the union movement through cultural activities at the Workers' Club, which became part of a broader strategy of implementing 'a three to four year program in the arts' (Crossin, cited in Ingleton 1989). A group of like-minded young union officials took up the challenge to enliven the May Day celebrations and also the image of the movement itself through cultural activities funded by the Art and Working Life program. Sympathetic community activists like Pitman and Elinor Boyd, who have had a long association with Darwin May Days, were also central.

The development of the community arts initiative dates back to 1986, when May Day concerts, partially funded by the Art and Working Life program were enabled by the connections that Robertson had established with local Aboriginal bands through organising concerts at the Workers' Club. More broadly, according to Crossin, the unions deliberately moved into the community arts movement, not only to enhance the May Day program, but also to seek new members when the newly-formed Media, Entertainment and Arts Alliance affiliated with the ACTU. Their strategy of 'deliberate infiltration' meant that 'all the major community and performing arts organisations in this town, for almost a decade, ... had strong union participation' at board level (Janet Crews has been President of the Darwin Theatre Company since 1989, and Didge McDonald has served as Chair of the Brown's Mart Board, for example) (Mark Crossin interviewed by David Watt, Darwin, 18 July 1997). As well, the NTTLC began investing time and money in arts projects across a range of artforms.

This 'community arts–led recovery' drew upon the network of community artists and arts-related organisations which had grown up around Brown's Mart and the Northern Territory Arts Council. This fertile ground helped to turn May Day into one of the best-known community arts events in the country, and a much-envied model in the southern states. Paddy Garrity, a Melbourne-based union arts activist who journeyed up to work on the 1991 May Day, wrote in an enthusiastic report:

The figures for involvement in Darwin's May Day Celebrations over the past few years are:

1987	150 people
1988	2,000
1989	3,500
1990	5,000
1991	6,000

Questions have to be asked and lessons learned, as to why Darwin, with a population of only 65,000, and no full time Trade Union Arts Officer (and reputation of being a non-union town), has over 6,000 people involved in 1991. And Melbourne (with a reputation of being the heart land of union militancy) has less than 2,000? [*sic*] participate in the May Day March. (Garrity 1991)

For Crossin, the victory over 'On the Beach', now a thing of the past, is not the only measure of success. The 1988 May Day, he claims, generated a thousand new members.

May Day 1988: The Gilruth March

As Garrity's figures show, the revived May Day started to take off in 1988. Planning for this event started soon after the 1987 march by a May Day Committee which met up to three times a week. The committee employed two experienced community artsworkers, Rick McCracken and Margaret Robinson, on a one-month contract to develop a funding proposal for a large-scale re-enactment of the 'Darwin Rebellion' in 1918–19. The historical subject was partially conditioned by the money available for history-based projects during the Bicentennial year (1988). But it also offered the opportunity to reclaim an almost forgotten history of the union movement and it fitted neatly into the recuperative brief of the Art and Working Life program.

When funding was obtained for a number of projects coalescing around May Day, McCracken and Robinson were taken on as project co-ordinators for fourteen weeks. The plans included a newspaper called the *Northern Standard* (in honour of the NAWU newspaper of the same name, which had at times been Darwin's only paper), the aims of which were described in a report from the May Day Committee to the NTTLC (25 February 1988):

1) to give rank and file unionists skills in all aspects of print media—writing, graphics, photography, layout, design and distribution. These skills are then available to individual unions.
2) to acknowledge the role of the original *Northern Standard* as a force generating cohesion within the Darwin community for issues of concern to organised labour
3) to provide a vehicle for organised labour's contemporary views to be put into the public arena

The newspaper that was produced in 1988 led to an annual May Day magazine which in 1994 won the Human Rights and Equal Opportunities Commission Award for print journals.

The 1988 program also included a dinner (which has become a May Day tradition), an exhibition of artworks produced by unionists in a series of

Puppet- making for the *March to the Future*, Darwin 1989. (Photo: Peter Matthew.)

poster-making workshops, the establishment of a May Day choir—a continuing feature of the celebrations—and a series of music workshops leading to The Rage, a concert on the Saturday before the march. The Rage was a young person's event which aimed to reach beyond the union's constituency and forge links with Aboriginal groups and bands. In the words of a May Day Committee meeting minute, this could offer a 'positive contact for youth with the trade union movement', an obvious plus given the movement's struggle to recruit from this area.

Central to the package of events was the parade and re-enactment. The Committee decided the content and form and employed two theatreworkers, Neil Cameron and Jan McDonald, and a musician, Natasha Moszenin, to put these plans into effect. Cameron and McDonald had worked together in Melbourne's working-class western suburbs at WEST Theatre Company, one of the most influential of the Australian community theatre groups which emerged in the late 1970s. Two bodies of experience informed Cameron's work. The first was from his time with Welfare State International, the pioneer of large scale, community-based outdoor ceremonial performances in Britain (Coult and Kershaw 1990; Kershaw 1992: 206–242). The second was his knowledge of community cultural development practice at Craigmillar, a poverty-stricken housing estate on the outskirts of Edinburgh where he worked in the 1970s. The Craigmillar Festival Society, established in 1964 by local residents, had run a series of arts-based activities as part of a community self-help program for a number of years. As a pioneering grass-roots venture in the use of cultural activity for community development, the Festival Society was a major influence on the development of community arts practice and funding policy in Australia and elsewhere (Crummy 1992; Watt 1995: 26–29). McDonald brought her experience as director of WEST's *Vital Signs* (discussed in Chapter 2), which had helped to establish the amateur-participatory model that came to dominate union-based community arts practice in the late 1980s.

Cameron and McDonald produced an event which had the same intentions as their earlier work at WEST (Cameron, 1993: 173–5). It converted a desultory march into a procession which included six 16-foot puppets, a 30-foot effigy of Administrator Gilruth and a steel drum band on the back of a truck as well as banners and flags. The latter had been made by unionists, their families and others at workshops advertised through the unions and in the press. The procession was led by a group of meatworkers with a puppet of union leader Harold Nelson. Five other puppets joined the march at different points along the route. Each represented a figure of the period, explained in pre-march publicity via a press release and a leaflet distributed through the unions. There was an injured Digger denied a pension by Gilruth unless he took the unpopular job of hangman. The union intervened to secure his pension when he refused to execute two Aboriginal men convicted of murder. The third puppet, Mrs Perreau, was described thus in the NTTLC leaflet:

With 10 children to feed and a farm failing to meet their needs, she and the family moved to Darwin. Pressures continued to grow until her husband could cope no more and ended his life by throwing himself off the wharf. She pleaded with the Administrator for help but was turned away. The Union came to her assistance and helped her support her family. Her harassment continued through an officer of the law who it is believed raped her. She shot the officer and was tried for murder. The public outcry that resulted secured her release.

Puppet four was W. J. Kirkland, editor of the *Northern Territory Times*, an outspoken opponent of Gilruth. The final two puppets represented, in turn, a group of barmaids who took Saturday afternoon off to celebrate the armistice, after being refused official permission to do so and were thrown out of work; and the police, to whom Gilruth had supplied arms.

The march proceeded loudly and colourfully through the streets to Government House, the scene of the original rebellion. Here it paused for a brief re-enactment of the 1918 confrontation with Gilruth (played, in a minor coup, by the current Administrator of the Northern Territory, Eric Johnson, who, according to Crossin, 'virtually paid for all the materials to build the effigy which we burnt—which was him') (Mark Crossin interviewed by David Watt, Darwin, 18 July 1997). Then it moved to Darwin's Civic Square where the Gilruth effigy was burnt, and this was followed by a family picnic. The re-enactment revived a forgotten labour tradition of acting out great events from revolutionary history, although Cameron was probably one of few people aware of the links to Nikolai Evreinov's *Storming of the Winter Palace* in Leningrad in 1920, the German union movement's *massenspeil* of the early 1920s and the pageants organised by the British Communist Party in the late 1930s (Leach 1994: 40–50; Davies 1980: 79–80; Wallis 1994, 1995).

The procession involved many more people than preceding May Days, and constructed a high-profile celebration of the union movement as a community, and of Darwin history. It generated local interest far beyond the union movement, an expansionist intent implicit in its planning. Barbara Pitman, a long-standing member of the May Day Committee in subsequent years, praised the NTTLC President at the time, Jamey Robertson, for his persuasiveness on the strategy:

> he felt that the only way to get a focus on the Gilruth uprising was to do it as a very big event, and quite rightly he said that this event ... was not only about union activity. It was about a *community* saying we don't want this and

we won't put up with it. (interviewed by David Watt, Darwin, 3 May 1996)

As a result, there was a conscious effort to reach people who may have had no association with the movement:

> Darwin people love a party and by and large it doesn't matter who's throwing it, they'll go—the fact that it was the union march didn't really make all that much difference, because quite cleverly ... the unions chose to involve a whole range of 'top people', like the Administrator [and the then Chief Justice]. That gave it a sense of being other than strictly within the union ranks. (interviewed by David Watt, Darwin, 3 May 1996)

As Janet Crews points out, the march mirrored the event it was designed to commemorate: 'The original rebellion was a community event led by unionists. This is why the historical re-enactment of the event in the form of the Gilruth march was something we wanted to involve the whole community in' (letter to David Watt, 24 February 1998).

The underlying assumption was that any association with the union movement was better than none. By celebrating the holiday as significant to more than its immediate membership, the union movement claimed a profile as a community organisation and demonstrated the NTTLC's willingness to embrace the strategies of 'social unionism'. May Day in Darwin has developed from these beginnings and now provides a focus for non-union groups wishing to have their say.

May Day 1989: The March to the Future

The success of the 1988 march led to plans for a concerted outreach program for 1989. The May Day Committee started meeting with arts groups in June ranging from Brown's Mart, the Darwin Theatre Company and Corrugated Iron Youth Theatre to the Timorese Association Cultural Group. It also met with a range of other organisations, including the Migrant Resource Centre and the Northern Land Council, in order to involve community and ethnic groups which, for various reasons, had previously shown little interest in the union movement. These groups were not easy to win over: some Asian groups, for instance, had been past victims of the racist elements of the Northern Territory union movement; others, like the Filipinos, Latin Americans and Indonesians, came from societies in which union membership was dangerous and even illegal. At a time of declining union membership throughout Australia, it was important to make these groups feel comfortable associating with the NTTLC.

As in 1988, the procession and theatre piece were the focal points among a number of events. The Cameron–McDonald team, emboldened by the success of the previous year and of Cameron's project *Fire on the Water*, submitted a detailed proposal to the May Day Committee on 17 March. The march was planned for the evening, rather than the middle of the day, so it could include a torchlight procession. A performance in Frog Hollow (on the site of Darwin's first high school) would follow and the darkness would enhance the use of lighting, smoke and flames. Finally, there would be a picnic and concert in the park. The proposal was accepted and the event went ahead under the title, *The March to the Future*.

Once again the procession included banners, flags, torches and bamboo and paper lanterns, made in workshops by artsworkers and volunteers along with several giant puppets also used in the performance. The atmosphere created by the procession was described as more like a 'carnival' than a traditional Australian May Day:

> With the warmth of the air and the heavy smell of kerosene mingling with the aromas of the Asian food stalls, the metallic drums beating out a Samba then a cascade of gongs like a gamelan, it could have been a festival night in Java, or La Paz. (Spunner 1989)

The NTTLC had encouraged community and ethnic groups, and a wide range of people were involved in the performance which was brief (about half an hour) but spectacular. It took the form of much carnivalesque performance in which foes meet and fight until good triumphs over the forces of evil. In this case an evil dictator (played at the last minute by then NTTLC President Mark Crossin), with two henchmen, an army of stiltwalkers and two monsters modelled on Chinese dragons, defended a tower full of imprisoned children. Families of the children accompanied by a huge 'mother' puppet (which had led the procession) battled with armies and monsters, released the children, captured the dictator, and set fire to the tower. The women carried shields decorated with symbols of their particular cultural grouping on bamboo poles with Maori, Timorese and Aboriginal symbols the most notable. The narrative was conveyed via a storyteller through a public address system, which also played music composed and recorded for the event. Flares, streamers, smoke bombs, burning torches, fire-eaters and theatrical lighting combined with the huge puppets, paper dragons and stiltwalkers, accompanied by the deafening noise of taped music and the steel band. Some 150 people performed, and the event used the skills of a core group of professional puppeteers, musicians and visual artists (Ingleton 1989). After the performance the park became

The March to the Future performance in Frog Hollow, Darwin 1989.
(Photo: Peter Matthew)

a fairground, and food and drink stalls competed for attention with performances organised by Brown's Mart on three different stages, each designed to cater for a different age group.

The event was a huge success in a number of ways: it bridged the gap between spectators and participants, one of Cameron's ambitions for this kind of work; it drew almost twice as many people as the previous year; it reached a number of ethnic and issue-based groups which had previously had little contact with the union movement, connections that have been maintained since; it drew national attention via media coverage; it offered skills training to a number of local artists who have gone on to further community-based work; and it put Darwin May Day on the map.

There were some in the union movement, though, who thought it had moved too far from the May Day 'tradition'. Peter Tullgren, Assistant Secretary of the Federated Miscellaneous Workers' Union (FMWU), for example, said this:

> I must say that May Day is a political movement and I believe it has to be seen in that light, and introducing a series of cultural events which tend to get more advanced and more involved every year I think detracts from that political message.

While he admitted that a lot of people were involved, he pointed out that:

> many of them are not necessarily trade unionists or trade union people. Now some might say 'Well that's good'. But it's taken what is principally a political march and a political event and turned it into a street party. (Cited in Ingleton 1989)

Barbara Pitman admits that Tullgren's *in principle* objection to the notion of a community arts-based May Day was shared by 'some union hard-liners'. It derives from the tension between demonstration and celebration implicit in the notion of May Day from its inception. It can also be seen as a rejection by an old-style unionist of the NTTLC's embrace of 'social unionism'. There were, however, objections from within the 'social unionism' camp as well.

Pitman herself felt that 'we'd totally lost the plot', more on artistic than political grounds. Her views probably coincided with those of Gillian Harrison, a highly experienced community artist, who wrote an evaluation report on the event in her capacity as an Australia Council Project Officer:

> To me the imagery and representation of women as either the big earth mama or the Thatcherite tyrant was offensive; the choice of the TLC Secretary for the role of the despot who conscripted and imprisoned children to use to his own ends was perhaps unwise; the script was weak, trite and blandly delivered; the overall celtic fairy-tale nature of the event, its visual presentation with procession and fire, seemed bizarre in a Darwin park on a hot night; there were no links with May Day or the trade union movement apparent to the audience. (Harrison 1989)

There was a more general dissatisfaction with the level of consultation. The 1989 project was more artist-driven than that of 1988 and a reiterated complaint was that unionists who had not been consulted about the content of the performance did not feel the same sense of 'ownership'. Cameron and McDonald inevitably bore the brunt of these complaints, but the struggle for control between artsworkers and the commissioning body has been a continuing one in Darwin, and is endemic to the whole community arts scene.

Central to the problem is a mismatch between the notion of the artist and the principle of what Tim Rowse has called 'decentralised patronage' as embraced by the community arts faction in the Australia Council (Rowse 1985: 24). Artists, particularly visual artists, are still trained on the romantic assumption that the production of art is the result of an intersection between skills, which can be taught, and 'talent', or even 'genius', which separates the 'artist' from the mere artisan, and certainly from the rest of us. No amount of rhetoric about 'ownership', 'empowerment' or 'community consultation' has ultimately broken the notion of 'art' as an individuated practice and the province of special people. As Barbara Pitman puts it:

> They're still being taught that you're an individual, that you're answerable to nobody, and somewhere out there there's a whole lot of money and somebody's going to pay you to just sit in a garret and do your thing. (interviewed by David Watt, Darwin, 3 May 1996)

The structures of patronage within the Art and Working Life program promoted a different social positioning of the artist, one that is implicit in the term 'artsworker'. AWL funding was given to the host body rather than the artist, in this case the NTTLC, who then *employed* the artsworker. When artists failed to see themselves as mere employees and assumed the right of control, it made no sense to the commissioning body who saw it as *their* project.

The NTTLC's response to this conflict was to set up a compulsory half-day seminar for all artsworkers employed on May Day projects, which was also open to volunteer workers. Designed to 'assist in your dealings with the unions as your clients in this project', it covered a range of issues, from the structure of the NTTLC and unionism in general to the position of the project within the Art and Working Life program. Of particular importance was a clarification of dispute- and grievance-settling procedures, which introduced artsworkers to a less anarchic mode of industrial relations than had sometimes emerged in earlier projects.

The disagreement, then, was not isolated to a battle between Cameron and McDonald and the NTTLC, and Pitman's experience as an Australia Council Board Member gave her a broader perspective on it:

> We sometimes set these artsworkers up to fail because we expect them to do two things. We expect them to have this impeccable process, which is enormously difficult—I mean the community is almost going to be your worst client, and a difficult client—and then we expect this really polished thing at the end. (interviewed by David Watt, Darwin, 3 May 1996)

Nevertheless, because of the unhappiness about the 1989 May Day content, the NTTLC rejected a proposal for 1990 from Cameron and McDonald, and decided on a different team. Although it proved a more successful process, there were difficulties along the way.

May Day 1990: Strong with the Women

Planning for 1990 began within weeks of the 1989 event, preceded by some back-room manoeuvring. Janet Crews, Chair of the NTTLC Women's Committee and, with Elinor Boyd, a central figure in the planning, described the push by NTTLC women: 'A lot of us made sure that we got elected to the May Day Committee for that year so that essentially we'd have the running of it and we'd control the agenda rather than being in a support role' (interviewed by David Watt, Darwin, 18 July 1997). The newly-elected Committee, inspired by a recent book on the role of women in Northern Territory history by local historian Barbara James, submitted a proposal, caucused via the Women's Committee, for a celebration of women in the development of the Territory. For Crews, the historical focus was particularly important 'in a place like Darwin where things have been wiped out every twenty or thirty years with a cyclone', which 'wipes out history as well' (interviewed by David Watt, Darwin, 18 July 1997).

Similarly important, after the experience of 1989, was the establishment of a collaborative relationship between artists and unionists in which the skills of each could be mutually useful. Crews noted that union officials:

> are good at organising and running the machine and making things happen and organising big events like meetings ... Artists have learnt a lot from us ... about how you mobilise large numbers of people around a particular objective ... [but] sometimes we're just absolutely hopeless at getting across concepts to people without sounding like boring old Stalinists. (interviewed by David Watt, Darwin, 18 July 1997)

It was thus a pressing concern that artists be offered a brief approved by the NTTLC meeting of 29 May, to allow time for further discussion.

It was accepted in principle, after resistance from some familiar sources, notably Peter Tullgren and the FMWU. The FMWU Branch Secretary wrote to the NTTLC following its acceptance of a more detailed proposal three months later:

> In the report [submitted to Council] reference is made to identifying 100 prominent women within the Labour Movement over the past 100 years.
>
> I would be pleased to receive your detailed answers to the following questions:—
>
> 1. Why is the identification restricted to women?
> 2. How was the number 100 selected?
> 3. What occurs if there are more or less than 100 identified?

4. Who determines the criteria for prominence?

5. How are the 100 to be identified?

6. Why is such a proposal even being considered?

This set the tone for some delicate negotiations.

The evaluation of the two previous years in early meetings produced a commitment to increase community involvement in constructing the event. It was resolved that a full script of the performance needed to be NTTLC approved, and that individual unions be consulted at all stages. A greater emphasis was also placed on employing local artists, and to that end a skills audit was undertaken. In the meantime, the Committee took what Janet Crews describes as 'a long shot' and asked Robyn Archer to be Artistic Co-ordinator. Archer had a substantial international reputation as a singer and recording artist (particularly of Brecht songs), and as a writer and performer of several highly successful cabaret-based theatre pieces. She was sufficiently enthusiastic about the project, particularly after reading Barbara James' book, to telephone from London and confirm her interest. Crews, Pitman and Boyd then wrote a successful grant application to the Australia Council to fund a procession and a performance event in Frog Hollow.

Archer's involvement began with a two-week visit in October and November 1989, during which she familiarised herself with earlier May Days, spoke to a network of unionists, artsworkers and representatives of interested community groups suggested by the May Day Committee, and interviewed women musicians interested in paid work on the project. She then produced a proposal, which she named 'Strong with the Women'. The document consisted of twenty-seven pages of suggestions for the procession and performance and a further seven pages listing technical requirements and offering plans for a stage including the placement of sound and lighting gear. This was presented to the Committee and then, in summary form, to the NTTLC. Her proposal drew on what she referred to as the 'remarkable successes' of the previous two years and added 'a new artistic emphasis on Music'. More controversially, and part of her brief from the Committee, was a 'particular thematic emphasis on Women' which was, in fact, to be more than just 'thematic':

> My aim is ... that the project should involve as many people as would like to be involved, bearing always in mind that the focus is to be on women. We should understand from the outset, that if men/boys wish to be involved then their participation is to be welcomed, but that for a rare change, they

may have to 'stand in the second row'. ... In no way should this event detract
from the achievements of working men; on the contrary I believe that allowing
this time and space to acknowledge and celebrate the unsung heroines,
mothers, daughters, comrades who have been there in a supportive role all
the time, is an ultimately ennobling experience for everyone. (Archer
1989: 1)

As musical director Bronwen Calcutt pointed out, the project was given
the broader brief of 'trying to foster women's music and women's
performance' rather than just to 'celebrate' women. This included the
establishment of an all-women May Day choir (Cited in Mason 1990).

Archer's proposal followed the formats established by Cameron and
McDonald—a procession, including puppets and costumes made in open
workshops, leading to an evening performance, concert and picnic in Frog
Hollow in which the puppets would be used. But she added an elaborate
consultative process. She proposed that the performance consist of a
sequence of episodes drawn from the history of women in the Territory, and
that the route of the march be determined by 'chosen points of significance
for Territory women past and present' to:

> be decided on by consultation between co-ordinators as to which subjects/
> characters/stories are best suited as the focus for a combination of a good
> large scale puppet or pack of costumed characters which can look great at
> the march and also be worked into a short large-scale performance later as
> part of the Picnic's main event ... Having decided on a particular figure,
> group and story, an appropriate point in the town can be chosen and this
> figure and/or group should join the march at that point. At the time of
> joining, members and spectators will see the figure/group simply as
> spectacle. The significance or story will be explained more fully later in
> performance. (Archer 1989: 2–3)

Her proposal offered a possible episode, drawn from James' book:

> You choose the figure of Ellen Ryan, game proprietor of the Vic Hotel, and
> a good representative of the enterprise and resilience of last century's
> Territory Women. There were many women involved in the history of pub-
> running, and Ellen Ryan always stood up for her workers. You research her
> life and find an incident or idea which would lend itself to a brief but
> effective dramatisation by puppet or group (because these dramatisations
> are to a large crowd at the picnic, they should be moved with large gesture
> and almost without words—certainly without 'speeches' as such). Perhaps

it is as simple as a dance (in the performance area in front of the music stage) of Ellen Ryan and the barmaids (perhaps women in the hotel industry would like to be involved) while onstage we have 'The Ballad of Ellen Ryan' or 'The Song of Mrs. Public House' (encompassing Ellen and May Brown and all the others—so the puppet becomes the archetypical pub-runner woman). Perhaps the little dramatisation begins with a chorus or dance of drunken miners. The large scale figure enters and cleans up the joint—they become more orderly drinkers. The background song can give some details.

Working backwards then, to the march, we have the route go through the Mall, or past the appropriate end, and these characters join the March. I have discussed with Barbara James that at some of these points we may be able to get sponsors to provide a commemorative plaque (the series design would be co-ordinated) that would be a permanent acknowledgement of the presence of great women in the town centre. The design should be attractive and have the effect that blue plaques in London do—in future people are simply walking along and come across this reminder of a woman's presence and role. In this instance it just so happens that 1990 is also the hundredth anniversary of the Vic Hotel, and Barbara feels sure that the present owners would start the ball rolling by financing the first plaque. This could be 'unveiled' by a woman of contemporary significance—no speech, just a one sentence announcement—then the figure and characters (barmaids or miners) join the march. Their story or significance is told later in the Picnic's main event. (Archer 1989: 3–4)

Indeed Archer listed twelve possible episodes (although offering less detailed plans than for this one, which wasn't actually taken up), running in chronological order from a dance enacting the local Larrakeyah women's creation legend to the present day. She recommended choosing eight of these, or alternatives should some not prove attractive. She suggested they be strung together:

by alternating between newly-developed group works, individual established [musical] acts, and dance or drama performances. The whole is drawn together by a gradual build-up on the music stage and environs of people and sounds. Once any musical act has done its individual turn (usually only one or two songs or pieces), it stays on the stage, and takes part each time the main theme returns. By the end, the main theme should be very large and loud. I re-emphasise that this main theme should be the musical equivalent of large scale puppet/mime. i.e. very simple words, often repeated, simple lines which can be very effective in combination with large numbers of singers and musicians. (Archer 1989: 6)

Archer thought the overall length should be sixty to ninety minutes, with individual episodes between five and seven minutes. This would have 'advantages in terms of keeping the crowd continually diverted and entertained, and in keeping the workload relatively small for everyone. The large effect is created by including lots of people' (Archer 1989: 8).

The concept meant establishing a team of artsworkers with clearly delineated roles and responsibilities. The central figures were Boyd as assistant director of the project, Bronwen Calcutt as musical director with the assistance of Alan Murphy and Michael Havir, Omar Pumar (a local with substantial theatre experience in Latin America) as director of the procession and performance, and Deb Humphries as visual artist. All except Calcutt were locals who had worked on earlier May Days. Individual episodes were to be placed in the hands of appropriate union or community groups, with Archer having constructed 'a large framework' in which others would work, so that 'the principal co-ordinators work with each other, the interested musical and theatrical groups, the Trade Unions, and the community to come up with the actual detail of both music and performance' (Archer 1989: 2).

She was at pains to point out 'the looseness of the structure' she was proposing:

> It really is up to co-ordinators to think about which bits, which subjects, which stories or characters, past or present, most interest them and which individuals or groups of people they want to work with—bearing in mind that the object should be to use everyone who would like to have a go, whether they have skills and experience or not. (Archer 1989: 10)

She was also careful to define her own position in the project as it evolved:

> I am under no delusions about the amount of time people have to devote to a project like this. Darwin is an extremely busy place, and both co-ordinators and performers/workers will be trying to fit this in amongst other commitments. It is for that reason that the process is beginning early, so that people can work things out at an early stage, and keep the work rolling along, so that by the time I return in April (three weeks before May 7), all decisions will have been made and work will be already in rehearsal at its own pace. I can do a certain amount of editing, advising on

'rewrites', and hands-on help in rehearsal, but I think my most effective role is in pulling things together as the bulk of the creative work originates and proceeds locally. (Archer 1989: 9)

The structure of the performance thus allowed a closer integration of the concerns and interests of participants than had been the case in 1989. Rather than a single theatre piece, Archer proposed a sequence of discrete pieces, individually written and shaped by two local writers, Jenny Vuletic (who had worked on earlier May Days) and Suzanne Spunner (a Melbourne writer with experience in community theatre living in Darwin at the time), in consultation with Pumar and the group which was to take responsibility for it. Calcutt's task was to tie these episodes together via reiterated musical themes, leading to a finale in which Archer envisaged 'the layers of sound which have been increasing each time a new individual performer or group comes on stage, will have reached something quite impressive to carry the main theme to its conclusion' (Archer 1989: 8).

Archer's plan suffered problems along the way which meant some compromises. Some men found the notion of playing second fiddle to women less than 'ennobling', and called, unsuccessfully, for the outright rejection of the proposal; a few maintained their hostility and stayed away. Others were concerned at the notion of a focus on women in the centenary year of May Day, as Crews explains:

> At one point [NTTLC Assistant Secretary] Rod Ellis advocated changing the theme from a focus on women and women workers to a celebration of the 100th anniversary of International May Day. By then we were too far advanced and too committed to revisit the underlying themes and ideas. But with growing support from other male unionists for Rod's proposal some negotiations had to occur through the May Day Committee as to how both ideas could be accommodated. Eventually they were—and quite effectively. (letter to David Watt, 24 February 1998)

The solution was to change the opening. Rather than the Larrakeyah creation myth the performance began with 'The Chicago Struggle' featuring the figure of Lucy Parsons, the widow of one of the four men executed following the Haymarket Incident. Lucy delivered a speech modelled on ones her real life counterpart had given at political rallies, explaining the origins of May Day and marking the centenary.

Ellis was sufficiently concerned about the antagonism created by the theme to write in a magazine distributed in the weeks before the march:

By participating in the parade and associated celebrations you will not only treat yourself and your family to a great spectacle and a load of fun but you will assist in a very positive way the essential work of the NT Trade Union movement.

In explanation of this claim he wrote:

Our society and the way we work has changed dramatically. The Australian model of anglo-saxon craft unionism has out-lived its usefulness. Union membership has fallen from 54% in the fifties to 40% by 1990. The Australian Trade Union movement faces the most serious challenge in its history. The movement must dramatically improve its organising base amongst workers—particularly women, young people and part-timers. It can no longer rely on workers joining a trade union because it is the right thing to do, rather unions must be able to better sell themselves, they must become more appealing. (Ellis 1990)

He need not have worried: Mark Crossin claimed 1990 was 'the best ... and by far the biggest May Day we've ever had' (interviewed by David Watt, Darwin, 18 July 1997). The march included unions, community groups like Amnesty International and Greening Australia, ethnic organisations and women's groups such as the Darwin Home Birth Association, the Women Lawyers' Association and the Women Pilots' Association. There were puppets and a Chinese dragon made for the performance, and more children than Crossin could ever remember at a May Day march. Many unionists carried new banners they had made with artist-in-residence Deb Humphries, who had been working for over a year on a separate union banner project which had been dovetailed into the May Day celebrations.

One insurmountable problem was the biggest tropical rain storm in twenty years. It didn't stop the march, but the performance was cancelled. Archer, putting on a brave face in an interview soon after, claimed:

You hear a lot in community arts about the process being more important than the product: well, we showed that was the case. The whole exercise had been such a buzz, it had involved so many people, that was what people will carry on. What we lost, was the icing on the cake. (Cited in Chesterman 1990: 45)

Crossin more frankly admits 'we were in tears' (interviewed by David Watt, Darwin, 18 July 1997).

The women pushed to re-stage the performance in the Darwin Performing Arts Centre, which meant some reworking, extra rehearsals and, above all, money. The NTTLC approached Chief Minister, Marshall Perron, with a request for $40,000. Previous appeals for support for May Day-related arts activities to the Northern Territory Office of the Arts had been flatly rejected and later requests were also turned down. Shane Stone, as Minister for the Arts, refused support in 1992 on the grounds that May Day 'amounts to nothing more than a political splurge designed to advance the political fortunes of another political party'. This time, though, the Chief Minister overrode the decision of his Arts Minister and gave them the money. Crews triumphantly described it as 'the only time unions in the Territory have ever got money from the NT government' (interviewed by David Watt, Darwin, 18 July 1997).

The piece was performed on 27 May, not in the fairground atmosphere of Frog Hollow after the march, but in a formal theatre; not to the expected audience of 10,000, after an elaborate campaign of pre-publicity and visits by spokespeople and performers to workplaces, radio stations, schools, offices of organisations like the Northern Land Council and government agencies like the Department of Immigration and Ethnic Affairs and the Aboriginal and Torres Strait Islander Commission, but to about 1,000 crammed into the Darwin Performing Arts Centre.

The show lived up to most of Archer's ambitions for it. Many of her suggested scenes had been taken up and Calcutt had produced a rich and varied musical score, incorporating a string trio from the Darwin Symphony Orchestra (the Fiddlewood Trio), a didgeridu and clapsticks, a gamelan, a percussion band, a synthesiser, her own accordion, a rock band and several choirs and small singing groups. The show was lavishly costumed and for its backdrop used the spectacular puppets which were taken upstage after being used in their particular scene.

The performance opened with a welcoming speech from NTTLC President Jamey Robertson. The Lucy Parsons character then told the story of the Haymarket Incident, the arrests, trial and execution of her husband and his comrades, and the international establishment of May Day. Her speech was accompanied by a Chinese opera singer softly singing the 'Internationale'. It finished with a few bars from 'Annie Laurie' before the performers moved upstage and off. The main band took up the central musical theme of the performance, 'Strong with the Women', which had been used as a chant during the march. Calcutt had set it to a range of different musics to suit each particular scene.

Next came the sound of the didgeridu and clapsticks as a large puppet Aboriginal woman was brought on for the 'Creation Story', which was narrated while a group of Larrakeyah women danced to a tape of indigenous singing. The women moved about the stage animating other performers, who 'became' features of the landscape, soon to be invaded by the 'colonials'. The transition to the colonial sequence was achieved musically as the didgeridu and clapsticks were drowned out by 'the sounds of thunder and lightning' from the band, which in turn faded to make way for the Fiddlewood Trio playing Percy Grainger's 'An English Country Garden'. As Grainger's music took over, the Aboriginal group confronted some colonists in nineteenth-century costume, men carrying flags and women carrying umbrellas, and then moved upstage to place their puppet before exiting. The colonial group danced to Grainger's song, sung by a small choir, the Orlando Singers. The 'Isolation Song' which followed, described the hardships of wives brought to an environment harshly different from their native 'green land'. As the song ended an amplified male voice (Ken Conway from Brown's Mart) said 'So there you have it, the Northern Territory is not a fit and proper place for children and white women'. In retaliation came a jaunty rendition, accompanied by the Fiddlewood Trio and Calcutt's accordion, of a rewritten 'The Wild Colonial Boy':

> I am a wild colonial girl
> No blushing English Rose
> And if there's work that needs be done
> I'll not look down me nose
> I've heard them say this 'no man's land'
> Is not for girls like me
> Well how in hell would they know where
> A girl like me should be?! (*Strong with the Women* 1990)

Two more verses completed the scene with a flourish and the performers moved upstage and off. Two of the direct consequences of colonisation were depicted by a pair of well-known songs, each with an accompanying tableau and a brief introductory narration. 'The Drover's Boy', written by Territory songwriter Ted Egan, told of Aboriginal women, kidnapped by the early cattle drovers, dressed as boys and used as assistants and sexual partners. 'Brownskin Baby', written by Bobby Randall, a local Aboriginal activist who had worked for the North Australian Aboriginal Legal Aid Service in the late 1970s, recounted the story of Aboriginal children stolen and placed on church-run mission stations. Each was accompanied by a mimed enactment of the events described, by performers picked out by a spot. Once again, as the sequence ended, the performers moved upstage.

The next episode was a narration drawn from documentary sources on the contribution of Chinese women to Darwin's development, symbolised by Granny Lum Loy, who single-handedly established a mango plantation in the 1920s. A puppet distributed mango seeds and members of Corrugated Iron Youth Theatre 'grew' from the seeds into small trees, all accompanied by Chinese music. A Chinese dragon, made and carried through the procession by a group of Chinese students, entered through the audience accompanied by flashing lights, fireworks and percussionists on both sides of the stage.

As this group moved offstage, once again leaving the puppet upstage, the lighting picked out a narrator:

> And dimly seen, as if she is seen through smoke, the invisible woman ... if you look hard enough, you can **just** make her out:

> The Chinese woman, trouser-clad
> Migrant woman, soaping laundry
> Aboriginal woman, cleaning up after white woman ...
> White woman, cleaning up after white man.
> Down the hallways and across the plains of the past,
> she hangs the washing, cleans the house, cooks the meals
> endlessly, tirelessly, always, all care, no pay,
> all day, every day, day in, day out,
> thanked if she's lucky

Meanwhile the choir re-entered and began to hum the tune of Bruce Springsteen's 'Working Life' and the narrator extended the notion of women's work beyond the domestic to 'the office, the hospital, the school, the factory'. The choir then sang some rewritten lyrics to the song. Performers entered, again with a puppet, during a hummed reprise of the tune. They enacted an elaborate slow-motion mime of various work processes, initially in isolation, but increasingly drawing into unified action as the choir sang another song:

> Step by step the longest march
> Can be won, can be won
> Many stones to form an arch
> Singly none, singly none
>
> And by union what we will
> Can be accomplished still

> Drops of water turn a mill
> Singly none, singly none (Trad. US; Music by Peter Seeger,
>   1948)

After another burst of 'Strong With the Women' came a spectacular scene in which a huge model of Amy Johnson's biplane, operated by members of the Women Pilots' Association, swept through the audience and onto the stage in a re-enactment of her 1930 landing in Darwin. The penultimate sequence showed a number of migrant groups arriving, performed by members of Timorese, Maori, Chilean and Colombian cultural groups. A Timorese song modulated into another version of the central musical theme which underpinned a 'choreographed statement of arrival, solidarity and survival' before the performers wound their way offstage to make way for a finale with the entire cast.

The puppets swirled across the stage enacting 'turbulence', 'as in war or cyclone' until they were brought to ground. The lights dimmed, and the choir picked up the final version of 'Strong with the Women'. This was what Archer had envisaged six months previously when she called for 'something quite impressive to carry the main theme to its conclusion'. It drew the entire company into a finale and included individual segments of rap lyrics from the Aboriginal women, the migrant women and the union women. It closed with the chant from the march, now richly musically layered:

> RISE with the women
> MOVE with the women
> SING with the women
> STRONG with the women.
> STRONG!

Such a description cannot do justice to the impressiveness or complexity of the music and choreography, or to the beauty of the puppets and costumes, or the spectacle generated by so many women from so many different cultural backgrounds all on stage together. Nor can it offer more than a taste of the excitement and sense of achievement generated by the project. Some had been working towards the performance for over a year, arguing it through the NTTLC; planning the hiring of artsworkers; writing grant applications; negotiating with those who had resisted the idea; securing the involvement of unionists and other community groups; organising rehearsals and workshops; coping with the disaster of the rained out Frogs Hollow performance; re-negotiating the performance for an indoor venue;

fighting to get it funded; and generally holding a huge venture together. Others had been working on their individual sequences for up to six months, grabbing time out of busy lives to go to rehearsals or workshops; reorienting skills they barely knew they had and learning new ones; encouraging their friends to participate; and working as a team for a project. They probably had no idea of its size until they saw it come together in the final rehearsals. The project was not only a triumph of collaborative work, but *theirs*, and a vindication of the NTTLC's commitment to culture as a mode of social and political activism. It was a very difficult act to follow.

May Days Since 1990

The NTTLC has found it impossible to mount anything as large as *Strong with the Women* since. Funding has become tighter, and fashions in funding have changed. Banner projects fell out of favour some years ago. The Australia Council will no longer fund processions without a substantial co-contribution from state government arts funding agencies and local authorities, and in the Northern Territory neither of these will subsidise what they see as political propaganda. The collapse of the Art and Working Life program in 1996, and the failure of the national network of Trade Union Arts Officers to argue for the devolution of Australia Council funds to the ACTU, has placed an extraordinary pressure on the NTTLC, which has never had the funds to employ an Arts Officer even on a part-time basis. As the emphasis of Australia Council policy has shifted back to older criteria of 'artistic excellence' and 'artistic innovation', and away from the social criteria of value which underpinned community cultural development funding, grants have steadily decreased to the point where the NTTLC has given up applying.

The NTTLC has also been aware of the fact that the forms of performance they utilised in the first three years of the revitalised May Days could only be carried so far. As Barbara Pitman put it:

> you can push these things to a certain level and then after that ... it does get a bit repetitive, and if you can't build on last year, don't do it. And when you do something that is truly spectacular and really vast then it's hard to keep building on that. (interviewed by David Watt, Darwin, 3 May 1996)

Mark Crossin saw the heavily funded May Days as 'developmental projects' and had 'never envisaged that we would always be propped up by external sources', but that unions would start to commit resources to the event (interviewed by David Watt, Darwin, 18 July 1997). The large-scale performance has thus given way to different emphases in the 1990s, on events peripheral to the actual march, like visual arts and photographic exhibitions, and a year-round interest in cultural activity.

May Days now are characterised by a large and colourful procession, incorporating the banners and other material from previous projects enhanced by new material produced through voluntary workshops, and an evening in the park, with food and drink stalls, a few speeches and a concert showcasing local performers. Attendances have massively increased since the early 1980s, and include an extraordinary array of groups, from unions, Aboriginal and other ethnically-based community groups, agencies and organisations like Amnesty International and Community Aid Abroad, green groups, anti-uranium mining organisations, arts organisations, gay and lesbian groups to the prostitutes' collective, all carrying placards in support of their individual causes and united under the particular theme chosen by the NTTLC for each year. These have ranged from the predictable, 'Unity in Labour' in 1991, to a consistent focus on unity in diversity, 'Many Voices—One Cry' in 1992, 'Promoting Unity—Respecting Diversity' in 1993 (a rally which concentrated on Aboriginal concerns, and was preceded by a 'Preparing the Ground' ceremony conducted by thirty Aboriginal women from the Lajamanu Yawulua Group), 'Families That Work' in 1994, 'Working for Tolerance' in 1995, and 'Workers' Rights—Human Rights' in 1996. In 1997 the first negative theme for an anti-racist rally reflected the beginning of hard times for the union movement in Australia as the Howard Liberal government presided over a resurgence in racism and the implementation of anti-union legislation.

This self-conscious emphasis on cultural diversity reflects a multicultural community, but it also places the union movement at the centre of it, as a natural rallying point for groups which may not have felt as happy about the connection a decade earlier. The NTTLC has managed to refashion itself in the popular imagination through the May Day projects, with obvious advantages in terms of recruiting beyond the traditionally strong areas of unionisation. In addition, as Didge McDonald points out, 'unions in the Territory are a lot more amenable to arts activity' than was the case in earlier years (interviewed by David Watt, Darwin, 17 July 1997). Thus, while the May Days have been reduced to a march and a concert, arts projects are part of the repertoire of unions throughout the year. The legacy of the big events is best measured in these terms: connections between artsworkers, arts organisations and unionists have been consolidated, unions see cultural work as a natural part of their armoury, and the union movement is seen as a natural ally for a wide range of dissident community groups. Darwin's May Days are an exemplary indication of the ways in which cultural work can make connections with community groups on the edges of the movement, and thus assist in the formation of the 'coalitions of resistance' upon which political activism will rely in 'New Times'.

Conclusion

Gravediggers of the Second International

The case studies here are part of a larger movement which is so localised and diverse that it cannot be surveyed in any exhaustive manner. Nonetheless, our analysis leads us towards some tentative conclusions with wider implications. We investigate strategic ventures in three countries which emerged in the late 1960s and early 1970s, at a high point of the organised labour movement. They went through similar negotiations with a labour movement descending into crisis because of international changes in the relationship between labour and capital. They also faced a changing intellectual climate which was both a product of and a factor in that shifting relationship. These experiences not only shaped the sorts of theatre they generated, but placed their work as part of a larger political project.

The Rise and Fall of 'Working-Class Culture'

The changing nature of the relationship between capital and labour forced a theoretical analysis in the discipline of labour studies clearly seen in the two editions, a decade apart, of Bryan Palmer's *Working-Class Experience* (itself a product of the same intellectual current which produced the theatre work we study). Originally published in 1983, this book was intended as a dissident intervention in Canadian labour history, which Palmer then saw as exclusively concerned with the *institutional* formations of labour. In his 1983 Preface, Palmer pointed out that his work marked a conscious break 'from previous attempts to survey the history of Canadian workers in its insistence that *working-class life extends beyond labour organizations and labour politics*', and that it stressed 'the totality of working-class experience' (Palmer 1992: 30). 'Class' was his focus of attention, and 'culture' his means of engaging with the *'human sensuous activity'* that experience engendered. Palmer introduced his book with a citation from the 'Thesis on Feuerbach' in which Marx described the lack of engagement with such activity as the 'chief defect of all hitherto existing materialism' (Palmer 1992: 28).

Palmer's 1992 Preface which looks back at the 1970s movement of new labour historians is characterised by a concern with the 'ambiguous and ambivalent realm' of 'working-class culture' which 'fractured the historical profession' in Canada (Palmer 1992: 13–14). The enemies at the time were:

> those who demanded that history must be narratives built on the accumulation of unproblematic evidence, innocent of theoretical (often 'foreign') insights, above the suggestion of the political projects of the contemporary moment, usually anchored in a pragmatic acquiescence to the long-established relations of a respectable, reform-oriented questioning of power and inequality. (Palmer 1992: 14)

Stephen Garton describes a similar, but earlier, divide in Australian labour history, between a founding group which tended to equate 'the organised working class with the working class as a whole', and a newer group which followed British precedents in studying the 'history of work and working-class culture' (Garton 1994: 47). In both Britain and Australia, labour history moved towards the emerging discipline of social history, largely via the claim, perhaps most clearly expressed by British New Left historian E. P. Thompson in *The Making of the English Working Class*, that class was not just a social category but an *event*, something which:

> happens when some men, as a result of common experiences (inherited or shared), feel and articulate the identity of their interests as between themselves, and as against other men whose interests are different from (and usually opposed to) theirs. (Thompson 1968: 8–9)

The new emphasis on 'human sensuous experience' and thus on 'culture' is clearly connected to the search for 'working-class culture' in theatre work of the 1970s and 1980s. Similarly, the swing to 'people's histories' and the development of oral history methodologies are linked to the emergence of the regional documentary as a theatrical mode in the 1960s and 1970s. The strategic ventures we examine, like the regional documentaries, all wrestled with the notion of 'working-class culture' and mostly found it elusive or even illusory. The life experience of a white, anglo male working in manufacturing industry no longer defines working-class culture if it ever really did. Feminists, social historians or those concerned with race and ethnicity unsettled what had become a convenient fiction just as labour organisations were drawn away from it by their own changing demographic.

In his 1992 Preface, Palmer admits to seeing the term 'working-class culture', as 'something of a misnomer' from which he has 'backed away' ...

somewhat' (Palmer 1992: 20). Yet he is critical of a tendency to jettison the notion too easily:

> Historians who have pioneered new and rigorous conceptual understandings of working-class experience adapt to the fashionable, if cavalier and simplistic, contemporary repudiation of Marxism and so-called 'essentialism', gravitating to the celebration of discursive identities, proclaiming confidently the end of nation, class, and, seemingly, history itself. (Palmer 1992: 15)

This over-enthusiastic 'celebration of discursive identities' underlies Baz Kershaw's remark, which began our study, about the 'promiscuity' of the political, which has rendered 'political theatre' little more than 'an historical construct' (Kershaw 1997: 255). 'Identity politics', while usefully corresponding to the self-identifications which people actually make, has served to destabilise class as a category.

Nevertheless identity politics has permeated many of the Left's attempts to remake itself for 'New Times', although mostly through the radical students of the late 1960s and 1970s recruited to the Left rather than organised labour. Theirs, of course, was not a conventional class politics anyway, but emerged from a plethora of single-issue campaigns (racism, the Vietnam war, environmental issues, feminism) which *some* chose, eventually, to draw into the ambit of an older class politics by seeking alliances with the organised Left. Jonathan Rutherford shows a common British trajectory: 'My past was in that moment in the 1970s: the 'free school' movement, anti-nuclear politics, men's anti-sexism, anarchism, and later the cultural politics of punk' (Rutherford 1990: 13). It led him to the Communist Party of Great Britain in 1983 where he discovered a clash:

> Its commitment to alliances, and the growing influence of a Gramscian politics of hegemony, introduced me to the contradictory and often fraught relationship which the more thoughtful parts of the organised Left had with the politics of difference ... Western Marxism's emphasis on big pictures, and the practice of 'reading off' the objective relations of class forces, couldn't address these emerging antagonisms. In shifting the parameters of politics to include personal and private life ... [the new social movements] undermined the Left's narrow conception of equality and exposed Marxism's inability to account for this new politics of the subject. (Rutherford 1990: 14–15)

The logical outcome for some was to repudiate class altogether. Palmer complains that in addition to 'the structures that oppress and exploit them', 'workers have [also] been divided and fragmented ... by their own acts and identifications, which have often privileged locale, race, skill, or gender over and against class' (Palmer 1992: 18). Yet, he says, there remains the gap between 'the objective presence of class as a relationship to the means of production' and 'the rarely developed subjective realization of a class consciousness that reflects a fully grasped understanding of the necessity of working-class revolution and the creation of a society in which class exploitation is eliminated' (Palmer 1992: 22). Although they are few and far between, such moments of realisation are still available:

> For all the cultural inertia of the working class, however, its apparent fragmentation, acquiescence, and accommodation could change with the drop of a hat or, more precisely, the drop of a wage, the demise of a skill, or the restructuring of a job. In confrontations that turned on such developments, cultural experiences might resurface and be moved beyond the passivity of a way of life to articulate a rejection of acquisitive individualism or affirm class identity in demonstrations of mutuality and collective aspiration. (Palmer 1992: 21)

For others, Rutherford among them, such (re)discoveries of 'solidarity' will depend on conditional alliances with single-issue campaigns, like those among the support groups which coalesced around the miners' strike in Britain in 1984–5 (Rutherford 1990: 18–19). The drive towards social unionism within the union movements of Canada, Australia and Britain suggests that organised labour is suffering a lack of confidence in the efficacy of a working-class culture.

The ventures we describe have had a close engagement with the union movement, which both produced and reinforced this intellectual trajectory. They have sought contact with unions as the site of 'working-class culture' and hoped to find there a political radicalism which corresponded to their own developing senses of politics. They mostly discovered that union activity was less exciting and certainly less radical than their initial contact in an inflamed situation had suggested. It did not take long, for example, for Banner Theatre to find itself banned by the Iron and Steel Trades Confederation for supporting rank-and-file unionists in their fight to keep the Corby steelworks open, or for Melbourne Workers Theatre to find itself at odds with union hierarchies at Jolimont Railway Workshop. The solidarity with local union activists that often pitted them in conflict with union bureaucracies provided a fertile ground for engaged work, but also revealed the deeper investments of a reformist labour movement in the fundamental alignments of class and ownership in Western society.

Class in the 'Cultural Ecology'

As the Fordist accord, which had long sustained the trade union movement, fell into decline, and union demographics altered with the movement of industries, capital and people across national borders, the idea of a working-class culture waiting to be found became increasingly untenable. Yet theatreworkers engaging with the real struggle of labour started here, embracing the perceived manifestations of a class-based cultural heritage, like the British folk song revival, 1930s agitprop and documentary theatre, the social realism of the Popular Front, and labour movement ceremonials like May Day. This search, mandatory in Australia through the Art and Working Life policy, meant exhuming cultural forms which would, it was often assumed, strengthen the social formations and class relationships that produced them in the first place. This expressed an understanding of form as productive relationship rather than transhistorical artefact, but it was ultimately illusory and contradictory. The revival of historical forms was an important sentimental mobilisation but it could not reconstitute the relations of militancy and class consciousness the revivalists read into them, so it ran the risk of becoming little more than an exercise in nostalgia.

In fact, it soon became obvious that resurrecting historical forms took artists away from the lived cultural and political experience of their intended allies, particularly as the apparent class consciousness of the early 1970s turned out to be illusory by the 1980s. Worse still, the exhumed cultures, which often reflected the male ethos of 1920s and 1930s manufacturing industry, embodied a sexism, racism and class essentialism highly unattractive to the new constituencies of the union movement.

The revivals worked best in marginalised cultures where an anti-colonial tradition produced local ('folk') performance forms that still expressed cultural resistance: we can see this in the use of 'mummering' by the Mummers Troupe in Newfoundland, (Brookes 1988) or in 7:84's exploitation of the 'ceilidh' in the Scottish Highlands in *The Cheviot, the Stag and the Black, Black Oil* (McGrath 1974). The important discovery was not that 'working-class culture' owned particular forms, performance traditions and indeed performance relationships, but that the point of contact between class experience, cultural form and oppositional politics was in specificities and differences rather than universalising texts. This made it possible to break out of the impasse created by the reductive assumption that both high art and popular ('mass') culture merely reproduced dominant 'bourgeois' ideology, and to move beyond attempts to recuperate a mythical independent 'culture'.

The discovery of the local often came as much from internal politics, particularly around gender issues, as it did from the realities of union work. The cultural work of the early 1970s, which moved from agitprop to a dazzling variety of community pageants, promenade plays, outdoor processionals, local documentaries, giant puppets and eventually Augusto Boal's Theatre of the Oppressed methods, developed along with, and was deeply influenced by, the emergent politics of gender, sexuality and ethnicity. We can thus posit a fairly direct line from the repudiation of 'working-class culture' as a transhistorical repertoire of aesthetic forms to more productive understandings of people's self-identifications. This can be traced through increasingly localised and dialogic adjustments in forms and methodologies. As Dave Rogers pointed out, 'the crucial thing' was 'to listen to what people say' (Cited in Beale 1997). Close and continuing contact with workers revealed that, even in manufacturing industry, not everyone was a white anglo male.

At the same time, the new politics of difference threatened the funding base of ventures which defined themselves as class-based. Destabilised both by 'New Times' theorisations which undermined assumptions about an unproblematised working-class culture, and by the apparently imminent collapse of the Fordist accord which sustained this perspective, the new cultural pluralism rewrote class as just another 'community' in a proliferation of 'cultures'. In the arms-length funding model that has sustained professional theatre for the last half-century in Australia, Canada and Britain, difference politics has widened the pool of professional artists even as subsidy dropped drastically. Arts juries and funding bodies routinely consider issues of gender, ethnicity and 'culture' (which often substitutes for 'race') in providing grants. The pie grows smaller, but the arts councils congratulate themselves for widening the sphere of potential recipients— without dislodging their deeper canonical assumptions. Nevertheless, engagement with difference politics can work to secure subvention, because the arms-length model is obliged to 'prove' its impartiality and largesse, most clearly through its apparent embrace of multiculturalism.

Yet widening the pool of professional artists also increases the number who are refused grants. The familiar vagaries of 'excellence' are invoked to explain refusals, but the real reasons are economic. Arts council peer juries routinely discover that they have not been summoned to decide who deserves a grant, but to draw the line between the haves and the have-nots when the money runs out. The artist who defines political engagement through class has little chance of claiming space in the undefined realm of 'cultural democracy' as the term is (mis)understood by cultural policy makers.

Conversely, the partisans of identity politics can invoke 'strategic essentialism', demanding recognition of a particular difference which defines who 'we' are. That is why the labels of oppression—sexism, racism, homophobia—carry talismanic force: they escalate the stakes in the negotiation, appropriation and accommodation of difference politics. For cultural bureaucrats, culturally activist art 'proves' the existence of a community, and thus of an audience, and a market. A dollar to Shakespeare, a penny to a queer theatre, and liberal democracy fulfils its mission. The funding of art is not merely a matter of economics, but a means by which the state helps construct its own monuments.

Class destabilises this equation. Unlike difference politics, class politics argues inclusivity of experience rather than fragmentation. It is worth noting that although the notion of contemporary arts funding derives from the Second International's call to uplift the toiling masses, it was quickly used to contain class struggle in the subsuming evangelical mission of 'the Nation'. This is particularly apparent in the *fin-de-siecle* national theatre projects in England and France, where, as Loren Kruger has detailed, theatre came to function as an institution of ideological legitimation (Kruger 1992). In the postcolonial settler societies of Australia and Canada, the alliance of cultural policy and national discourse developed much later, and was given urgency by the apprehension of class conflict on the domestic front of the Cold War. The historic Royal Commission report recommending the founding of the Canada Council in 1951 cautioned that while the war secured military victory, it was now time to look after 'cultural defences' (*Royal Commission* 1951: 275). Systematic arts funding was instituted in the English-speaking democracies to combat the spectre of artists and intellectuals joining the ranks of the Left—as they had in the 1930s. In the rhetoric of national community, 'the glories of the garden' as the Arts Council of Great Britain famously put it, or the quest for a postcolonial 'true Canadianism' that impelled the Canada Council, explicit engagement with class politics was seen as divisive and worse, juvenile. Liberal democracy deployed the language of cultural democracy, and entered into a long and contentious accommodation with 'community' politics. The conflation of 'community' and 'nation' is sustainable only as long as class is either unmentioned, as it tends to be in Canada, or redefined as a cultural locus.

Class was mentioned in the Art and Working Life program in Australia which, as Gay Hawkins points out, was initially defined by its proponents in oppositional terms (Hawkins 1993: 97). It was a strategic attempt to use community arts rhetoric to unsettle the conflation of 'community' and 'nation'. Much of the recuperative work we have cited—most notably that of Burn and Kirby—happened with substantial support from a faction within the Australia Council as Council publications rather than arts projects. These Council pamphlets and occasional publications (of a historical or theoretical nature) exhorted unions to use the program for their own end, as in the following, for example:

> The continuing threat of rising unemployment, the fight to maintain real wage levels and the quality of working conditions, the defence of the industrial rights of working people, the indiscriminate introduction of new technology and its impact on jobs and the economy, the erosion of welfare levels and services ... these are issues absorbing the energies of trade unionists and the Art and Working Life program can and should contribute to those struggles. (*Caper 18*: 6)

The program was thus an inevitable focus of a Liberal-National Party Waste Watch Committee which accused it of funding political propaganda. This pressure contributed to a steady redefinition of the program and increasingly 'class' was rendered as another locus of 'community'. Difference politics took their toll on the program as 'class' was marginalised by the proliferation of 'communities' and 'cultures'. It became apparent that much funded under the program would have been eligible under the broader category of 'community'. By 1996 the program was removed from the books with barely a whimper from the nationwide network of trade union arts officers, some of them by then more concerned with issues of aesthetics than political instrumentality. While this is disappointing, more significant is the unions' reluctance in many cases to pursue the opportunities the program offered, either at the time or subsequently. The 1998 confrontation between the Maritime Union of Australia and the government could certainly have done with some Ground Zero–style media manipulation. But, with the honourable exception of Melbourne Workers Theatre's recently-formed Rapid Response Team of volunteer artsworkers, which has appeared at a number of union and other rallies and demonstrations, theatreworkers were nowhere to be seen.

The system of public subsidy in the arts always ultimately rests on the primacy of 'excellence' as a shifting term to signify whatever is needed. In the highly politicised world of arts funding, 'excellence' can mean the Royal Shakespeare Company, a rap artist in a community hall, or a community development project with a group of teenage delinquents. But no matter the differences, the real meaning of 'excellence' is almost inevitably that the work in question has a set of aesthetic values that can be identified and defended if necessary (as it was in the United States with Robert Mapplethorpe). To the cultural bureaucrat, class-based art provides no such digestible aesthetic theory. Attempts to theorise class aesthetics have either proved intellectually bankrupt (for example, socialist realism), or have been so historically specific that they cannot be translated.

If class-engaged art articulates struggle, and identifies the interests of the state with class oppression, it produces a condition that the cultural model of liberal democracy cannot accept—in theory, because it repudiates the fiction of the national community (richly diverse perhaps, but nonetheless united), and in practice because it locates cultural bureaucrats as part of the problem, when most see themselves as progressive, even radical, partisans in the cause of cultural freedom. Consequently, class-engaged work has no place in what the Canada Council (when it refused Ground Zero an operating grant for 1998) called the 'cultural ecology' of 'the community', awkwardly conflated with 'the nation'. This of course comes as no surprise; what may be surprising is that so many theatreworkers should have succumbed in the first place (however cautiously) to the cult of dependence on public funding and its promise of a life on the margins of 'the theatre profession' as constructed by the arts councils in Australia, Canada and Britain.

Many of these disenfranchised theatreworkers were already disillusioned about unions as agents of social change and custodians of working-class culture. But if single-issue politics exposed the crisis of class-based politics in the professional theatre, they also revealed political possibilities in the sphere of social unionism. We are left with a question which we hesitate to answer: can artsworkers carry on this work only by repudiating the narrative of professional theatre into which cultural politics briefly implicated them?

Strategies of Enactment

Two of the ventures we have examined have kept their distance from the professional theatre, and a third, the NTTLC's May Day, was never part of it. Melbourne Workers Theatre is our only example of a venture that used the idea of the theatre *company* as an ongoing ensemble of employed artists working together, and even this was quickly eroded by the exigencies of project-based funding. Melbourne Workers Theatre, like so many others (Banner and Ground Zero included), consists of a paid administrator and a nucleus of mostly unpaid 'members' who develop projects, obtain the funding and hire the project-specific artsworkers (which may include themselves) to carry it through. The company is now basically committed to performing plays for in-theatre venues, albeit alternative ones, for an audience established through workplace performance. It views itself as a maker of multicultural art for worker audiences, a less instrumentalist view than that of either Banner or Ground Zero. In Melbourne Workers Theatre's continuing enactment of lived multiculturalism, the representation and the process of making it are equally important political interventions. The venture's emphasis in performance on textuality and narrative is part of the process of *constructing*, at least on stage, an always strategic and contingent working-class culture, albeit more sophisticated now than in what Patricia Cornelius described as its 'workerite' beginnings.

In contrast Banner and Ground Zero are more explicitly instrumental. Banner Theatre has been an amateur venture for much of its long life, seeing performance as an extension of political activism, moving from picket line to full-blown performance and back again, substantially untrammelled by the pressure to conform to a model amenable to funding bodies. Ground Zero has sustained itself more like a small business, and developed the most eclectic modes of work of our case studies, from the strategic use of street performance as media opportunity ('streeters') to custom-made videos for internal use by union educators, to more conventional 'plays'.

Of particular interest to us in both cases has been how local engagements and discoveries were formalised into institutional structures. For both Banner and Ground Zero, political need and artistic possibility define the work, but the institutional solutions developed to realise it brought forth a corporate identity—'the company'—that changed their political relationships. To sustain the original mission in changing circumstances is invariably complex, the more so over time as new generations of artists who do not know the political conditions of its founding come on board. The 'company' in this way takes on a life of its own and becomes the site of its own political struggles and contestations.

The idea behind our use of the term 'strategic ventures' is to separate the actual process of political and artistic work from the notion of the 'company' as a supra-individual structure enforced by the realities of cultural policies. The Canada Council, for example, explicitly funds 'companies, not individuals', even though, as in the case of Ground Zero, the difference may only be a corporate seal. As a mechanism which facilitates the meetings of unions and theatreworkers, the company model has been at times an effective strategy. But as our case studies show, the strategic reliance on the company model is inherently unstable because the 'company' tends to consist of little more than a skeleton administration, and usually a loose alliance of volunteers who decide which strategic venture to take on next, negotiate the funding and recruit the workforce. The notion of a class-based 'company' has therefore never been a sustaining fact, but a fiction which is perhaps tacitly accepted by funders as well. Both Banner and Ground Zero have managed to move between constituencies, grasping opportunities for strategic interventions when they occur and funding them (mostly) through sources other than arts councils.

There are, of course, differences between the two ventures which reflect the distinct cultural and economic climates and histories of political engagement. Whereas Banner's history is firmly rooted in British working-class militant socialism, Ground Zero demonstrates the trajectory more common in Canada, where theatreworkers come to politics through the theatre itself, and mostly align with the social democratic centre of the New Democratic Party. Consequently, Ground Zero's field of possibilities and its performative eclecticism have been framed by its ability to negotiate with activist institutions in the organised social justice movement. Political geography also accounts for some of these differences: the higher density of population and the history of political struggle in the British industrial Midlands establishes a very different set of possibilities and tactics than in Alberta or rural Ontario. Banner can use its long-established union connections to attempt to link the likes of the Exodus Collective and Reclaim the Streets, on the one hand, and unions, or at least rank-and-file union activists, on the other. As single-issue radical activists move beyond anarchism and recognise the power of organisation and social mobilisation, Banner can draw them into dialogue with rank-and-file union activists. Through shows like *Sweat Shop* and *Criminal Justice*, the venture has attempted to construct a cross-generational alliance that fuses the militancy of a generation that grew up on folk songs with a new generation more at home with CD-ROMS. This has led to productions characterised by a broadness of sweep in which the show becomes a framework for a number of narratives loosely linked by a central thematic concern. The old Banner slide show extends to highly elaborate manipulations of digital images, and the folk song revival moves into a wide range of amplified musical styles in an attempt to reach new and different audiences and draw them into dialogue with an older militancy. Banner and Ground Zero both perceive their role as strictly *instrumentalist*—they construct implements for the use of their strategic partners.

Finally, and superficially most oddly in a book ostensibly on 'theatre', the Darwin May Day celebrations mark a more deliberately instrumentalist use of performance in the service of the labour movement than even Ground Zero or Banner. With artsworkers employed as consultants on the development and implementation of projects rather than generating them from inception, this work is closely controlled by the organised labour movement, which displays in this case a rare understanding of the political possibilities of cultural work. The NTTLC's exploration of the strategic importance of social unionism, a product of the pre-eminence of public sector, white-collar unions in a small, multicultural city, led to a series of projects and alliances developed through the liberating impulses of festivity and celebration. The re-occupation of public space and the affirmation of diversity re-enact a sense of solidarity, and demonstrate in the most visible manner the effectiveness of activist alliances.

Instrumentalist Performance and Opportunities for Dialogue

Taken together, these strategies of enactment and representation refute the false humanism of the Second Internationalist theory of cultural delivery, which assumed the pedagogic necessity of a bourgeois intelligentsia in educating and re-humanising the working class. As the gravediggers of the Second International, these ventures are all concerned to construct performance events *through* which their strategic partners speak rather than theatre where artists speak *to* the 'working class' or 'the people'. The clear instrumentality of the NTTLC's use of performance to enliven an old labour movement ceremonial and offer a point of alliance for a broad range of dissident groups is reflected in similar commitments in the work of Banner and Ground Zero. Even in the case of Melbourne Workers Theatre, an avowed case of making theatre for working-class audiences, this instrumentality is reflected in the attempt to construct a working-class culture as part of a larger political project through close consultative mechanisms, rather than the simple application of assumed class-specific forms.

This entails a commitment to *dialogue* as a central means of generating performances. From Ground Zero's contingent alliances with 'coalitions of resistance' to Banner's commitment to the primacy of 'actuality', and Melbourne Workers Theatre's recourse to the interview as the central source for dramatic narratives, these ventures are built on listening and transmuting what they hear into performances. At least as importantly, and most clearly in the Darwin May Days, performances are intended to provoke further dialogue, both between the strategic partners on particular projects as they are developed and within and around the performances themselves.

All four of the strategic ventures we have examined share Dave Rogers' 1992 perception of the 'disarray' of the 'old battalions of the working class', and his search for a new 'unifying politics to bring together the very different and separate strands and sites of struggle that characterise the 1990s' (Rogers 1992: 25–6). All have, to differing degrees and in different ways, embraced the politics of 'New Times', and become the site of connections between single-issue struggles and progressive elements of the union movement. There is a place for the labour movement in these 'New Times', but only if it aspires to a central position in this 'unifying politics', as it must. As Bryan Palmer has written:

> for all the capacity of these movements and causes to galvanize vocal world-wide protest, they lack the economic teeth to chew into those forces that profit from oppression, ecological devastation, and war-mongering. A real social unionism would indeed link up with these sectors, but it would rightly stress the extent to which only mobilizations led by the working class and backed by the working-class capacity to stop the productive forces of advanced capitalist society in their tracks have the actual power to transform social relations. (Palmer 1992: 372)

Our case studies suggest methods by which performance may now contribute to the work the unions need to do to re-establish themselves as a nodal point for political resistance.

On the basis of the evidence we have seen, ongoing alliances between the energy of single-issue campaigns and the organisational power of unions will entail three corresponding movements. Firstly, theatreworkers will need to move away from the fiction of the professional theatre and the patronising legacy of the Second International, a move emphatically made already by some, and which arts funding cutbacks have made for others. Secondly, there will need to be a corresponding resistance on the part of workers to an institutionalised labour movement that is more focused on protecting jobs and increasing wages in individual unions than on the larger issues that transcend particular union constituencies. Thirdly, single-issue groups will need to engage with unions and it will not be an easy dialogue, as environmentalists try to find common cause with loggers and miners, for example. The different consultative modes developed by the ventures studied here have had some success in consolidating the communities of interest with which they have chosen to work. Real political effectiveness will now depend on their strategic skills in creating opportunities for building alliances, and the organised labour movement's recognition of those skills. If there is a productive future for theatres in the labour movement, it will lie in the tactical use of the ability of theatreworkers to create sites for the necessary dialogues, either within the event of performance or through the processes of its generation.

Abbreviations

ACTU Australian Council of Trade Unions
AFA Alberta Foundation for the Arts (Canada)
APG Australian Performing Group
ARU Australian Railways Union
AWL Art and Working Life (Australia)
AWP Artists in the Workplace (Canada)
AWU Australian Workers' Union
BCCCS Birmingham Centre for Contemporary Cultural Studies (UK)
BLF Builders Labourers Federation (Australia)
CBC Canadian Broadcasting Corporation
CCDC Community Cultural Development Committee (Australia)
CEP Communication, Energy and Paperworkers (Canada)
CLC Canadian Labour Congress
CND Campaign for Nuclear Disarmament
CPSU Community and Public Sector Union (Australia)
CPTA Canadian Popular Theatre Alliance
CUPE Canadian Union of Public Employees
CUSC Combined Unions Shop Committee (Australia)
CUSO Canadian University Services Overseas
FMWU Federated Miscellaneous Workers' Union (Australia)
GZP Ground Zero Productions (Canada)
GZP Papers L.W. Conolly Theatre Archives, University of Guelph
ICU Intensive Care Unit (Canada)
ISTC Iron and Steel Trades Confederation (Canada)
IWW Industrial Workers of the World
MWT Melbourne Workers Theatre
NAWU North Australian Workers Union
NDP New Democratic Party (Canada)
NTTLC Northern Territory Trades and Labour Council (Australia)
NUM National Union of Mineworkers (UK)
NUR National Union of Railwaymen (UK)
OAC Ontario Arts Council (Canada)
OCHU Ontario Council of Hospital Unions (Canada)
OHA Ontario Hospitals Association (Canada)
PTT Popular Theatre Troupe (Australia)
ROSAC Retention of Steelmaking at Corby (UK)

SEQUEB South East Queensland Electricity Board (Australia)
SPSI Serikat Pekerja Seluruh Indonesia (All-Indonesian Workers Union)
TGWU Transport and General Workers' Union (UK)
TUC Trade Union Congress (UK)
UTLC United Trades and Labour Council (Australia)
WTM Workers' Theatre Movement

References

Ackers, Peter, Chris Smith and Paul Smith, eds. (1996) *The New Workplace and Trade Unionism: Critical Perspectives*, London: Routledge.

ACTU. (1987) *Future Strategies for the Trade Union Movement*, Melbourne: ACTU

ACTU/Trade Development Council. (1987) *Australia Reconstructed*, Canberra: Australian Government Publishing Service.

Alcorta, F.X. (1984) *Darwin Rebellion 1911–1919*, Darwin: Northern Territory University Planning Authority.

Allen, Douglas. (1980) 'Glasgow Workers Theatre Group and the Methodology of Theatre Studies', *Theatre Quarterly*, 8, 36: 45–54.

Archer, Robyn. (1989) 'Mayday 1990: Strong With the Women', Submission to NTTLC May Day Committee.

Aronowitz, Stanley. (1989) 'Working Class Culture in the Electronic Age', in Ian Angus and Sut Jhally, eds, *Cultural Politics in America*, New York: Routledge: 135–150.

ARU Gazette. (1991) [Australian Railway Union] March.

Bacon, Nick and John Storey. (1996) 'Individualism and Collectivism and the Changing Role of Trade Unions' in Peter Ackers, Chris Smith and Paul Smith, eds. *The New Workplace and Trade Unionism: Critical Perspectives*, London: Routledge: 41–76.

Banner Theatre. (1974) *Collier Laddie* typescript, Banner Theatre files.

—— (1976) *The Saltley Gate Show*, typescript, Banner Theatre files.

—— (1980) *Steel*, By Fran Rifkin and Pete Yates, typescript, Banner Theatre files.

—— (1994) *Sweat Shop*, by Dave Rogers, typescript, Banner Theatre files.

—— (1995) *Criminal Justice*, by Stuart Brown, typescript, Banner Theatre files.

Barker, Clive. (1961) Letter to trades unions, 30 August 1961, Charles Parker Archives, Birmingham Central Reference Library, CPA/1/8/7/1.

—— (1992) 'Alternative Theatre/Political Theatre', in Graham Holderness, ed., *The Politics of Theatre and Drama*, London: Macmillan, 18–43.

Barrie, Shirley. (1991) Preface to *Straight Stitching*, in Alan Filewod, ed., *New Canadian Drama 5: Political Dramatists*, Ottawa: Borealis Press

Beale, Sam. (1997) 'Raising the Banner', in *Squall*, Autumn.

Bessai, Diane. (1992) *Playwrights of Collective Creation*, Toronto: Simon & Pierre.

Boal, Augusto (1979) *Theater of the Oppressed*, London: Pluto Press.

—— (1992) *Games for Actors and Non-Actors*, London: Routledge.

—— (1995) *The Rainbow of Desire: The Boal Method of Theatre and Therapy*, London: Routledge.

Booth, Karen. (1987) 'Putting political theatre back on the tracks', *Melbourne Times*, 27 May.

Bouzek, Don and Loree Lawrence. (1990). 'The Ground Zero Model.' *Canadian Theatre Review* 63: 5–9.

—— (1984). *Waves.* Unpublished typescript. GZP Papers.

—— (1986) Letter to Department of National Revenue, 7 May. GZP Papers.

—— (1996.1) Interview with Scott Duchesne, Toronto, June. GZP Papers.

—— (1996.2) Letter to Caroline Lulham, 17 November. GZP Papers.

—— (1999.1). 'Industrials for the Social Services', *Canadian Theatre Review* 99: 10–15.

—— (1999.2) 'Rag, Tag and Bobtail', *Canadian Theatre Review* 99: 55–81.

Bovell, Andrew. (1987) *State of Defence* typescript, MWT files.

—— (1990) *The Ballad of Lois Ryan*, in *Australasian Drama Studies* 17: 85–116.

Bowdler, Rhoma. (1975) Interview, *The Miner*, October/November, 5.

Bradby, D. and J. McCormick. (1978) *People's Theatre*, London: Croom Helm.

Braun, Edward. (1979) *The Theatre of Meyerhold*, London: Methuen.

—— (1982) *The Director and the Stage*, London: Methuen.

——, ed. (1969) *Meyerhold on Theatre*, London: Methuen.

Brenton, Howard. (1975) 'Petrol Bombs Through the Proscenium Arch: Interviewed by Catherine Itzin and Simon Trussler', *Theatre Quarterly*, 5, 17: 4–20.

Bridson, D.G. (1971) *Prospero and Ariel: The Rise and Fall of Radio: A Personal Recollection*, London: Victor Gollancz Ltd.

Brookes, Chris. (1974) 'Useful Theatre in Sally's Cove', *This Magazine* 8, 2: 3–7.

—— (1988) *A Public Nuisance: A History of the Mummers Troupe*, St John's: ISER.

Burke, Peter. (1979) *Popular Culture in Early Modern Europe*, Sydney: New South Wales University Press.

Burn, Ian and Sandy Kirby. (1985) 'Historical Sketch', in *Working Art: A Survey of Art in the Australian Labour Movement in the 1980s*, Sydney: Art Gallery of New South Wales: 54–95.

Burn, Ian. (1982) 'ACTU National Conference: Art & Working Life', *Art Network* 5: 38.

Burvill, Tom. (1986) 'Sidetrack: Discovering the Theatricality of Community', *New Theatre Quarterly*, 2, 5: 80–89.

—— (1998) 'Playing the Fault Lines: Two Political Theater Interventions in the Australian Bicentenary Year 1988', in Jeanne Colleran and Jenny S. Spencer, eds., *Staging Resistance: Essays on Political Theater*, Ann Arbor: University of Michigan Press: 229–246.

Cameron, Neil. (1993) *Fire on the Water*, Sydney: Currency Press.

Canada. (1951) Royal Commission on National Development in the Arts, Letters and Sciences, 1949–1951. *Report*, Ottawa: King's Printer.

Capelin, Steve, ed. (1995) *Challenging the Centre: Two Decades of Political Theatre*, Brisbane: Playlab Press.

Caper 5. (1980) *The Arts at the Workplace*, Sydney: Community Arts Board of the Australia Council.

Caper 13. (1981) *Art & Working Life: A Survey of Cultural Work Produced By and For the Trade Union Movement*, Sydney: Community Arts Board of the Australia Council and the Australian Council of Trade Unions.

Caper 18. (1983) *Art & Working Life: Cultural Activities in the Australian Trade Union Movement 1983*, Sydney: Community Arts Board of the Australia Council and the Australian Council of Trade Unions.

Caper 19. (1983) *Working Class, Working Culture: The Workers' Cultural Action Committee of Newcastle*, Sydney: Community Arts Board of the Australia Council and the Workers' Cultural Action Committee of Newcastle Trades Hall Council.

Caper 23. (1984) *Loco: A Play By Sidetrack Theatre*, Sydney: Community Arts Board of the Australia Council.

Chambers, Colin. (1989) *The Story of Unity Theatre*, New York: St. Martin's Press.

Chance, Ian. (1989) 'The Northern Territory', *Lowdown*, April: 11–32

Cheeseman, Peter. (1970) *The Knotty*, London: Methuen.

Chesterman, Colleen. (1990) 'Robyn Archer Talks About Women's May Day in Darwin', *refractory girl*, No. 37: 45.

Clarke, John, Chas Critcher and Richard Johnson, eds. (1979) *Working-Class Culture: Studies in history and theory*, London: Hutchinson.

Condé, Carole and Karl Beveridge. (1990) *Class Work*, Toronto: Communication and Electrical Workers of Canada.

—— (1998) *Political Landscapes*, Toronto: Gallery TPW [Toronto Photographers Workshop].

Coppieters, Frank (1975) 'Arnold Wesker's Centre Fortytwo: A Cultural Revolution Betrayed', *Theatre Quarterly*, 5, 18: 37–54.

Cornelius, Patricia. (1993) *Last Drinks*, typescript. MWT Files.

—— (1987) *Dusting Our Knees*, typescript. MWT Files.

Coult, Tony and Baz Kershaw, eds. (1990) *Engineers of the Imagination: The Welfare State Handbook*, London: Methuen.

Crick, Michael. (1985) *Scargill and the Miners*, Harmondsworth: Penguin.

Crowley, Frank. (1986) *Tough Times: Australia in the Seventies*, Richmond: William Heinemann.

Crummy, Helen (1992) *Let the People Sing! A Story of Craigmillar*, Newcraighall: Helen Crummy.

Cumberlidge, Claude. (1987) (Secretary, Waterfront Workers' Federation), Letter to Victorian Minister of Transport, 11 August. MWT Files.

Dare: 1997 (1997) *National Community Cultural Development Conference: Transcripts*, Sydney: Australia Council.

Davies, Andrew. (1987) *Other Theatres: The Development of Alternative and Experimental Theatre in Britain*, London: Macmillan.

Davies, Cecil W. (1977) *Theatre for the People: The Story of the Volksbuhne*, Austin: University of Texas Press.

—— (1980) 'Working-Class Theatre in the Weimar Republic, 1919–1933: Part I', *Theatre Quarterly*, 10, 38: 68–96.

Davis, Julie. (1994) 'Our Own Stories', *Our Times* 13, 4 (Oct/Nov): 15

DiCenzo, Maria. (1996) *The Politics of Alternative Theatre in Britain, 1968–1990: The Case of 7:84 (Scotland)*, Cambridge: Cambridge University Press.

Ellis, Rod. (1990) In *May Day Magazine*, Darwin: NTTLC.

Endres, Robin and Richard Wright. (1976) *Eight Men Speak and Other Plays from the Canadian Workers Theatre*, Toronto: New Hogtown Press.

Ermolaev, Herman. (1977) *Soviet Literary Theories 1917–1934: The Genesis of Socialist Realism*, New York: Octagon Books.

Evans, Gary. (1991) *In the National Interest: A Chronicle of the National Film Board of Canada from 1949 to 1989*, Toronto: University of Toronto Press.

Evatt Foundation. (1995) *Unions 2001: A Blueprint for Trade Union Activism*, Sydney: Evatt Foundation.

Ewer, P, W. Higgins and A. Stevens. (1987) *Unions and the Future of Australian Manufacturing*, Sydney: Allen & Unwin.

Farrell, Frank. (1981) *International Socialism and Australian Labour: The Left in Australia*, Sydney: Hale & Ironmonger.

Ferris, Paul. (1972) *The New Militants: Crisis in the Trade Unions*, Harmondsworth: Penguin.

Filewod, Alan. (1987) *Collective Encounters: Documentary Theatre in English Canada*, Toronto: University of Toronto Press.

—— (1992) 'The Canadian Popular Theatre Alliance: A Potted History', *CPTA Newsletter*.

—— (1998) 'The Mummers Troupe, the Canada Council, and the Production of Theatre History', *Theatre Research in Canada* 19, 1: 3–34.

Fisher, Trevor. (1986) *Charles Parker: Aspects of a Pioneer*, Birmingham: Charles Parker Archive.

Fotheringham, Richard, ed. (1987) *Community Theatre in Australia*, Sydney: Currency Press.

Fox, Len (1966) *The History of May Day in Australia*, Sydney: Sydney May Day Committee.

Freeman, Jane. (1989) 'Disconcerting opening night', *Melbourne Times*, 11 October.

Freire, Paulo. (1972) *Pedagogy of the Oppressed*, Harmondsworth: Penguin, trans. Myra Bergma Ramos

Garrity, Paddy (1991) 'Report on Darwin May Day Celebrations 1991', unpublished paper held by NTTLC.

Garton, Stephen. (1994) 'What Have We Done? Labour History, Social History, Cultural History', in Terry Irving, ed., *Challenges to Labour History*, Sydney: University of New South Wales Press: 42–62.

Gauntlett, Mark. (1993) 'Funding "Australia"', *Canadian Theatre Review*, No. 74: 12–17.

Goddard, H. and L. Layman. (1988) *Organise*, Perth: Trades and Labour Council.

Goldstein, Malcolm. (1974) *The Political Stage: American Drama and Theatre of the Great Depression*, New York: Oxford University Press.

Goorney, Howard and Ewan MacColl, eds.(1986) *Agitprop to Theatre Workshop*, Manchester: Manchester University Press.

Goorney, Howard. (1981) *The Theatre Workshop Story*, London: Methuen.

GZP. (1990) *Where's the Care?* videotape. GZP Papers.

—— (1991) *The Business of Health*. Prompt script print-out. GZP Papers.

—— (AFA 1998) 'Artistic Director's Letter.' Alberta Foundation for the Arts application. GZP Papers.

—— (AWP 1990) OCHU/ Ontario Arts Council 'Artists and the Workplace' application. GZP Papers.

—— (Care 1990). *Where's the Care?* production typescript. GZP Papers.

—— (CC 1992) 'Artistic Director's Letter.' Canada Council application. GZP Papers.

—— (OAC 1994) 'Artistic Director's Letter.' Ontario Arts Council application. GZP Papers.

—— (CC 1997) 'Administrator's Letter', Canada Council application. GZP Papers.

—— (OAC 1998) 'Artistic Director's Letter.' Ontario Arts Council application. GZP Papers.

—— (CC 1999) 'Artistic Director's Letter.' Canada Council application. GZP Papers.

—— (CUPE, n.d.) 'CUPE/Hospital Workers Popular Theatre Project.' Typescript draft. GZP Papers.

—— (Diary, n.d.) Personal research diary, Don Bouzek. GZP Papers.

—— (Forum, n.d.) 'Cultural Workers Community Forum, Draft #1.' Typescript. GZP Papers.

—— (OAC 1993) 'Popular Theatre Workers Retreat: Statement of Principles'. [Included in 1993 Ontario Arts Council application] GZP Papers.

—— (OAC 1995) 'Artistic Director's Letter.' Ontario Arts Council application. GZP Papers.

—— (OCHU 1991.1), 'OCHU Bargaining Tour' communication package. GZP Papers.

—— (OCHU 1991.2) Peterborough focus group transcript. GZP Papers.

Hall, Stuart and Martin Jacques, eds. (1988) *New Times: The Changing Face of Politics in the 1990s*, London: Lawrence & Wishart.

Hall, Stuart. (1988) 'The Meaning of New Times', in Stuart Hall and Martin Jacques, eds., *New Times: The Changing Face of Politics in the 1990s*, London: Lawrence & Wishart, 116–134.

Hammersley, Martyn and Atkinson, Paul. (1995) *Ethnography: Principles in Practice* (Second edition), London: Routledge.

Harrison, Gillian (1989) 'Report to NTTLC May Day Committee', unpublished paper held by NTTLC.

Hawkins, Gay. (1993) *From Nimbin to Mardi Gras: Constructing Community Arts*, Sydney: Allen & Unwin.

Herbert, Kate. (1992) 'Retrenchment blues lack strong punch' *Melbourne Times*, 9 September.

Hewison, Robert. (1986) *Too Much: Art and Society in the Sixties 1960–1975*, London: Methuen.

Hillel, Angela. (1986) *Against the Stream—New Theatre in Melbourne 1936–1986*, Melbourne: New Theatre

Hobsbawm, E.J. (1964) *Labouring Men: Studies in the History of Labour*, New York: Basic Books.

—— (1983) 'Mass-Producing Traditions: Europe, 1870–1914', in E. J. Hobsbawm and T. Ranger, eds., *The Invention of Tradition*, Cambridge: Cambridge University Press: 263–307.

Hodge, Dino. (1993) *Did You Meet Any Malagas? A Homosexual History of Australia's Tropical Capital*, Darwin: Little Gem Publications.

Hoggart, Richard. (1958) *The Uses of Literacy*, Harmondsworth: Penguin.

Hudson, Roger. (1971) 'Towards A Definition of People's Theatre', *Theatre Quarterly* 1, 4: 2, 100–101

Hyman, Colette A. (1997) *Staging Strikes: Workers' Theatre and the American Labor Movement*, Philadelpia: Temple University Press.

Ingleton, Sally (director). (1989) *May Day*, video documentary in the series *What Do You Really Do For a Job?*, Sydney: SBS Television.

Itzin, Catherine. (1980) *Stages in the Revolution: Political Theatre in Britain Since 1968*, Methuen: London.

James, Barbara. (1989) *No Man's Land: Women of the Northern Territory*, Sydney: Collins.

James, Bob and Len Fox. (1989) 'May Day in Australia', in Andrea Panaccione, ed., *The Memory of May Day: An Iconographic History of the Origins and Implanting of a Workers' Holiday*, Venezia: Marsilio Editori: 753–4.

James, Robert. (1993) *Carnival, Discipline and Labour History: An Historiographic Study of the Meaning of Eight Hour Day, May Day and Other Labour Demonstrations in the Hunter River District, 1860–1940*, Unpublished PhD, University of Newcastle, Australia.

Jellicoe, Ann. (1987) *Community Plays: How to Put Them On*, London: Methuen.

Karpf, Anne. (1980) 'Charles Parker and the Radio Ballad', *Radio Month*, 2, 5: 14–15.

Kelly, Owen. (1984) *Community, Art and the State: Storming the Citadels*, London: Comedia.

Kershaw, Baz. (1992) *The Politics of Performance: Political Theatre as Cultural Intervention*, Routledge: London.

—— (1997) 'Fighting in the Streets: Dramaturgies of Popular Protest, 1968–1989', *New Theatre Quarterly*, 13, 51: 255–276.

Kidd, Ross, and Nat Colletta, eds. (1981) *Tradition for Development: Indigenous Structures and Folk Media in Non-Formal Education*, Berlin: German Foundation for International Education and International Council for Adult Education.

Kidd, Ross. (1979) 'Liberation or Domestication: Popular Theatre and Non-formal Education in Africa', *Educational Broadcasting International*, 12, 1: 3–9.

—— (1984) *From People's Theatre for Revolution to Popular Theatre for Reconstruction: Diary of a Zimbabwean Workshop*, The Hague: CESO.

—— (1985) '"Theatre for Development": Diary of a Zimbabwe Workshop', *New Theatre Quarterly*, 1, 2: 179–204.

Kirby, Sandy, ed. (1996) *Ian Burn, Art: Critical, Political*, Nepean: University of Western Sydney.

Kirby, Sandy. (1991.1) 'An Historical Perspective on the Community Arts Movement', in V. Binns, ed., *Community and the Arts*, Leichhardt: Pluto Press: 19–30.

—— (1991.2) *Artists and Unions: A Critical Tradition*, Sydney: Australia Council.

Knowles, Richard Paul. (1992) 'Sources of Interest: Some Partial Histories of

Mulgrave Road: Groping Towards a Method', *Theatre Research in Canada*, 13, 1 & 2: 107–119.

Kolakowski, Leszek. (1978) *Main Currents of Marxism*, vol. 2, trans by. P.S. Falla, Oxford: Clarendon

Koorier. (1990) 'Koories and Work – a Play', June.

Kruger, Loren. (1992) *The National Stage: Theatre and Cultural Legitimation in England, France, and America*, Chicago: University of Chicago Press.

Laxer, James. (1997) *In Search of A New Left: Canadian Politics after the Neoconservative Assault*, Toronto: Penguin.

—— (1998) *The Undeclared War: Class Conflict in the Age of Cyber Capitalism* Toronto: Viking Press.

Leach, Robert and Roy Palmer, eds. (1978) *Folk Music in Schools*, Cambridge: Cambridge University Press

Leach, Robert. (1975.1) *How to Make a Documentary Play*, Glasgow: Blackie and Son.

—— (1975.2) *The Wellesbourne Tree: A Musical Documentary Play*, Glasgow: Blackie and Son.

—— (1989) *Vsevolod Meyerhold*, Cambridge: Cambridge University Press.

—— (1994) *Revolutionary Theatre*, London: Routledge.

Lesnick, Henry, ed. (1973) *Guerilla Street Theater*, New York: Avon.

Levine, Ira. (1985) *Left-Wing Dramatic Theory in the American Theatre*, Ann Arbor: UMI Press.

Littlewood, Joan. (1995) *Joan's Book*, London: Minerva.

Lloyd, A.L. (1969) *Folk Song in England*, London: Panther.

Lockwood, Douglas. (1968) *The Front Door: Darwin 1869–1969*, Adelaide: Rigby.

Lunn, Eugene. (1982) *Marxism and Modernism*, Berkeley: University of California Press.

Lyne, Allen. (1987) 'Art and Working Life – Bourgeois Theatre in Overalls?' in R. Fotheringham, ed., *Community Theatre in Australia*, Sydney: Currency Press: 47–52.

MacColl, Ewan. (1973) 'Grass Roots of Theatre Workshop', *Theatre Quarterly*, 3, 9: 58–68.

—— (1985) 'Theatre of Action, Manchester', in Raphael Samuel, Ewan MacColl, and Stuart Cosgrove, eds., *Theatres of the Left 1880–1935: Workers' Theatre Movements in Britain and America*, London: Routledge & Kegan Paul: 205–255.

—— (1986) 'Introduction: The Evolution of a Revolutionary Theatre Style', in Howard Goorney and Ewan MacColl, eds., *Agitprop to Theatre Workshop*, Manchester: Manchester University Press: ix–lvii.

—— (1990) *Journeyman*, London: Sidgwick and Jackson.

Macintyre, Stuart. (1998) *The Reds*, Sydney: Allen & Unwin.

MacKinnon, Niall. (1994) *The British Folk Scene: Musical Performance and Social Identity*, Buckingham: Open University Press.

Mackney, Paul. (1987) *Birmingham and the Miners' Strike: The Story of a Solidarity Movement*, Birmingham: Birmingham Trades Union Council.

Marsh, Arthur. (1980) *Trade Union Handbook: A Guide and Directory to the Structure, Membership, Policy and Personnel of the British Trade Unions*, Westmead: Gower.

Marsh, David (1992) *The New Politics of British Trade Unionism*, London: Macmillan.

Marsh, P.C. (1987) (Secretary, Victorian Trades Hall Council), letter to MWT, 1 May.

Martin, D'Arcy. (1994) 'When Artists Meet Unions', *Our Times* 13, 4: 21.

—— (1995) *Thinking Union: Activism and Education in Canada's Labour Movement*, Toronto: Between The Lines.

Marwick, Arthur. (1996) *British Society Since 1945*, Harmondsworth: Penguin.

Mason, Sally (producer). (1990) *Women Today*, Darwin: Office of Women's Affairs, Chief Minister's Office, Territory Television Productions.

McCaughey, James. (1987) 'Dusting Our Knees', *New Theatre: Australia*, 6.

McGrath, John. (1974) *The Cheviot, the Stag and the Black, Black Oil*, London: Eyre Methuen.

—— (1981) *A Good Night Out*, London: Eyre Methuen.

McKay, George. (1996) *Senseless Acts of Beauty: Cultures of Resistance Since the Sixties*, London: Verso.

Mewett, Peter. (1988) 'Darwin's "Beercan Regatta": Masculinity, frontier and festival in North Australia', *Social Analysis*, 23: 3–37.

Mills, Deborah. (1986) 'An Evaluation of the Australia Council's Art and Working Life Program', June [ts].

Muir, Kathie. (1986) 'Art and Working Life', draft report to UTLC of South Australia.

Murray, Robin. (1989) 'Fordism and Post-Fordism', in Stuart Hall and Martin Jacques, eds., *New Times: The Changing Face of Politics in the 1990s*, London: Lawrence & Wishart: 38–53.

MWT. (1989.1) *Bulletin no. 6*. MWT Files.

—— (1989.2) 'Who We Are, What We Do', information leaflet, 27 July. MWT Files.

—— (1990) *Theatre From the Shop Floor* (publicity pamphlet) MWT Files.

—— (1992.1) Press Release, September. MWT Files.

—— (1992.2) 'Schedule of Projects.' MWT Files.

—— (1992.3) Union Support Group minutes, 12 August. MWT Files.

—— (1992.4) Union Liaison Worker Report. MWT Files.

—— (1992.5) *Annual Report* . MWT Files.

—— (1993) *Annual Report.* MWT Files.

Nugent, Ann. 'Drama on the factory floor, *Canberra Times,* 8 October.

Ontario Hospital Association. (1990) 'Results of OHA's Survey On Impact Of 1990/91 Hospital Funding Allocations.' (Unpublished report) GZP Papers.

Paget, Derek. (1987) 'Verbatim Theatre: Oral History and the Documentary Method', *New Theatre Quarterly,* 3, 12: 317–336.

—— (1990.1) '"Oh What a Lovely War": The Texts and Their Context', *New Theatre Quarterly,* 6, 23: 244–260.

—— (1990.2) *True Stories? Documentary Drama on Radio, Screen and Stage,* Manchester: Manchester University Press.

—— (1995) 'Theatre Workshop, Moussinac, and the European Connection', *New Theatre Quarterly,* 11, 43: 211–224.

Palmer, Bryan. (1992) *Working Class Experience: Rethinking the History of Canadian Labour 1800–1991,* Toronto: McClelland and Stewart.

—— (1994) *Goodyear Invades the Backcountry: The Corporate Takeover of a Rural Town,* New York: Monthly Review Press.

Palmer, Roy, ed. (1971) *Room for Company – Folk Songs and Ballads,* Cambridge: Cambridge University Press.

—— ed. (1972) *Songs of the Midlands,* Wakefield: EP Publishing.

—— ed. (1973) *The Painful Plough,* Cambridge: Cambridge University Press.

—— ed.(1974.1) *Poverty Knock,* Cambridge: Cambridge University Press.

Palmer, Roy. (1974.2) *A Touch on the Times,* Harmondsworth: Penguin.

Panaccione, Andrea (ed.). (1989) *The Memory of May Day: An Iconographic History of the Origins and Implanting of a Workers' Holiday,* Venezia: Marsilio Editori.

Parker, Charles. (1961) Letter to Clive Barker, 12 September, Charles Parker Archives, Birmingham Central Reference Library, CPA/1/8/7/1.

—— (1963) Letter to F. W. Skinner, Halifax Council of Social Service, 26 July, Charles Parker Archives, Birmingham Central Reference Library, CPA/1/8/8/2.

—— (1972) 'The Radio Ballad', unpublished article held in the Charles Parker Archive, Birmingham Central Reference Library, CPA/1/2/7/2.

—— (1974) *New Statesman,* October

—— (n. d.) Unpublished notes on *The Battle of Saltley Gate,* Banner archives, Box 6, Birmingham Central Reference Library.

Peetz, David. (1998) *Unions in a Contrary World: The Future of the Australian Trade Union Movement,* Cambridge: Cambridge University Press.

Perrot, Michelle. (1984) 'The First of May in France, the birth of a working-class ritual', in P. Thane, G. Crossick and R. Floud, eds., *The Power of the Past*, Cambridge: Cambridge University Press: 143–171.

Pettiona, Greg. (1987) (Course director, Hospital Employees Federation No. 1 course, 15–19 June 1987), to MWT. n.d. MWT Files.

Pilkington, Doody Scott. (1992) Letter to the editor, *The Sentinel*, 8 June.

Piscator, Erwin. (1978) *The Political Theatre*, New York: Avon, trans. Hugh Rorrison.

Powell, Alan. (1996) *Far Country: A Short History of the Northern Territory*, Melbourne: Melbourne University Press.

Radic, Leonard. (1992) 'Sexploitation and angst in the skin trade', *The Age*, 14 May.

Reeves, Andrew. (1988) *Another Day Another Dollar: Working Lives in Australian History*, Carlton: McCulloch Publishing.

Reid, Mary Anne. (1997) *Not a Puppet: Stories From the Frontier of Community Development*, Sydney: Australia Council

Reynolds, Vicki. (1995) *Daily Grind*, in *Australasian Drama Studies*, 26: 101–140

Rifkin, Jeremy. (1996) *The End of Work: The Decline of the Global Labor Force and the Dawn of the Post-Market Era*, New York: G. B. Putnam's Sons.

Rogers, Dave. (1991) 'Ewan MacColl – End of an Era?' *Political Song News*, 11: 4–6.

—— (1992) 'Banner Theatre', *Theatre Ireland*, 28: 21.

Rowse, Tim. (1985) *Arguing the Arts*, Ringwood: Penguin.

Russell, Robert. (1988) *Russian Drama of the Revolutionary Period*, New York: Macmillan.

Rutherford, Jonathan. (1990) 'A Place Called Home: Identity and the Cultural Politics of Difference', in Jonathan Rutherford, ed., *Identity: Community, Culture, Difference*, London: Lawrence & Wishart: 9–27.

Sager, Eric. (1993) *Discovering Darwin: The 1930s in Memory and History*, Darwin: Historical Society of the Northern Territory.

Sainer, Arthur. (1975) *The Radical Theatre Notebook*, New York: Avon.

Salverson, Julie, *et al.* (1998) 'Popular Theatre Workers Retreat. Peterborough 1992 – The Hi-Lites.' *CPTA News* (Summer): 1–2.

Samuel, Raphael, Ewan MacColl and Stuart Cosgrove, eds. (1985) *Theatres of the Left 1880–1935: Workers' Theatre Movements in Britain and America*, London: Routledge and Kegan Paul.

Sansom, Basil. (1980) *The Camp at Wallaby Creek: Aboriginal fringe dwellers in Darwin*, Canberra: Australian Institute of Aboriginal Studies.

Saville, John. (1988) *The Labour Movement in Britain*, London: Faber and Faber.

Scannell, Paddy. (1986) '"The Stuff of Radio": Developments in Radio Features and Documentary Before the War' in John Corner, ed., *Documentary and the Mass Media*, London: Edward Arnold: 1–26.

Schechner, Richard. (1992) 'Invasions Friendly and Unfriendly: The Dramaturgy of Direct Theater', in Janelle G. Reinelt and Joseph R. Roach, eds, *Critical Theory and Performance*, Ann Arbor: University of Michigan Press: 88–106.

Schulz, Katheryne. (1994) 'Labours of Love: Carole Condé & Mayworks 10th Birthday', *Our Times* 13, 4: 26.

Schutzman, Mady and Jan Cohen-Cruz, eds. (1994) *Playing Boal: Theatre, Therapy, Activism*, London: Routledge.

Scott-Norman, Fiona. (1992) *InPress*, Melbourne: 201, 27 May.

Seyd, Richard. (1975) 'The Theatre of Red Ladder', *New Edinburgh Review* 30: 36–42.

Seymour, Anna. (1996) 'Culture and Political Change: British Radical Theatre in Recent History', *Theatre Research International*, 21, 1: 8–16.

Shevtsova, Maria. (1995) 'Other cultures, other classes: Patricia Cornelius on writing for the Melbourne Workers Theatre', *Australasian Drama Studies* 26: 141–152.

Simpson, J.A., ed. (1978) *Socio-cultural Animation*: Strasbourg: Council of Europe

Sinfield, Alan. (1989) *Literature, Politics and Culture in Postwar Britain*, Oxford: Basil Blackwell.

Spunner, Suzanne. (1989) Review for Australian Broadcasting Commission, transcript held by NTTLC.

Stephen, Ann and Andrew Reeves. (1985) *Badges of Labour Banners of pride: Aspects of Working Class Celebration*, Sydney: Museum of Applied Arts and Sciences and Allen & Unwin.

Stourac, Richard and Kathleen McCreery. (1986) *Theatre as a Weapon: Workers' Theatre in the Soviet Union, Germany and Britain, 1917–1934*, London: Routledge and Kegan Paul.

Strong with the Women. (1990) Prompt copy held by Janet Crews, NTTLC, Darwin.

Sutton, Pollyanna. (1987) 'Theatre on factory floors', *The Good Times*, 22 January.

Taylor, John. (1991) *Immigration and Its Labour Market Impact in the Northern Territory*, Canberra: Australian Government Publishing Service.

Taylor, Karen Malpede. (1972) *People's Theatre in Amerika*, New York: Drama Books.

Thompson, Clive. (1998) 'State of the Union', *Report on Business Magazine* [insert in the Toronto *Globe and Mail*], April: 72–82.

Thompson, E. P. (1968) *The Making of the English Working Class*, Harmondsworth: Penguin.

Thompson, Paul and Theatre Passe Muraille. (1975) *The Farm Show*, Toronto: Coach House Press.

Thomson, Helen. (1992) 'Last Drinks', *The Australian*: 9 September.

Turner, Graeme (1990) *British Cultural Studies: An Introduction*, Boston: Unwin Hyman.

Vela, Irene. (1993) '"A Muso—And a Bubble and Squeak As Well!": Making Music with John Romeril', in Gareth Griffiths, ed., *John Romeril*, Australian Playwrights series; Amsterdam/Atlanta: Rodopi.

Wallis, Mick. (1994) 'Pageantry and the Popular Front: Ideological Production in the 'Thirties', *New Theatre Quarterly*, 10, 38: 132–156.

—— (1995) 'The Popular Front Pageant: Its Emergence and Decline', *New Theatre Quarterly*, 11, 41: 17–32.

Watt, David (1990.1) '"Art and Working Life": Australian Trade Unions and the Theatre', *New Theatre Quarterly*, 6, 22: 162–173.

—— (1990.2) 'Introduction, *The Ballad of Lois Ryan*', *Australasian Drama Studies* 17: 86–90.

—— (1991) 'Interrogating "Community": Social Welfare v. Cultural Democracy', in V. Binns, ed., *Community and the Arts*, Sydney: Pluto: 55–66

—— (1995) 'The Popular Theatre Troupe and Street Arts: Two Paradigms of Political Activism', in S. Capelin, ed., *Challenging the Centre: Two Decades of Political Theatre*, Brisbane: Playlab: 13–33

Watt, David and Graham Pitts. (1991) 'Community Theatre as Political Activism: Some Thoughts on Practice in the Australian Context', in V. Binns, ed., *Community and The Arts*, Sydney: Pluto, 119–133

Widgery, David, ed. (1976) *The Left in Britain 1956–1968*, Harmondsworth: Penguin.

Willett, John, ed. (1964) *Brecht on Theatre*, London: Methuen.

—— (1959) *The Theatre of Bertolt Brecht*, London: Methuen.

—— (1986) *The Theatre of Erwin Piscator: Half a Century of Politics in the Theatre*, London: Methuen.

Williams, Jay. (1974) *Stage Left*, New York: Scribners'.

Williams, Raymond. (1958) *Culture and Society 1780–1950*, London: Chatto & Windus.

Work Place Arts. (1989) 'Artists in the Workplace: Example Projects', Toronto: t.s. pamphlet.

Index